D0594178

MODERN BRIDES
& MODERN GROOMS

A Guide to Planning Straight, Gay, and Other Nontraditional Twenty-First-Century Weddings

MARK O'CONNELL, LCSW

Foreword by Liza Monroy

SKYHORSE PUBLISHING

Skyhorse Publishing books may be purchased in bulk at special discounts for sales promotion, corporate gifts, fund-raising, or educational purposes. Special editions can also be created to specifications. For details, contact the Special Sales Department, Skyhorse Publishing, 307 West 36th Street, 11th Floor, New York, NY 10018 or info@ skyhorsepublishing.com.

Skyhorse® and Skyhorse Publishing® are registered trademarks of Skyhorse Publishing, Inc.®, a Delaware corporation.

Visit our website at www.skyhorsepublishing.com.

10 9 8 7 6 5 4 3 2 1

Library of Congress Cataloging-in-Publication Data is available on file.

Cover design by Danielle Ceccolini
Cover illustration by Dan Parent

Print ISBN: 978-1-62914-583-9
Ebook ISBN: 978-1-63220-049-5

Printed in the United States of America

"We are weaned from our timidity
In the flush of love's light."
—Maya Angelou

"Those who dream by day are cognizant of many things which
escape those who dream only by night."
—Edgar Allan Poe

"The sharing of joy . . . forms a bridge between the sharers which can
be the basis for understanding much of what is not shared between
them, and lessens the threat of their difference."
—Audre Lorde

for Justin

Contents

Foreword

You could not ask for a better partner for the important jour-ney upon which you're about to embark.

And I don't mean your fiancé (though I'm sure your fiancé is wonderful and that's probably a huge part of why you're reading this).

I'm talking about actor-artist-psychotherapist-husband-author Mark O'Connell, and the journey is but the first step of an even larger one ahead: planning your wedding—and the whole life that follows. Mark's particular combination of multi-hyphenates makes him the most ideal expert and guide. In a day and age in which there's no boilerplate, no one-size-fits-all definition for what a wedding can or should be (same goes for marriage), Mark emphatically invites you to create your own. It's *your* big day, but his concrete ideas, guidelines, and marvelous suggestions are sure to help along the way. From the practical—dealing with a limited budget, handling contracts and meddling mothers—to the more psychological and emotional elements of asking for help and support, the myth of sexual death in marriage, why not to trust anyone who tells you to "just be yourself," the book in your hands is so much more than a wedding guide.

And who better to write such a transcendent guide than a multi-hyphenate who also happens to be *in* a happy marriage?

Wait, make that: a happy, complex, multifaceted, and *real* marriage, one that has gone through tests of time, acceptance, and various shades of legality. (On previously mentioned budget limitations: "Limitations are liberating . . . Same-sex couples are experts on limitations, having been denied the right to marry for so long . . .")

Whether you identify as gay, straight, or somewhere in between, in these pages you'll come to realize some essential, distilled truths about your own nature (see the "Engulfed or Abandoned" quiz) and the human psychology that factors not only into wedding planning, but upon which entire relationships are built. You will find yourself surprised and delighted by the stories, case studies, personal anecdotes, ideas, and advice between these pages. I was, and my own wedding (. . . um, the third and hopefully final time on this go-round that I'll ever be a bride) is more than a year behind me.

I was married three times by the age of thirty-three, a fact I have always been reticent to openly discuss, but it serves a point here: in a testament to this book's universality, I could have put *Modern Brides & Modern Grooms* to good use in planning any of my three extremely different weddings: 1) at twenty-two, to my gay best friend (to keep him in the country and with me) at a Vegas quickie ceremony presided over by an Elvis impersonator, 2) at twenty-four, to a high school boyfriend turned investment banker at Manhattan City Hall followed by a Mayan ceremony on a Mexican beach that no one could understand (turns out no one could understand the marriage, either) and 3) at thirty-three, to my perfect third-time's-a-charm-er in a beautiful redwood grove in California surrounded by friends and family.

I share this to emphasize that no matter what circumstances surround your relationship or what kind of wedding you want, Mark's perspective and advice will prove invaluable to working out the kinks and having not only your dream wedding, but better communication with your significant other, family, friends, and in-laws. It takes a village to make a wedding, a celebration and ritual that ultimately is, as Mark writes, a performance: "Weddings are theater, and acknowledging this will focus your planning. I know . . . there are sometimes religious components, cultural traditions, and family values to these affairs to consider. But no matter how you slice and dice it, a wedding is a piece of theater: an entertaining, ritualistic, transformative event."

With any performance, then, comes being watched. One becomes, albeit fleetingly, a celebrity. Never before have I read a wedding book that tackles the subtle complexities of "preparing to be watched." As an actor, Mark covers all the performative aspects of weddings and guides us through them starting from the proposal: Mark and his husband Justin, also a multi-hyphenate (lawyer-writer), created "Proposal Week," spinning cliché proposal traditions into something new, fresh, and completely their own. (Mark and Justin's story is also at once both fairytale-like and completely, utterly human. "On Justin's thirty-fourth birthday, he awoke to a cake of himself as a king, sitting atop a mountain of multicolored cupcakes, which was based on a weird dream he had shared with me when we were twenty-two"—this is an excellent couple.) I love the practical budget chart at the end, which is Mark and Justin's own.

So dive in, read on, and venture forth on your own journey into wedded bliss. As Mark writes, "There's a whole lot of theater ahead of you—happy, sad, and everything in-between."

With this book, a little luck, and a lot of love, you'll be well-equipped to navigate it all.

—Liza Monroy
author, *THE MARRIAGE ACT: The Risk I
Took To Keep My Best Friend in America
and What it Taught Us About Love*
Santa Cruz, CA

Introduction
Marriage equality has arrived, and it's not just for "the gays"!

This book is for those of you hoping to create a personalized wedding that dignifies your relationship, your individuality, the mutual recognition between you and your partner, and the equality you share—whether you're of the same or opposite sex.

Weddings are evolving across the board, and so too is the freedom and fun in planning them. Ceremonies (even religious ones), are now more a proclamation of love and commitment, on equal terms, for all couples—and less a public ritual during which one man drags a woman out by the hair and throws her at the feet of another man. In a little over a hundred years, brides have grown from being property to proposing, and now they can also watch their lesbian and gay friends enjoy conjugal kisses (under the law!).

When my husband, Justin, and I were married in 2006, at the age of twenty-nine, I found myself both moved by the past and roused to engage with the future. My gay uncle, Dan—who was twenty-nine in 1986, when SCOTUS ruled that same-sex sex was not a Constitutional right—took me aside during our reception and told me, with the sincere shimmer of a tear in one eye, "I wasn't sure I'd ever see a day like this."

Meanwhile several of my straight female friends responded with enthusiasm to the custom-made ceremony Justin and I had crafted out of cherry-picked text and music, emphasizing our love and friendship as equal but separate. My gal pals were somewhat ambivalent about having weddings—concerned about the aforementioned inequities that have historically stained these events—but after seeing ours, they were inspired and emboldened. These ladies have since collaborated with their partners to create magnificently distinctive nuptials of their own, honoring their unique loves, while also liberating their guests by exploding tradition—e.g., I was a bridesman for each of them.

Modern weddings are indeed becoming more and more queer. By *queer* I don't necessarily mean LGBT, but more inclusively I refer to anyone busting out of stale societal norms to get some fresh air. Modern weddings include, but are not limited to: the straight Catholic couple who read a Dan Savage piece about marriage equality at their ceremony; the faithfully Jewish straight bride who married a non-religious, gender-nonconforming groom; as well as the variety of interfaith, interracial, and binational weddings I've had the pleasure to attend—not to mention all those weddings of couples who actually, genuinely, like each other . . . and who want their truth to outweigh tradition.

This isn't to say we don't stand to inherit anything useful from traditional marriage. Obviously the very idea of throwing a kick-ass party of exhibitionism, romantic-ideals, and righteous-symbolism is derived from them. And now, with DOMA's demise, couples of the gay and lesbian variety share equally with straights in the economy of instant marriage recognition: including the option to do a Vegas-style quickie, but more importantly, the ability to answer the frequent cocktail party question, "When were you married?" lickety-split.

I can't tell you how many times I've been tripped-up in the headlights of that question, as though I'd been pulled over on the highway after having a stroke: "Well officer, we had a wedding in 2006 in Massachusetts (we're New York residents), but Mass didn't recognize out-of-state weddings at the time (Thank you, Mitt Romney) and the *New York Times* refused to announce it as a wedding (even after we long-windedly explained), so we tried to do it legally during a visit to San Francisco in 2008—we were first to register at City Hall the day the Cali Supreme Court ruled in favor of same-sex marriage (prior to *The Terminator* intervening, and Proposition 8)—but the law hadn't been implemented yet, so we went back to Mass in 2009 to legalize it (when they finally allowed out-of-state weddings), with only my mom and the random, all-purpose officiant witnessing as we stood in the rural outdoors, in front of an enormous rock (alluding to the hopeful end of some disaster film, like *Deep Impact)* and, thanks to Governor Patterson, it was sort of recognized in New York at that time, and was then officially reciprocated when same-sex marriage became legal in our home state in 2011, but we haven't had another ceremony yet, and if we do, we won't announce it in 'the *Times* 'cause we're still smarting from that first rejection, but at least now we know *for sure* we want to be together. So . . . does that answer your question?"

I've compared our marital quest to getting a PhD (it takes about seven years, after all)—except, when you finally get your PhD, your family is almost too happy to call you "*Doctor*," whereas, at this point, ours is sick of recognizing our marriage. Now, seven years after we tied the knot (the first time . . . it's quite an unwieldy knot by now . . .), couples like us can finally chitchat about their nuptials with ease—one date, one location, and a lithe display of smile-teeth—like any straight Tom, Dick, or Britney Spears.

While that's all very well, we should remain conscious of the salvational creativity that carried us through all those years of hearing "No!" Rather than accommodate *anyone* else's expectations for how your wedding should look (e.g., black tuxes and lacy white gowns at the altar resembling iconic cake-toppers or automatons with political ambitions), we can look back on the richly imaginative problem-solving that allowed us to claim meaningful marriages in the face of adversity and against all odds—and now we can do it with the law, society, and *joie de vivre* on our side.

Rather than guiding you to a "new normal," I hope this book emboldens you to create a "new"—a new of your own. Your wedding is a performing art, as is your marriage itself. Both require you to creatively collaborate in surviving conflicts, supporting each other's dreams, and building together a life that is livable. As an actor and a psychotherapist, I can tell you that approaching your wedding like a performing artist will help you achieve these goals and engage with inevitable obstacles along the way.

This is a guide to help you have a wedding on your own terms—and take the people you love along with you for the ride.

Part of that goal is about navigating more than just the practical challenges of menus and DJs. Deep down, weddings are about navigating some of the deepest emotional relationships of your life, with the people closest to you.

In the chapters ahead, I explore those kinds of relationships and challenges by telling personal stories: the story of my wedding and the challenges I faced, and wedding stories from my friends and family. (Look out for the brave, inspiring, hilarious, challenging, and moving connubial journeys of Lyn and Jorge, Sharon and Emily, Dani and Jamie, Connie and Steve, Corky and John, Bill and Michael, Lindsay and Paul, Emily and Brandon, Jesse and Danny, Lily and Bart, Winnie and Mason, Allie and Wyatt, Jamie and Sean, B., Julie, Tabitha, Yasmine, Rachel, Evelina and more). I share with you not models, but trials, errors, and stories of the willingness to carve out more life-space, love-space, and wedding-space than we've ever had before.

Through these stories, this book prepares you, the modern bride or modern groom, for understanding better who you are, what your Big Day is all about, what you want from it, and why you want those things.

Ultimately this core work or "emotional road map" to your wedding will help you express yourself confidently through the right dress or tux or shoes (or loincloth) or flowers or song or any other practical detail of your day that will make it authentically yours.

I hope these pages inspire you to make use of what we've all learned in our long fight to marry who we love and to create an event that authentically expresses you, your intended spouse, and both of you as a couple—whether you're L, G, B, T, Q, straight, or none of the above. This is the wisdom, the joy, and the gift of modern brides and modern grooms.

Part 1

First Comes Love . . .

1 To Have and to Hold Conflict: The Ironies of Waiting, Fighting, and Choosing

I know what you're thinking:

A gauzy white light reveals a shimmery altar. Your love's face appears, elfin, glowing. You both smile, gently, achingly, as you lock eyes, each with a Great Gatsby, I'm-only-thinking-about-you sort of gaze. Your family and friends look on, blissfully agape, as though you're Olympic champions about to claim the gold—they want nothing more than your happiness, in this moment and forever. You kiss. You are transformed.

Maybe you weren't thinking that exactly, but something close? This vision is a conjugal fantasy, but it's also very real. You will experience its essence, in some form, during the course of your wedding. It will be true, but it won't stand alone. You'll face multiple truths at once.

Irony in Love's Fire

Everything true about weddings is also untrue. They're as hot and cold as Katy Perry, and as ironic as Alanis Morissette. They connect us to one family while tearing us from another, delight us with gains as we grieve losses, and buoy us to new identities while old ones crumble beneath us. As my yoga teacher Nancy would have said it, weddings "balance on a core that rocks from side to side." The tensions, conflicts, and disasters that eventually afflict marriages tend to arrive when we deny their foundational irony—their rocky core. So before you even think about getting married, consider what you're signing up for—an endless search for balance on imbalance. Having said that, its very bittersweetness is what makes the marital process so delicious and acquiring a taste for it early on can help make it last. (I write this having been with my husband for fifteen years.)

Your wedding is so much more than just that "party of your life" that you're "supposed" to have and want—and which many people plan with half a brain. No. It's an opportunity to practice the exquisitely painful joy of creative collaboration, something you'll need to make use of for the rest of your lives together. I promise you, it hurts so good. Everything from buying a home, raising a child, or co-running a business involves an alert negotiation of subjectivity, a debate of ideals, a push and pull of suggested narratives. Your wedding is a fertile opportunity to hone the craft of co-leadership by creating a memorable event that expresses you both. But before you begin this process, you'll want the ironies to sink in, and that means time and practice— both of which same-sex couples are particularly used to, having waited for legal recognition of our chosen partnerships for so long.

Many of you opened this book because you've already begun planning a wedding, so you might not be interested in hearing about waiting. You may skip this section, if you like.

Although, even *you* might take the time to consider a few things about your couplehood: How do you communicate? How do you collaborate? How don't you? Have you spent enough time together? Have you spent enough time apart? The answers to these questions are the best wedding planning guide you'll find, and they'll continue to serve you in all your major projects, obstacles, and transitions as a couple.

The Newlywed Bus to Nowhere

Let's talk about the iconic 1967 film *The Graduate* for a moment. The finale, during which Dustin Hoffman charges recklessly into Katharine

Ross's conventional wedding, has become a prototype for climactic scenes of *nuptials interruptus,* dramatizing the modern sentiment "love conquers all." The scene radiates with an angsty fire, like impulsive sex that will not/cannot be tamed; sex without foreplay or contemplation. The choppy editing and slightly out-of-sync, seventies-horror-film-style audio (remember those weird shots of Anne Bancroft's angry teeth?) contribute to the hasty, violent passion. Katharine Ross's vacant eyes ever-so-slowly blossom to excitement at the sight of her anti-suitor, as though she is a "doll" from the "valley" or a "Stepford wife" (which she would famously play several years later). The lovers escape the adverse crowd, whom we see whacking them on the head—again, choppily, abruptly, seventies-horror-film style.

And finally they escape. To the bus. Free. They each take a breath of relief. And then . . . each tries to look at the other. Tension. Uncertainty. "Now what?" All they have is each other, and they've only just met. With this as their foundation, how will the couple resolve conflicts later? The only conflict resolution strategy their parents have modeled for them is "escape"—i.e., excessive drinking, sleeping with the neighbor's kid, crashing weddings.

Apart Together

Consider this: "I love you because you keep going away." That doesn't sound right. A friend of ours who was in a verbally abusive relationship shrieked this at me years ago in response to some couples' advice I had given when she had asked me what kept Justin and I together, and more specifically, why we never screamed at each other. I gave her one answer—just a guess really, because who the hell knows for sure—which was that we were often in different cities (he was in law school in Boston, while I studied acting in Providence) and constantly pursuing our respective passions and goals. I suggested that maybe the distance made our hearts grow fonder, and that our apartness, our separate development, somehow magnetized us back together, again and again. She didn't buy it. Like many of us, she hoped for something simpler. She wanted a magic bus that would rescue her and her boyfriend from an abusive relationship and chauffeur them to one that was mutually attentive and loving. An instant, romantic panacea (*romantacea?*) that would keep them together forever.

Conflict and Recovery

I still believe what I said is true, that our searching separateness kept Justin and me together. But that doesn't mean we were above screaming at each other. Hardly. We just cleverly did it behind closed doors. (Not every day, but . . .) That was the advantage of renting separate apartments during our first years together in Manhattan; we always had our own private sanctuary to recover from disagreement when it devolved into tantrums. When we moved into our first apartment together, my mother's Westchester home became my new safe haven, as it was only a Metro-North ride away.

> ### *Now's the time to fight, and to fight big.*
>
> By which I mean to verbalize your core conflicts to each other, not tear at each other's hair. Don't wait for a time when these fights are harder to resolve and there's more to lose.

If you don't have messy conflict before you're married, you *will* do it later, only one of you will end up leaving for good. The way you both learn to recover from the fights—the refuge you seek from the storms—will be the muscle you'll use to build your wedding and your marriage.

By the way, when I use the words "*resolve*" and "*recover*," I'm not referring to all the running away I used to do. We can think of those episodes as adjustment tantrums, the kind you might have upon beginning a new fitness program. The muscle of which I speak is one that takes time to cultivate, one that requires you to be brave by being vulnerable, and as researcher Brene Brown says, to "say I love you first."

It's the muscle that Justin flexed when he approached me—one closeted teen to another—at Simon's Rock, an early admissions college for misfits (me) and geniuses (Justin). It's the muscle I flexed seeking his company on campus at night, and the one he flexed in return, sharing his attraction for me—though I rejected him out of fear. It's the muscle I rediscovered six years later, seeing him on MTV's *The Real World* and writing him a letter of apology (a love letter?). And the muscle he found to respond. We shared this muscle to hop the Bonanza bus and surprise each other with spontaneous visits (across state lines). We used it to make up after every almost-breakup. Justin used it to skip exams to be with me after my father passed away, and I used it, years after we were married, to abruptly leave a new job to be with him when his mother was ailing from cancer. We would not have had space to grow if we impulsively hopped on a bus together at sixteen. We relied on this well-cultivated strength to create our wedding—the symbolic birth of our lives as a creative, collaborative pair.

Your Choice

It's tempting to get married while your love is new, when it all seems simple and unblemished, when everyone's still excited about you, when they all want you to do it. But the story of choosing a spouse based on peer (or cult) pressure never did end well—am I right, Katie Holmes?

Those of us who are lesbian or gay don't have a history of being forced to marry our same-sex counterparts, so there's no need to start now, no matter who you choose to marry, and that goes for everyone. Long-term queer relationships, of all stripes, have always been based on making a choice. We've risked physical attack, stigma, and in many cases, excommunication from our families to make these choices. We've waited years for our love to be recognized properly and have used the time to learn the landscapes of our own minds and hearts, the genesis of these choices. We've been very much alive, alert, and awake in making them, and the choice to get married needn't be an exception. Even those of us who are not gay or lesbian might do well to assume this position, these stakes, and the mindfulness of choosing and fighting for a marriage that reveals your truth more than tradition.

If you're ready to plan your big performance, then great! However, I recommend a few rounds of rehearsal before you take the stage. Get familiar with your role, and that of your scene partner, and learn together to survive the ironies in love's fire before you commit to this choice.

2 Fail! Again, and Again: The Curse, and Blessing, of Elizabeth Taylor

The first queer wedding I ever attended was that of my aunt Connie to Richard the Third when I was ten. What made it queer? 1) It was Connie's third (hence my nickname for Richard); 2) Richard was from Canada (i.e., it was a binational affair, and he was inscrutably polite); and 3) we never saw or heard from Richard again after that night (things certainly could have ended worse with a name like Richard the Third). Oh! And 4) my mother let me out of the house in a peacock green jacket, white slacks, cotton-candy shirt, and shimmery yellow tie (a Key West lounge singer ensemble) suggesting that she knew I was queer, and that such garish attire was appropriate for this queer event.

Now wait, before you get all judge-y about Connie's queer, third wedding, you might consider the fact that Elizabeth Taylor attended Connie's "normal" first wedding in 1976.

Elizabeth Taylor, as you may know, was not only one of the greatest goddesses of the screen, but was also famous for her serial marriages—her own brand of queerness. After Connie hung out with Liz during wedding number one (and presumably after getting hexed by ol' violet eyes), Connie went on to marry six more times, twice to her fifth and current hubby. You might recall that Ms. Taylor did such a thing. There's a bit of "stranger than fiction" to this story, and it has certainly evoked its share of laughter in my family over the years—not least because of its extreme contrast with the crazy luck of my parents. They got to be "normal" in their long-lasting marriage, while also being very much in love.

But I must tell you that at sixty-one, after many a wedding, Connie is now happily married, happily living, and doing so in a way I can only hope to emulate at her age. Not only are she and Steve—her husband of almost twenty years—joyously creating theater together, but they equally create life together. A lot of it. They travel, read, cook, dance, play, and revel with Connie's daughter and son in-law. The matrimonial road was rocky for Connie, but she abided, and eventually found a balance on its rockiness.

Wedding Anxiety Disorder

Unfortunately for Elizabeth Taylor, she began getting married in 1950, when what I call Wedding Anxiety Disorder (WAD) was at a peak for American ladies. Wedding anxiety derives from a history of kinship that has been less than kind to women, described by anthropologist Claude Levi-Strauss as women being shuffled between clans; or as I said in the introduction to this book, dragged out by the hair by one man and thrown at the feet of another. This traumatic history permeates modern society and modern women who, even today, receive messages that if they don't get hitched—before they're, I don't know . . . twenty-five or something—they're done for! This social norm has had the power of a malicious dictator or vicious virus; it infected its way into Liz's head, who transferred it to Connie years later. And as with any oppressive norm we internalize, it took years to free themselves from it.

Though WAD still lingers on, we now acknowledge it, sometimes playfully (does Beyonce's song "Single Ladies" ring a bell?). The WAD contagion has affected countless people, goading them into premature marriages as if to legitimize both the couples and the individuals—giving them free passes to *Normal's Arc* to be spared the *Misfit Apocalypse*. Under this pressure, one is expected to nab the first person who seems promising, sort of close her eyes, cross her fingers, and invite everyone she's ever met to watch her prepare for eternal, normative bliss—tightly holding her eyes closed and fingers crossed, even after the limousine (or bus) pulls away.

Elizabeth Taylor seemed to be saying something like, "Alright. I'll try to live within this framework, and if it doesn't work, I'll try again, and if I fall flat on my face, I'll get up and do it again, and again. And you see that attractive, independent minded young woman over there? [meaning Connie], I'm going to take her with me." Elizabeth and Connie both tried bravely to live within those contagious rules. Though they were met repeatedly with disappointment, their brazenly, queer commitment to these failed efforts exposed the punishing history of marriage norms for the rest of us. We glean from them great lessons: namely, that it is necessary to fail in relationships if we ever want them to grow.

> ### Fail
> "Fail Again. Fail Better," wrote Samuel Beckett.
>
> We too can and should fail before expecting relational success. Get curious about the ways you have failed your partner, or (s)he has failed you thus far. If nothing is phoning in, you may want to postpone the wedding until something does. You'll both be better off having failed each other, acknowledged it, and survived it together before taking the connubial leap.

I speak from experience. Justin and I founded our relationship on a steaming hotbed of failure. As bullied—and consequently failed—high school students we found each other as "refugees" in 1993 at sixteen, on "the island of misfit teens" known as Simon's Rock College. *Project Runway's* Nina Garcia would have kicked us out for our failed attempts at "styling": torn stonewashed jeans, half-shaved/half-long-hairdos, flannels, Birkenstocks, acne. More significantly, we also failed to be out. Few openly gay teens were at that time. Same-sex marriage wasn't legal; there was no internet to learn how much "better" it would get;

Ellen had not yet declared "Yep, I'm gay!"; homosexuality was largely associated with AIDS. To be gay was to fail.

But somewhere in that melancholic abyss there was life. Beyond our sad appearances, the dark cloud of our shared abjection and fear, there was ineffable laughter, recognition, and desire. Being together felt like "home." Never did I feel this more potently than one rainy late night while walking on campus. I was lonely, all alone. Seeing him in the distance, I called out willfully, from the gut, "Justin?"

Late nights, fluent exchanges of giggles, too many cigarettes (regrettably; please don't try this at home), and the warm rush of freely being ourselves consumed the first two weeks of college. As with most things done as a teen, we did too much too soon, and when Justin bravely tried to take things further, whilst sitting on a rock one fateful night—"I guess I'm attracted to you."—my inner bully quelled our queer pleasure, like a first responder to a disaster. I had an emotional breakdown. (Fail.) I was sent home. (Double fail.) Justin was advised not to talk to me by the dean, and so he didn't. (Triple axel fail.) It would be six years before we'd speak again.

The years between sixteen and twenty-two are fertile for failing again, and better. During that time, each of us found our own way out of the closet, into our bodies, and onto an expedition of intimacy. Independently, we learned a ton about desire: longing, seeking, tasting, having, breaking, and being broken. What better time to vacillate between euphoria and despair than while your hormones are ablaze? Then one night, while watching *The Real World: Hawaii* with friends, there he was on the TV: same honey-brown eyes, same alluring sense of humor, same subversive, silver tongue, only now he was a hot, hip young adult, as opposed to an awkward teen. I called out willfully, from the gut, "Justin!"

One letter (composed to the desperate sounds of Dido), and several epic all-night phone calls later, we erupted into the shameless, torrid lovers we never, ever could have been in college.

Cue the months into years of long-overdue PDA—"A" for "affection" and for "arguments." Mortifying arguments (once while having a very expensive dinner, with his boss). We acted out "the breakup scene" countless times; you know, the one where a pouty-lipped starlet stands in a doorway, raises her voice, and then lowers it, for effect, ending it all "for good." I jest, but it felt bad. Bad. Eviscerating. I can still recall how difficult it was to be vulnerable. To say what I really wanted, which was to be with him but also to be seen and heard by him. It was excruciating to apologize, to negotiate, and to compromise. But whenever we did, we were that much more able to tolerate the other's nagging flaws. (This is what I referred to in the last chapter as conflict and recovery, and what some psychotherapists call *rupture and repair*.). Only then could we find our way back to the late night sanctuary we had founded at sixteen.

In short: Pre-marital public tantrums are a must. Fighting is a form of figuring out. Let yourselves survive a great hitch before getting hitched.

Now, had we been straight, our adolescent love-play might have occurred by day, without shame to tear us apart, and our mutual feelings easily could have skyrocketed us prematurely into marriage—an impulsive bus ride to nowhere. After all, the high school sweetheart scenario my parents modeled for me was absorbed into my mind as the epitome of "normal" and, therefore, desirable. They were wed at twenty-two, having been one another's first love, and somehow remained laughing, kissing, and dancing until the day my dad died. (My brother's high school girlfriend Kim used to say, "I want to go in there," referring to my parents' bedroom, as we could always hear them guffawing behind the door.).

But you, me, and the statisticians all know that though my parents inhabited a "normative" marriage—e.g., straight, kids, loving, liking, lasting—they were, and would in fact still be, outliers among couples. By inherently failing to be "normal," or rather by virtue of being gay, Justin and I were arguably protected from the inevitable disappointment of unmet expectations/of not being my parents. Our queerness provided us an open, unexplored field through which to blunder, make discoveries, and sculpt out space. Our space.

> Don't try to emulate the "normals" in your life: those happy few who "made it," "got away with it," and did not seem to fail. This will only be in vain—unless, of course, you alone are the anomaly who consistently wins the stuffed toy from that machine with the vexing claw.

Avuncular Wisdom

I didn't look to my parents for a roadmap to plan our wedding, nor am I sharing such a thing with you now. Though I certainly invite you to consider the good fortune of my parents' traditional, romance, this being a book inspired by queerness, I instead direct your attention to the trials of Aunt Connie, by proxy of Liz Taylor. Eve Sedgwick, the queen of queer theory, called this type of inherited wisdom "the avuncular": a relationship with aunts/uncles/adult relatives who are not parents directly above you in the family tree and who may represent non-conforming sexualities.

Connie took a lot of heat during her years under the Liz spell, and I surely feared association with her as a result. But as I grew older, recognizing my inevitable bad fit in a normative world, I saw her journey anew. I appreciated the necessary boldness of dreaming, trying, taking risks, and sometimes separating from the pack to seek life—even at the cost of ridicule. I learned the exquisite beauty of failure. The permission it gives you to try your wings, to fall, fall again, and in falling better to fumble your own way into flight. Failure forces you to take your own side, to love yourself better, and to increase your capacity for loving other people.

Fortunately our social customs continue to evolve, providing more room for fumbling, however discouragingly slow the process. Compare

Elizabeth Taylor to contemporary screen goddess Julia Roberts, who was engaged a handful of times but only married twice. There is more opportunity now for women in particular, but for us all, to experiment, to make bids for love, to get rejected, and fall flat many, many times, before marriage is even considered. And we have the brazenness of women like Connie and Liz, in part, to thank for this freedom.

Our marriages don't have to be social traps, they can set us free. They needn't hide us, but can instead expose our desires and choices. They needn't sedate us, but can wake us. And all of this becomes possible if we have room to fail before we fly.

3 Between Paradise and Prison: Navigating Families and Tribes

"What? Are you getting married?" my uncle Dan said, with snark. It was 2001 and I called him to plan a visit. (We actually spoke on phones in those days to make such arrangements, as opposed to texting; to think that 2001 once symbolized "the future!") Pride weekend was coming up in New York City. We were new in town, and Justin fancied the idea of meeting and hanging out with my gay uncle—a la Eve Sedgwick's notion of the avuncular. Dan was clearly less interested in hearing how thrilled I was to be dating Justin ("for over a year!") and more so in teaching me how to be a "gay man."

Now, Dan's tutelage was no doubt a form of privilege: he generously invited us to his house on the Fire Island Pines, "The Uncle of All Gay Meccas." A mecca that can only be reached by waving goodbye to the land of Long Island and taking a ferry ride. My first time on the ferry there was erotically baptismal: a shimmery, watery ritual that opened the world fresh as we transited from the land of the "normal" to the island of the "queer." Marriage has a similar impact.

> Weddings are a symbolic ferrying from family to family, tribe to tribe, place to place. Those whose families and tribes (or the tribes of their partners) are very different from one another find such a transition not without the pain of loss, even while being led blissfully to a new life.

I'm lucky in having overlap between family and tribe in the form of my uncle, but at the time, there was still the inevitable feeling of moving through an open door as the other closed.

For many of us, doors slam in varying forms of rejection. In my case, my father had recently passed away from a heart attack. This feeling of rejection, this "slam," was not my father's doing, but I felt it in the chill of his absence. The one year he spent getting to know Justin was fun for them both; at last, someone was around who shared my dad's interest in history and politics. I'll never know how those relations would have evolved, and the grief and wonder still lurk in my heart, as they did that summer as we stepped off the ferry.

"Welcome to the island, boys," spoke a hushed, mischievous male voice. As Dan welcomed us to his Buddhist temple of a house, we were greeted by several forty-something men sitting in a row (in my memory, their colorful speedos formed a perfect rainbow). Later, we explored the island unchaperoned; our own private *Idaho, Eden,* and *Blue Lagoon.* The unadulterated smiles beaming on us promised freedom and play. For some, the visual buffet of buff is the elixir of the Pines, and I'm not above looking, depending on my mood. But for me, the more crucial tonic was the sense that on this island I would never, ever, get beaten to death for being gay. As we frolicked together about the sand and the boardwalks by moonlight, I could almost hear the reeds whisper reassuringly to me while the nearby sounds of the ocean held us.

Then suddenly, the joyful act of norm-busting became a little too normal. One afternoon, Dan and his speedo-clad posse accompanied us to the beach. No sooner had we laid down our towels were we surprised by an abrupt bit of pedagogy: the speedos were off before I could breathe. . . There it was, uncle Dan's "dandan"—either a thin noodle or a large sea beast, depending on whether you're speaking Japanese or reading *The Arabian Nights*—lying on the ground looking up between his legs, it reminded me of that famous scene in which Indiana Jones falls shockingly into face-off with a cobra. "Trunks off," spoke Dan the Great and Powerful. "That goes for the hot tub, too."

I hadn't really hung out with my uncle before—so to speak. Though when I was nineteen, he did see me act in two sexually charged, yet professional, plays—one in which I was completely naked—so one might expect he'd envision and accept me as out, proud, and queer in my own way. One would be mistaken. Intent on my indoctrination into his (our?) community, he needed to impose on me the character of Naive, Newbie, Nephew—from the sticks.

The rules kept coming at us. "No sitting together at dinner. Mix it up. What are you, *sticky*?"—meaning, to my uncle's friends, "monogamous."

In some ways the Pines is one of the most normative enclaves I've ever seen. Rich, white, straight men have simply been replaced by rich, white, gay men who tend to enforce their own brand of homogeneity. To be not-male, not-white, not-muscled, not-butch (they *try* to be strict about that one, but I mean, come on . . .) too-clothed, or monogamous is to carry the whiff of something foreign or "exotic." This is not the only truth, of course, but true it is, and it made me wince at first taste. The contradictions of the Pines bring to mind Italy's historic "gay" island of San Domino. In the late 1930s, Mussolini used it to internally exile homosexuals, though ironically many of the men found the island to be a paradise on which they could freely play, have sex, and love—it was simultaneously a paradise and a prison.

I couldn't understand why these men were dislodging the prison bars of normal only to replace them with more bars—albeit in rainbow colors. Isn't that like establishing a club on the island, calling it Stonewall, and then arresting couples who dance with only each other all night? Now, surely they felt victimized by Justin and me in return, as we were contaminating their hard-earned fresh air with oppressive heteronormative toxins—e.g., ideas of monogamous romance and love.

> *Such are the conundrums of kinship and kindredship, however, and wherever we find it.*

How do we avoid a *them versus us* scenario? How do we stay connected to our communities as we seek our own lives? How to

> stay true to lives that are livable without disavowing our strongest allies, influences, and supports?

If I was frustrated with Dan and company it's not because I was right and he was wrong. It was that I wanted him to recognize my heart and mind. Being with Justin, committed to Justin, was my nude beach, my naked hot tub, and my queer. We had both found our own different paths to self-fulfillment and self-realization.

(You should know that Dan's brother, my uncle Phil, is a gay football-fanatic, Florida Republican! And is also quite lovable. So you see, we all view our tribes, and find comfort there, in our own individualized way.)

Living in the Spaces

Throughout the years, Justin and I have come to truly value the Pines, and Dan. His house is the family home I've known the longest at this point in my life (see "Irony" in chapter 1). We've developed a deep appreciation for this avuncular connection, even if we sometimes don't feel seen within it. The island can be our own unique paradise and, at the same time, a place that belongs to various other folks from whom we've let ourselves learn and be changed. And when the fit just isn't good, we have our senses of irony and humor to help us survive. Psychoanalyst Philip Bromberg might say we've learned to live "between the spaces" of communal expectations and individual dreams.

The in-between space we occupy on the island recalls The Little Mermaid, caught between worlds. Though she was given a "happy," normative ending by Disney—as if marrying her into a legged, land-bound life completely resolved her identity crisis—Hans Christian Andersen's original character is fated to an ever-after as sea foam, to live in a melancholic space between identities of land and sea. She's not easily seen, heard, or understood, but has the freedom to exist in all of her truth. Similarly, the island is a place we can be monogamous, not unlike my parents, and revel like my uncle at the same time. A place where by day I can share an exuberant, erotic, social space with other men—a freedom I lacked as a boy—and by night take introspective walks to the beach, during which I continue to feel close to my father, listening to the silence of sea foam.

> ### The sea is not a bad theme for your wedding, actually . . .
>
> The ebb and flow suggesting the space between identities, traditions, and preferences. A space that is both melancholic and festive. If the mermaid aesthetic is not your style, you might consider drawing from Shakespeare's *The Tempest*: an island wedding where past and future co-exist by way of dancing sprites, ethereal ghosts, monsters, the sorcery of a creative mind, and the tears of those who are shipwrecked—lost, but also found. Recognized at last.
>
> Take the idea, it's yours. I won't tell you how to go about it; you can make it your own.

But just one moment.

To be fair to that administrator of "gay rules" I call Uncle Dan, you should know what I've come to realize about him: he did see me all along. On numerous occasions, I've heard renditions of my "love story," embellished and sentimentalized each time anew, by one or another of his friends. Never from Dan directly, but that's okay. It's sometimes hard for kin to acknowledge you face-to-face. Often that's not because they want to regulate and punish you. They really just want to be recognized, as well. You see, just as I had wanted to be seen by Dan, I finally understand that he wanted, and also deserved, the same from me.

And I do see him. I see a man from a large blue-collar family in the Bronx who formed adaptive identities: e.g., on the island of Manhattan and that of the Pines as a successful professional, lover, loyal friend, and as a very generous uncle. I see someone who is happily unmarried.

*Let's not forget that marriage isn't a goal for everyone,
nor need it be. There are countless ways to have love
in your life.*

Dan has it in the form of travel, a passion for history, culture, and people, among many other things I won't pretend to fully understand or trap in a label.

If we listen carefully enough, we can hear the unspoken wisdom of our kin.

From Dan we can learn to celebrate love that does not need an institution or a name. Just as we flash our kin with our wish for marriage, they in turn may want to flash us with celebrations of their own.

At Dan's fiftieth birthday party, for example, a scattering of his family and his tribes assembled for one mosaic moment of recognition. And there was a magnificent cake, provided by his ex-boyfriend, with whom he maintains a close and loving relationship. A photo of young Dan was scanned onto the icing. Naked. And queer in his own way.

4   How to Fail Better: Identifying Emotional Roles, and Learning to Play Them

"I don't want it to be like an Elton John concert," declared my mom, fearing we would have a *big fat GAY wedding*! She glared in my eyes intently, as though Justin was not there beside me.

We were at a cafe in Italy—in the midst of traveling with our mothers—and this comment set us off. In the flicker of a second, I felt engulfed by my mom while Justin felt abandoned by her. In other words, she spoke as though *her* feelings—her experience, her world—completely trumped mine, and as though his ... well, she wasn't even thinking about his feelings.

And by the way, we had no plans to walk the aisle in sequined suits a la Elton (although, so what if we had?). We weren't even engaged. My mom had simply found a chance to emote anxiety that had little to do with us, and everything to do with her. You see, we were all tossing out wedding ideas over coffee, just for fun. And in a moment of inspired, creative, weirdness—totally joking—Justin shared a vision of our moms processing side-by-side, wearing enormous chess-themed headpieces, singing in baritone dirge-voices, "Ha-ppy We-dding Day." Justin's unencumbered imagination frequently tickles me. But it apparently doesn't work so well on my mom.

Flummoxed and desperate, I struggled to locate my feelings and bring them to life—spattering words without focus or direction: "Who? What? Elton John?" While Justin quietly darted his feelings like razor sharp arrows through intense eyes.

I bit recklessly into a pastry—one of those over-stuffed puffs with custard bursting at the seams. Talking and chewing, I clumsily flailed a cluster of feelings at my mother, hoping something more than custard would stick. Hoping she would magically awake to realize her comment was unfair and then apologize, thereby releasing me from the tight grip of her dominating narrative. I get like this when my emotional truth is trapped—like Rapunzel in a tower—while someone with bigger, stronger, louder emotions stands guard (especially when that "someone" is my mother).

Meanwhile, Justin aggressively slurped down his cappuccino, feeling shut out. As I carried on, he carefully strategized a plan to make himself known to my mother, and to me. To scale the tower walls, break in, and be my rescuer so he would no longer be alone. His first step was to try telling me to calm down—which is always a big mistake. *I would not!* Then he asked my mom, "What exactly are you worried about?" It was a reasonable question that might have resolved the miscommunication had she answered it (and if she perhaps asked a few questions in return). Instead, she pushed full-steam ahead with her fear: that our wedding would deviate too far from the norm; or rather from *her* idea of the norm (i.e., an event her cousins "would understand"). Justin was whacked off the tower walls before he could find his footing.

Though my mother was at the center of this clash, it clearly encapsulates the core emotional conflict between Justin and me—the one that rears its head whenever we argue and particularly when we plan events. If I were to visualize it, it would look something like this: me doggy-paddling in tempestuous waves for emotional life, while Justin, crestfallen that I'm wasting time in the water, sits waiting for me, alone, on board his lifeboat. And actually, I bet it's not unlike what goes on between you and your significant other.

Emotional Roles

The sooner you identify who's who and get a handle on it (without involving a third party), the smoother your wedding planning will be. I know, easier said than done. Believe me I know.

So, why didn't we just tell my mom to *back off*? After all, it was our hypothetical wedding she spurned—like a trespasser in our home, taking a moment to denigrate the curtains. But to focus on my mother and her loose lips is to overlook the emotional reverberations she triggered in Justin and me. Reverberations that show up, within and between us, again and again and again.

We stayed too long at the cafe before parting ways, everyone disgruntled (save for Justin's mom, Sandy, who wisely teased us rather than get involved). Tension pervaded Justin and me for the rest of the day like a dark cloud. And as we walked the Spanish Steps and threw coins in the Trevi Fountain, we wished it would simply evaporate.

Here's the dilemma: we were both inconsolable. We needed to use each other to feel better, but we didn't know how. Both of us were too afraid to be vulnerable; to share, listen, and reflect back how this episode had affected us.

I wanted Justin to rescue me from my mom; to assert my feelings and preferences on my behalf. But I also didn't, fearing he'd re-engulf me with his own feelings and preferences. Deep down, what I really wanted was for him to help me discover and harness my own unique point of view and help me define it so clearly that I could gracefully extricate myself from my mother without throwing a tantrum. And of course I wanted him to read my mind to spare me having to say all of that.

Justin, on the other hand, wanted to rescue me from my mom and assert his feelings and preferences on my behalf. But he also didn't, fearing he'd have to work this hard—abandoned by me—every time he wanted his feelings known. More so, he wanted me to rescue myself from my mother, so I could then acknowledge his feelings—how she had hurt him by shutting him out.

Instead, I remained lost and he remained hurt. Both of us stagnant, incapable of taking in the beauty around us. Had we been able to recognize each other's emotions—to be mutual mirrors—we could have saved ourselves from my mom's unsolicited two cents.

Before we can resolve the emotional conflicts that make us feel crazy and unseen, we need to better understand them. They are much ado about primary attachments—moms, dads, folks if you will—and that delicate balance between connection and separation.

Defining Your Emotional Roles

Psychologist Harville Hendrix writes that children whose folks emotionally engulfed them overcompensate in adulthood by pushing people away—he calls them *isolators*—while children left feeling emotionally abandoned overcompensate as adults by constantly forging closeness—he calls them *fusers*. He also says these kids marry their opposites. If they learn to verbalize their feelings effectively, together they can get to the other side of their engulfment or abandonment. At the same time, they find security in their partnerships, while also feeling less unresolved with their folks.

Now, I despise categorical thinking more than most (e.g., books of the *Men Are From Jupiter, Women Are From Neptune* variety, which only apply to a very limited number of romantic pairs). But I've learned that identifying emotional roles in romantic relationships that are somewhat flexible, and which reasonably account for nuances, can help clarify our specific emotional needs, thereby increasing safety, communication, and the ability to negotiate within a relationship. To accomplish this, it is helpful to identify each of our "characters." As actress Mary McDonnell says, "Great characters develop out of restricted situations.

When people feel the limitations of life, something else takes over that's specific and colorful." Much like acting, defining our roles can be helpful in expressing emotion to our partners and listening to their emotions in turn. Through this process, we increase our capacities for collaborative, creative problem-solving.

As limiting as it sounds to be a "type," identifying with an emotional role can help you to reflect on who you are and what you've got to work with. Like my yoga teacher Nancy says, "We find freedom within the boundaries of a pose." I gleaned this precious pearl of wisdom for myself in an acting class when I was a gawky teen. Wearing a mask (to temper the ego a bit), I was instructed to look in a mirror and create a character. As much as I hated seeing unflattering parts of my body, it was empowering to face the raw materials. To see what was actually available for creative use—as opposed to what I wanted/hoped/imagined there to be. And to acknowledge what was not there, as well. The defining limitations of our emotional attachment roles can be equally liberating. Keep in mind that every couple I've ever encountered—socially and as a therapist—has one of each role between them. That's right: Every. Single. Couple. You are not the exception, I promise. (Give me ten minutes of your time at a party, while Justin rolls his eyes, and I'll make you a believer.) I like to call the roles *The Engulfed* and *The Abandoned*, focusing on their emotional essences as opposed to their actions.

The Engulfed and The Abandoned

If you're the Engulfed, the overall impression your caretakers left on you was emotional engulfment. You have a harder time asserting preferences than your partner, tending to go along with her/his feelings and preferences. You more frequently seek time alone than your partner to get your bearings. At the same time, you want your partner's support as you learn to assert your wants and wishes. You are like a yo-yo that seeks to travel far from your partner's grip, while also being securely attached.

If you're the Abandoned, the overall impression your caretakers left on you was emotional abandonment. You prefer to be in control of the events involving you and your partner. You tend to reach for your partner when you want her/his company. You have no problem clearly asserting your preferences or limitations to her/him. At the same time, you want your partner's support as you learn to let go and lean on her/him. You are like the hand that keeps the yo-yo secure as it travels in the air, hoping you can one day develop enough trust to switch roles.

It isn't always obvious who's who on the surface, which is why I like this model so much. It's not necessarily about gender, finances, class, race, social power, personality, or demeanor.

Of course some couples experience a variety of engulfments or abandonments due to job or career status, immigration status, language barriers, and other life chances. And also, I should acknowledge that in childhood we've all obviously been abandoned in one form or another, and we've all experienced some version of engulfment. But what this model seeks to zoom in on is the unique and highly specific ways in which each of us formed intimate emotional bonds—interpersonal attachment styles—at a very early age. Identifying with one role or the other really only serves us in that it increases our capacity for effective emotional communication.

The two roles are magnetic and complementary, which is how you and your partner ended up together, but they also threaten each other. Like a wandering oyster and free-floating sea particle, you got together, proceeded to aggravate one another, and are in the process of (potentially) forming a thing of iridescent beauty. Knowing and accepting which of you is which can provide emotional safety and security as you learn together to survive life's inevitable ruptures.

Here are a few personal examples that may help you determine who's who (though every engulfed or abandoned shows herself differently): I tend to give a vague, waiting-in-the-wings/"catch me if you can" sort of vibe. This, I guess, comes from learning to attach by giving up the emotional spotlight to my . . . ahem . . . caretakers. I'm like a celebrity assistant, or one of those E! Hollywood reporters who are always like, "It's hard for Oprah." My T-shirt might say, "Where am I?" I'm the Engulfed. Justin, however, tends to come across like a heat-seeking missile aimed precisely at who and what he wants. I guess this is from a childhood of depending on himself to secure emotional bonds. He's like a solo performer who picks an appealing fan from the crowd to join him backstage for post-show cocktails. Justin's T-shirt might say "Where are you?" Justin is the Abandoned.

Getting it?

When I tried explaining this to an intensely cerebral friend, he replied, "Aren't there people who survived childhood so well that they're now too strong to be engulfed or abandoned?" Nope. And besides, relationships would be a whole lot less interesting if that were true. (This friend is an obvious *Engulfed*, by the way: *Abandoneds* tend to be tired of asserting a "strong" identity, hoping instead to be relieved from this post, while *Engulfeds* tend to spend lifetimes fixating on their oft-unsatisfied wish to be seen as emotionally "strong.") If we didn't walk around with raw, messy, imperfect needs pressing against our seams, there would be no drive to find someone to contain us, love us, grow us—someone who also lets us do the same for them.

Engulfed/Abandoned Quiz

This quiz will determine whether you are the *Engulfed* or the *Abandoned* in your relationship. This is not scientifically based and is not intended to brand you in a category. The intention is to approximate your emotional essence in the relationship; I always observe two distinct ones in each romantic pair. Once you know who's who, you and your partner can better recognize each other's emotions, improve your communication, negotiation, and conflict resolution. (Rather than simply dismissing one another as being "crazy.")

You are more likely to . . .

1) A. Screen your partner's calls, or tend to call her/him only when you have news.
   B. Call your partner just because you want company.

2) A. Defer responsibility for most things.
   B. Automatically take responsibility for most things.

3) A. Let your partner be the buffer between you and your family.
   B. Be the buffer between your partner and her/his family.

4) A. Be incorporated into her/his world.
   B. Incorporate her/him into your world.

5) A. Hope your partner reads your mind.
   B. Make your feelings and preferences *very* clear and without apology.

6) A. Feel like you are occupying the tent of your relationship.
   B. Feel like the pole holding up the tent of your relationship.

7) A. Take for granted that your partner will be there.
   B. Make an effort to keep your partner by your side, or risk losing her/him.

8) A. Feel chased and/or rescued by your partner.
   B. Chase and/or rescue your partner.

9) A. Be indifferent or okay with the design, the state, and the rules of your home.
   B. Make and insist upon the design, the state, and the rules of your home.

10) When you say, "*We* like [blank]," or "*We* do [blank]," you really mean . . .
    A. "My partner likes [blank]" and "My partner does [blank]."
    B. "I like [blank]" or "I do [blank]."

Give yourself a point for every question you answered with "B," adding an extra point if you answered question #1 with "B" and subtracting a point if you answered question #1 with "A." If your total falls between 0 and 5 you are likely an *Engulfed*. If it is between 6 and 12 you are likely an *Abandoned*.

By identifying and accepting your attachment role, you allow yourself to be vulnerable, but with clarity, and to be on equal footing with your partner (as neither of the roles is more powerful, or desirable, than the other). Both roles force us to take emotional risks and to say "I love you" first.

Both roles imply need. If your needs are mutually acknowledged and authentically expressed, neither one of you can rise above the exposure of emotional nakedness. In this place together, you can cultivate safety: to feel, to talk, to be, to set boundaries with intrusive family members . . . and to collaborate.

This will prove handy when you start making choices about wedding logistics: date, location, aesthetic, guest list, budget . . . The list of practical concerns is infinite, but there's really only one Mother of All Conflicts, and all the practical stuff never really gets resolved until you address it.

In our own wedding, for example, I learned to acknowledge the emotions underlying Justin's deal-breaking requests for very, very specific ceremonial text and music—even when the choices seemed arbitrary to me—while he learned to support my tedious creative process, taking care not to shut me down as I slowly churned out my preferences—which was tricky, as I changed my mind. About everything. A lot.

To get better at this process of communication, Harville Hendrix suggests a listening tool, not unlike mirroring exercises developed by the acting teacher Sanford Meisner. The idea is to listen as your partner describes a feeling, a desire, or concern, and to repeat it back to them—neutrally, without attitude or interpretation. This slows down your communication process. It maintains focused attention on one of you at a time. That way the listener doesn't interrupt and smother the speaker with their own version of events before the speaker has had a chance to be recognized. The next step is to validate the speaker's statement and then to empathize with it. Then you switch. That's it.

Exercise

Scene 1

Abandoned: "When you walk out the door, mid-argument, it feels like an icy rejection."

Engulfed: "I hear that when I walk out the door, it feels like an icy rejection."

Abandoned: "That's right."

Engulfed: "That's got to hurt. I get that. Especially given your childhood."

Scene 2

Engulfed: "When you fixate on me walking out the door, I feel smothered."

Abandoned: "I hear that when I fixate on you walking out the door, it feels like you're being smothered."

Engulfed: "That's right."

Abandoned: "That's got to be overwhelming. I can understand that. Especially given your childhood."

This example is a bit stiff, but as any good actor would do, you would play each of these actions in your own way, keeping it simple and direct. Through this process, the Engulfed might learn to grant the Abandoned assurance the next time (s)he walks out the door, while the Abandoned might acknowledge the Engulfed's need for space.

These scenes do not require severe emotional intensity. (When your home becomes an endless run of *Who's Afraid of Virginia Woolf?*, you might be working too hard.). Sometimes your partner may not be ready for this kind of talk, in which case you might say, "I love you. I'm here to help. And I'll wait."

Peter and Wendy

A couple I'll call Peter and Wendy came to me for therapy because their incessant verbal sparring seemed irreconcilable. Peter was in his late thirties, worked full time as a teacher, was divorced, and had a ten-year-old daughter—Tink—who stayed with him every other week. Wendy was in her early thirties, had only lived in the United States for a few years, and was taking night classes and supporting herself with a full-time job while applying for citizenship. Wendy found that to feel connected to Peter meant listening and holding the cyclone of stress he'd bring home from work each day. By the time it was her turn to complain, Peter would tune out—or, more stinging for Wendy, he would turn his attention to Tink, if she was there. Whenever Tink would visit, Peter would take her to Central Park where they would race, go to the zoo, or ice skate while Wendy lagged behind. Back at the apartment, Peter and Tink would endlessly play card games, board games, and video games, while Wendy sat alone—having been told that they needed their "special time."

When we began implementing the dialogues, it wasn't easy to get Peter and Wendy to use "I" statements as opposed to "You" statements. So many of their first attempts sounded like this: "Peter, am I your mother?! You dump on me then play with your toys!" Or this: "Wendy you are so goddamn controlling . . . when will you leave me alone?!"

Eventually they began saying things like, "Peter, I know Tink is important to you, and I want to grant you that. I just want to have special time with you as well. I need your support," and "Wendy, I know you feel left out, and I want to work to give you better support and include you in more of my life."

Some of the solutions they came up with included picking several nights a month for Wendy/Peter special times, several nights for Peter/Tink special times, and a few other times when they would all play games together. After a year of treatment, Peter and Wendy appropriately shut me out, leaving me with a card that read, "Thank you for helping us love each other better."

Valentoymes

Now, not all couples benefit from this approach—either due to the extreme nature of their conflict or because one or both of them lacked the willingness to be vulnerable.

Such was the case for a couple I saw for therapy whom I call *Valentoymes*—which was how the woman referred to "Valentine's Day," in her indiscernible, New York–metro accent. At the first session, she explained that each year her boyfriend promised to buy her an engagement ring for *Valentoymes*, but never delivered. As it was early February, she was anticipating her annual let-down (abandonment). "You know what I'm gonna get fa *Valentoymes* this yee-ah? A loy detectah test." [Translation: Lie detector test.] "Ya know whoy? Cuz he's been f—kn moy sistah who lives upstay-yahs. And ya know what? I don't have a sistah; she's dead ta me!" Just then the boyfriend, who had been quietly engulfed, burst out with, "I took the loy detectah test. Three yeeyahs ago. And I payassed!" The woman smirked, slowly fixed her big hair with sharp, colorfully-decaled nails, then stingingly whipped back with, "Ya didn't payass. It was inconclusive . . ."

Needless to say, the dialogue exercises didn't work for them. And after three sessions, they left treatment for good. Their prognosis remaining . . . inconclusive.

Which isn't to say they didn't continue to enact their little scene of vicious engulfment and barbed abandonment on anyone who would listen for years of unfulfilled *Valentoymeses* to come. Or that they are even still together. But if they are, they certainly have not moved through their significant wounds without first learning to listen to each other.

Steve and Sonia

The greatest challenge for many couples is to take the emotional risk of really listening and really sharing with one another without a third party to dump on, implicate, argue with, or use for therapy.

My brother Steve and his partner, Sonia, overcame this challenge through trial and error (as opposed to taking my incessant advice). They got super serious, super fast, and within a year of coupledom moved into a house in the burbs—just like Sonia's friends, who had husbands and babies. (Guess which one of them is the Abandoned . . .) When you visited their place, you would play their favorite game, which involved working out all of their couple conflicts in front of you—turning lunch into an episode of *The People's Court* on a good day and *Jerry Springer* on a bad one. To their credit, they eventually made a brave and bold move out of the house and into separate apartments in the nearby city, all while maintaining their relationship. They only recently moved back into a house together after about five years of living apart. During that time, they both did tremendous emotional work: learning to be vulnerable, honest, and empathic in their communication. I can honestly say that it is now a delight to visit their home. And as I write this, I have learned they are engaged!

Of course, a third party is not always a bad thing for couples in conflict; as in the case of Wendy and Peter, therapy is necessary at times. But couples therapy is most effective when used to practice better communication between the couple. When both the Engulfed and the Abandoned are stuck endlessly ranting at the therapist—the third party—something needs to change.

Rapunzel and Prince

I'm thinking now of a young couple I worked with whom I'll call Rapunzel and Prince. After a decade of marriage, they were now considering divorce. Rapunzel reported feeling trapped (engulfed), as though in a tower, wanting Prince to rescue her, but refusing to let him in. While Prince, tired of failed rescue attempts, waited for Rapunzel to join him on the grass below (abandoned), losing faith that she would ever make it down on her own.

Unlike *Valentoymes*, these two had gotten so good at avoiding their own feelings that it was often hard for me to get a sense of their conflict. Sessions would begin with them both calmly, placidly staring at me. Then after ten minutes of light humor, I'd have to dig in with prying questions. Eventually one of them would start complaining to me about the other, looking at me and me alone the whole time. But this never happened without me first pulling some teeth.

As months approached a year of treatment, they were still complaining, while avoiding eye contact with each other and any version of the dialogue exercises—both inside and outside of sessions. When I asked how they felt about one another, they would only say "indifferent." Meanwhile I grew increasingly frustrated with them both, and told them so, explaining that I was modeling how to put feelings (of frustration in this case) into words. I explained that their job now was to tell me to shut up, back off, and begin doing the work with each other. They eventually got there, but not without a push and a lot of practice.

With practice you too will be able to tell third parties to back off. You'll get better and better at recognizing your partner's feelings and at being his/her mirror. Eventually you'll say this sort of thing to her/him on demand: "Yes, I know you need time to verbalize your feelings. I know you expect me to bulldoze over you like your mother does, and that makes you angry," or "Yes, I know you fear I'm not capable of taking care of you, that you'll always have to take care of me, like you take care of your mother."

> *And speaking of mothers, I must say, mothers get such a bad rap in this world, so to clarify, I'm not blaming ours for making us imperfect.*
>
> As I said earlier, we're all imperfect, and we bring that to every relationship. (Besides, if we're to buy into this theory, I should thank my mother for my engulfment, without which I'd have never attached to Justin.) The detective work we do in unraveling "The Case of *The Engulfed* and *The Abandoned*" isn't about "whodunit?" We assume that life does it to all of us and so blame is irrelevant. It's about how it was done, how it has affected each of us, and how we can work with what we've got to be more effective communicators, with partners and also with parents.

The ten-day trip to Italy we took with our mothers was pivotal in this regard.

Justin and I had been together for about six years and wanted to do some traveling. As budget-conscious, early-career Manhattanites, our options were limited. As a super unresolved engulfed/abandoned pair, there were no options . . . without the moms. Both of them were coping with unforeseen golden years of singlehood: my father had died four years earlier, and my mother-in-law Sandy had divorced Justin's father two years before that. The unknown had colonized them—we all go queer or deviate from the norm sooner or later. Their lives were unmapped in mainstream society as Meryl Streep had not yet vindicated their demographic in blockbuster cinema. So as young men with a high level of mom-attunement, we found an opportunity to grant several wishes at once. We booked a budget trip to Rome, Florence, and Venice—a classic "antipasti" tour—with moms in tow.

A little skinny on our moms: in addition to engulfing and abandoning us, they are two of the most loving people ever to grace the planet. They also had striking similarities: though my mom descended from Italian immigrants, and Sandy from New England WASPs, they were born two days apart, married on the same day and year, and gave birth to me and Justin respectively two months apart. (I may have to write another book taking astrology into account.) They were also both psychologists who worked in schools and sported similar, silver, pixie cuts along with big earrings. Their family and friends always depended on each of them for emotional support. Where they veered from total twin-ship was in their own distinct forms of emotional expression, stemming from their different cultural and family histories. Sandy learned to take the emotional back seat, while my Mom tends to drive. I'm sure you can make the links to how these mothers impacted Justin and me respectively.

They were both supportive of our romance, though their overlapping hopes and fears cast a shadow over us—beginning with their first impressions. During our months of phone courtship (after that six-year hiatus I mentioned), Justin and I excitedly showed each other off to our moms using any media at our disposal—this was pre-Facebook. Justin took Sandy to see me in a Farrelly Brothers movie titled *Outside Providence*, in which I had one scene—just one—playing a cruel intentioned prep-school senior who horribly humiliates a freshman. Sandy was enthralled. Meanwhile, I showed my mom an episode of *The Real World: Hawaii* in which Justin intervened to get treatment for an alcohol abusing roommate. My mother was not impressed, "Mark! He kicked Ruthie out of the house. Are you sure you can trust him?"

Despite my Machiavellian character in the film, Sandy idealized me; and despite Justin's altruistic behavior on the show, my Mom feared him. Whereas Sandy hoped I would take care of Justin (perhaps believing he'd then be more equipped to care for her), my Mom dreaded he'd tear me away. All the while, they both truly did want us to be happy. But these things are complicated.

And if you really want complicated, then travel to Italy with your moms for ten days and have them share a room. Not only did I find myself engulfed by two moms as we wandered through the Forum and the Vatican, but I also got to hear from Justin how my Mom left the windows open all night and how his mother nearly froze to death. As we marveled at The David and the Uffizi, Justin got to feel abandoned by two moms and also hear from me how his mom was eating cookies in the middle of the night and how all the crackle and crunch gave my mother migraines.

Back then, we didn't know about Harville Hendrix or attachment roles or mirroring exercises. All we knew was that something needed to change. We began by giving each other space to share how the moms affected us. "I feel invaded when your mom pinches my butt," I told Justin, which he was able to hear without coming to her defense. He in turn said, "I just feel like I'm invisible to your mom because I can't get pregnant," to which I validated and offered empathy. We also decided to try keeping our conflicts between us, thus denying our mothers opportunity to interfere with our "stuff" and forcing each other to take ownership of it.

By the time we got to Venice, we had found a sense of security between us, recognizing the other's unresolved neediness. Venice is a wonderful place to celebrate all things ironic, as its decay and decline coexist with its beauty. It's also very small, yet you can easily get lost amidst all the stairs and tunnels, especially if you're alone—which is why it's always better to do Venice in pairs.

A Venetian-themed wedding might be fun . . .

Mysterious masks on all the guests—to temper the egos a bit— and the two lovers alone unmasking at the altar, finding naked solace in each other, amidst all the colorful chaos.

Had we found such solace earlier in our journey, back at the cafe in Rome, I might have responded to my mom differently. I might have said, "Mom, I hear you saying you want to be part of our wedding. And I'm glad. We'll promise to touch base with you when the time comes. Right now we're just having fun." Then I would have smiled at Justin, touched his shoulder, and changed the subject.

Here's what we did instead.

We chose to stay a few more days in Venice, to enjoy the sinking city sans moms. We focused lots of attention on them during our last morning as a group, reviewing the laughs and the ruins and the sumptuous meals we had all shared. The dawn in San Marco Square was particularly golden as we walked them to the water taxi, sending them off into the shimmery ocean. We waved. For a moment, they looked away, and then turned back. We were gone.

By the end of that year, we were engaged.

Part 2

The Vision

5   All the Wedding's a Stage: Let "Why?" Be Your Guide

"Let's get married next year."

We were visiting the Simon's Rock campus, where we first met. The Berkshire trees and fresh nip of September conjured our private, sixteen-year-old nights. (Lighter memories at last reigned over the dread, doubt, and angst that had originally pervaded that time.) We were taking turns pushing each other on a rope swing hanging from a tree; a staple must-do at the college. I don't remember who said it first or if those were the exact words, but this was where and how we decided. Then one of us asked, "What next?"

If I could go back in time and offer us a bit of counsel—mid-swing—I'd advise us not to get too thrown by each of the bumpy little "what"s, "where"s, and "how"s along the way, and instead to let the "why?" be our guide.

"Why?" is the first question great theater directors ask before working on a play. Why this play? Why now?

> *Weddings are theater, and acknowledging this will focus your planning.*
>
> I know, I know—with these affairs there are sometimes religious components, cultural traditions, and family values to consider. But no matter how you slice and dice it, a wedding is a piece of theater: an entertaining, ritualistic, transformative event.

Consider how legendary director Peter Brook describes theater: "deliberately constructed social gatherings that seek for an invisibility to interpenetrate and animate the ordinary." He says that good theater creates phenomenal moments of recognition between people: "What has been up till then individual experiences become shared, unified." He could just as easily be talking about weddings.

Each of us is driven in our own unique ways to have such an event. Ask yourselves why you want this ritual, this convergence of invisible and visible, of private and public. Ask again and again. The process of asking will lead the way.

It will keep everyone on your side, for one thing. People expect to be entertained and transformed at any performance, and it feels better if they know why they are there. You know what it's like to drop a bundle of cash on a Broadway play only to cringe in the bad stink of perplexity? "Why did he write that? Why was it produced? Why did they invest millions of dollars, and their time? My time? Everybody's time? Why?!" You don't want your wedding to be like that.

Ask yourselves "Why?" ahead of time, as a mantra, and you'll avoid a theatrical stink-bomb, no matter how large or small, extravagant or simple, expensive or affordable your nuptials will be. As my acting teacher Brian used to say, "You can be as big or as small as you want, so long as you're specific."

Keep in mind that great theater is independent of overworked sets, frilly costumes, or pyrotechnics. One of the best productions I've ever seen featured nothing more than Fiona Shaw covered in sand to the neck—just her talking head and a pile of sand, for three hours. Astounding. She had asked herself *why* the story needed to be told, and so delivered it to us with great clarity and immediacy, from the neck up. And you know what? I would have been captivated had it lasted another three hours. Liberate your mind: your wedding can be just the two of you and five friends in an empty room and still be magic—if you are armed with specific intent. If you ask *why*.

Why will also help you decide what to cut, who to cut, and what to say to those who buttinsky their way into your planning. *Why* will be the bones of the occasion, making it easy to narrow down options—of location, for example—as you'll have a clear frame on which all the dressings must fit. Having ours in the Berkshires, for instance, was a no-brainer.

> ***Now's the time to toss around some ideas—fun ideas, outrageous ideas.***
>
> There are no wrong answers. Make room for cheesy childhood fantasies, images that move you, thrill you, even if they include oppressive norms. Just get them all out on the table so you know what you've got to work with. Then together you'll be able to distill all that inspiration down to the foundation of your performance, the *why*.

Why Wedding? Why Now?

As my friend Nando puts it, weddings are "just about status." He says, "She just wanna get the five-story, twin-tower-cake, and show all her friends what she got." And you know, he's got a point. Few can afford a big wedding these days. A 2013 study calls modern marriage a "middle-class luxury," saying a lack of steady employment makes most people too concerned with their own survival "to provide materially and emotionally for others." This understandably makes many wonder if the ones getting hitched are just grandstanding.

But getting married for status is not only done by gratuitous, blingy show-offs. Those in poverty have also caught on to nuptial privileges, even if it is a struggle to fulfill many of the responsibilities that come with it. While working in a community mental health clinic in Manhattan, for example, I had a homeless client who married her girlfriend so they would be "upgraded" to a family shelter. This provided them more safety, privacy, and space than before. So yes, there are a variety of reasons people of all stripes seek the social privilege of marriage.

Although, I suspect that many, if not most, wedding-bound couples are after something more than status, despite appearances—something invisible and hard to define; something more than "Here's what I've got. Take that!"

I believe we have drives that transcend the reductiveness of "happy endings," even though riding into the sunset—*The End*—has been the most popular way to discuss weddings throughout the centuries. I suspect there is a more ineffable and commonly shared drive to marry within many of us. I think we viscerally experience this drive every time we break off from families, and start to form new ones.

For example, critical of the Marital Status Game as he may be, Nando says he does want to get hitched to his boyfriend "for the legal protection," he said at first; in light of their status as a bi-national couple. But as we talked further, he revealed he wants something more than "sitting around a desk signing papers on a random afternoon." He wants a proposal. Not "a rock that anchors your hand to the floor . . . I wouldn't be with a school teacher if that's what I wanted." But there's an inexplicable fantasy he wants to enact, perhaps a security that transcends residency or finances and is deeper than a vapid declaration of "Look! We're soulmate, twin-flames, forever!" An inexplicable *something* he searches for words to describe. The specific words Nando eventually does find will be the lynchpin of his wedding—and perhaps reveal he is more alike than different from the married folk of whom he's sometimes critical.

Many couples I spoke to, especially straight ones, simply thought having a wedding was a way to move forward. To become adults. To segue into a new phase of life together. To be witnessed, validated, and celebrated as a couple. And to garner support as an established nuclear family prepared to raise a child.

Angus and Summer

As it turns out, getting married to raise a kid in a "secure home"— i.e., with two legally bound parents—is seemingly the most popular,

America's Sweetheart answer to the question of *why*. Even if romantic love doesn't share top billing at the event.

For instance, when my older brother, Angus, and sister-in-law, Summer, were married after almost a decade together—and after entering their reception to the tune of the *Mission Impossible* theme—their officiant explained their choice to marry by saying, "Angus wanted to start a family." (As a testament to their ceremonial intent, Angus and Summer are terrific parents to two radiant girls.)

My mind cracked wide open on this topic a few years ago during dinner at the home of an opposite-sex married couple we know. My seat at the table was directly facing two enormous *Warholian* portraits of our hosts' two tween girls. Late in the evening, we were engaging in meaningless chatter, contemplating whether the actor/choreographer Joel Gray might be gay. (It was really late) I pondered, "Hmm, he *does* have a daughter . . ." (As I said, it was really, really late.) The husband, a former figure skater—just giving you the facts—replied coolly, intently, with a flicker of raised-eyebrow and a breathy, effeminate tone, "That's neither here nor there." Then he stared at me. The *Warholian* portraits also stared over his shoulder, all of their eyes boring into my skull. A quick chill down the spine and I stood corrected, informed, and improved:

Everyone's deal is unique.

No judgments here. It's all good.

> The reasons we get all connubial with each other are personal, various, and distinct—though some are more on-trend than others. You'll save a ton of stress, confusion, arguments, embarrassment, and grief if you know exactly what yours are before making any plans.

Marriage as Preservation of Self and Community

My friend Yasmine says she originally chose to be married mostly for the sake of her future kid. But she discovered that having the palpable love and safety she's cultivated with her husband David mirrored back to them by family at her ceremony was deeply meaningful to her. Yasmine is motivated by her faith in Judaism and finds it particularly important to be married; to create a family for the survival of the Jewish people. As we discussed this drive for survival, she referenced the Holocaust.

Given Yasmine's *why* for getting married, it would seem there is much more in common between marital goals of traditional Jews and those who are LGB or T than many often think. There's the shared history of course: those considered to be homosexual were also prisoners in Nazi Germany; the "Pink Triangles" and the "Stars of David" suffered in the camps together. I'm always stung when this historical trauma, this link between us, is disavowed. For example, during the High Holidays, I'm often approached on the streets of Brooklyn by several Orthodox men of all ages, asking, "My friend, my friend. Are you Jewish?" Whenever I say, "No, but I'm gay. Are you gay?"—which is every time—the response is one of disgust. (Even one time in Chelsea, the heart of NYC gay life, of all places.) They respond as though my intention is to insult—which is insulting to *me*—as opposed to my real intention to provoke laughter, to provoke thinking, and make a bid for kindred connection using their very method.

Unlike traditional Jewish families, same-sex parents, of course, don't necessarily have children of the same tribe or minority status. But all of us have identities and loves we want to protect, to be recognized, and to survive. Women and men who don't have their own children are connected to nieces, nephews, students, patients, and various other lives they help to grow. And those little ones in turn hold them in mind, carrying on their dignity.

Like Jamie McGonnigal, for example, a voice actor on *Pokémon*. It was important to him that his young fans know that he married his husband, Sean. He wanted them to see "[t]hat you're just as likely to have that happy ending when you're gay. Growing up in a different time, no one told me that—and I assumed I'd live a life devoid of real love and certainly marriage." McGonnigal emphasizes the importance of letting all young people know that their lives are filled with possibility. He also provides a great example of how those of us outside of "normal," traditional, procreative, heterosexual marriages contribute greatly to young lives.

(Harvard professor Niall Ferguson's odious comments about "gays and childless people" who "don't care about future generations" is an unfortunate, ignorant, yet all too commonly perpetuated fallacy.)

We can all agree that a wedding symbolizes the birth of a family unit, whatever form that may take. The word *family* means a lot of things; not only raising one's own children.

Lesbians, Jews, gays, Native Americans, persons of transgender, African Americans, Chinese Americans, Mexican Americans, and many others have a shared queer history of abjection and genocide—even in our own country—as well as a history of identity we do not want to be forgotten. And all of us—including white, straight couples—are more alike in wanting marriage than we are different, even though our identity labels can be deceiving. And on that note, I'd like you to know that Yasmine's husband identifies as "queer."

Now for my own big Wedding Why: I just wanted my story to be known and easily understood. Nothing more, nothing less.

Yes, there were, of course, all the legal things—the documents and protections. But that part didn't really matter, since our marriage was not legal in our home state of New York at the time or in Massachusetts where we were wed. (The Massachusetts governor at the time, Mitt Romney, had unhelpfully resurfaced an antiquated law banning out of state marriages.)

> *I was naive about all the legality then. You should try your best not to be.*
>
> Boring as it may seem now, it packs a theatrical punch down the road when you're denied a hospital visit for your partner of thirty years, or abruptly torn from your home of thirty years after your partner dies, or—adding insult to injury—your partner's family, whom you've been very close with for thirty years, suddenly claims assets that have been in your possession for most of your life. And just when you think "My family would never do that," try to remember the infectiously persuasive power of norms, to which even the best intentioned of us fall prey.

After we were married, every time my mother introduced Justin to people with, "This is Mark's . . . um . . . partner?" we had words. By contrast, every time she sent cards to my brother's home addressed to "Angus and Summer O'Connell" *before* they were married . . . I asked questions. These things may seem small, and her actions weren't the real problem. Where these actions were born in the mind is what bothered me. In her mind, norms ruled with the force of a relentless emperor. Her mind automatically organizes itself with a normative template. It looked to normative "rules" instead of the truth of the relationship at a desperate moment. All of our minds are susceptible to that sleepy bodysnatching spell of norms, which is why we must wriggle ourselves awake and demand recognition. To my mother's credit, she has allowed her mind to be influenced by my self-advocacy and now refers to Justin as my husband.

Legal protections are still a crucial consideration to the *why* of your wedding, though the striking down of the Defense of Marriage Act in 2013 has certainly awakened many people to the notion of marriage recognition. Legal protections and social introductions for same-sex spouses, and perhaps spouses in general, have since become less com-plicated. And a story less complicated was really all I hoped to achieve when we decided to get married.

I wished for my invisible truth to be made visible. Not just the words that would be used, but also the silent symbolism of our lives together. Not just the story told on that one day in that one moment, but one that would move with me and with us through major life events. Rituals of social and theatrical quality sometimes have this power. Peter Brook describes the effect of such an event:

"For a moment, a life of a completely different nature was tasted . . . And the transformation and the taste—and the confidence—it gave could take place again and again whenever the audience came together in the special circumstances of a performance."

Such a performance took place unforgettably at my father's funeral in 2001. When I stood with my mother and three brothers in the spot-light, I could feel the audience of familiar faces witness the truth of the moment. A truth that was larger than the sum of every individual in the church—the theater—and larger than the text in the paper that read, "Stephen O'Connell has died. He leaves behind a wife and three adult children." Something silent, undeniable, and indelible happened. This was how I wanted the story of Justin and me to be experienced, known, and remembered.

I wanted the love that dare not speak its name to emerge from the shadows and shout its name in the brightest white light.

As we wandered the fresh grass of the Simon's Rock campus—having decided to marry—we found the rock where he first shared his teenage attraction to me and where I had rejected him coldly—with adolescent nasality and a self-loathing lack of eye contact. There are few things better in life than having another go at something big. We assumed the same positions. This time I looked at him and, mirroring back his bold line to me from years ago, said, "I guess I'm attracted to you too."

6 Make Your World the Real World: Dreams, Creativity, and the Virtues of Being Wrong

"The things I draw come true."

That's from the theme song of my favorite childhood TV show, *Simon in the Land of Chalk Drawings*. (You may know it better from Mike Myers's classic parody on SNL: "I like to do drawrings.") It was about this boy who created his own world with a piece of chalk. And I *loved* it. It helped me plan my wedding, and it can help you plan yours.

> ### Remember
>
> Your dreams and your creativity will solve most of your wedding problems and help you find your truth along the way.

Like Simon, when I was five years old, I tried to create my own world with a piece of chalk. Yellow chalk. I was trying to draw the yellow brick road on my block in the small village of Millerton, New York. You know, so I could be Dorothy and skip off to see the Wizard. I think I only got through about twelve bricks, but hey, I tried. I did better with my wedding and did manage to make my dream to rejoin with Justin a reality.

I've learned to see the limitations in my life as advantages. Had I actually grown up on a yellow brick road, for example, it might have been fun for a few minutes, but I'd probably lose interest. Without the need to create the yellow bricks, I'd lack that feverish impulse to churn fantasies into realities with my little piece of chalk. The need to create keeps us engaged, alive, and makes the world—newly changed by our impact—far more fun and rewarding to live in than before.

So, I hate to say this, but if you're Barbie and Ken, with perfect families, a huge budget at your disposal, and a top event planner spouting on about standard etiquette and what's "on trend," your *project wedding* is gonna be a snooze fest. I'll wager a guess that's not the case for you, dear reader.

> **Take an inventory of your personal wedding limitations.**
> **Within them, you'll find creative liberation.**

Early in our planning, several people asked questions along the lines of "What do same-sex couples do for . . . *blah, blah, blah?*" Some of the men on Fire Island I mentioned earlier might have concrete answers to such questions. But for me, the beauty was that there were no standards, traditions, or rule books for us. It was just us, and our creative minds. Your minds will be your greatest assets as well.

People dish out similar advice in a variety of ways. There's the familiar quote from the 1989 film *Field of Dreams,* "If you build it, they will come." And the self-helpy, cultish programs that tell you to paste an image over your bed so it will come true. And, of course, all the meditation gurus tell you to put an "intention" out into the world. I guess I'm saying something similar. . . .

It's all you.

The point is that most of what you'll need will really come from within you.

Which is to say you don't have to *do* too much at this point. Defer the *doing.* For now, just *be.*

And take notice.

What lights up your eyes? What gives you goosebumps? Your inspiration is there already, floating around your mind. And all those impressions—even the weird ones, especially the weird ones—will inform you. What colors, songs, memories, or indulgent fantasies of the future are calling you? (If you got nothing, you can always check back in with your *why.*) This is a time for creative gestation. Just imagine how much better those *Project Runway* designers would be if they were allowed a whole month of sketching and pondering fabrics at Mood before even touching a sewing machine.

Being versus Doing

Listen to yourself. This was a revelation to me while training to be an actor. After years and years of acting for survival in my rural high school—doing my best to pretend I wasn't an effeminate male who liked boys—I learned about the *doing* of acting. And knowing how to *do* can be extremely useful if you're warding off bullies as a teen, playing Shakespeare in an NYC parking lot as an adult, or receiving guests at a wedding or funeral at any age. (I've done all that.) But we can easily over*do* to the point of being inauthentic.

As an actor, I realized that my closeted youth had taught me to overact my way through life. To *do* way too hard. Too much *doing* makes a lot of noise, but shuts down the real fireworks. There's so much juicy potential between actors and real people when *doing* is removed—when our instincts and desires are allowed to *be*; to emerge and flow. When I think of my attraction to other men, there's life in my life and in my art. Far more life than my lamely attempted—belabored—high school performances as a "dude" who wanted to bang "chicks." (And, ironically, I was able to play the roles of straight lovers—such as Romeo, not in a parking lot—much more truthfully and effectively when in touch with my natural desires.) The well of your own dreams and desires is bountiful and at your disposal when you get out of your own way. Don't *do, be*. Don't *act, reveal*.

To *reveal* means to follow the flow of your desire, your instincts—a great practice for dancing, singing, speaking, and myriad public expressions you're bound to engage in on your nuptial day. But hopefully that's a ways off. For now, all you have to reveal is your vision, your dream of how it could be.

I always find the following acting exercise helpful—in concept—when getting in touch with instincts, desire, and vision.

Try This

Simply stand alone in front of an audience—real or imagined—even if it's just your cat. Absorb the eyes of your scrutinizers. Notice how you feel. Follow your impulse to move, however you will. Do whatever feels truthful, however odd it may be. Now tell them a story—the story of your wedding perhaps—in whatever way, and at whatever pace feels right.

I described the concept of this exercise to a gay client who wanted to come out to his family but was unsure how to go about it. His immediate response was, "I'd be no good at that exercise since I have no talent." I explained that talent wasn't the point. The point was that, without any expectations, each participant finds her unique way to make her story known—her truth—in her most impassioned, alive, authentic way. . . .

You needn't be afraid at this stage in your planning. This is a time for play, without consequences.

Yasmine and David

Yasmine and her husband David, for example, played with the image of the chuppah, which led them to a personal, meaningful, and innovative wedding. The chuppah is the canopy under which spouses are traditionally married in a Jewish wedding, symbolizing their new home together. Yasmine and David made their home their chuppah, and their chuppah their home—by which I mean the cozy-one bedroom Upper West Side apartment they share. Their visions of family beaming at them in their nest were literally brought to fruition. All of the plates, silverware, and decor purchased for the nuptials became furnishings for their apartment. Not only did they consolidate spending, but they followed their imaginations to an event of great personal significance, which enlivens their every day—e.g., whenever they put fresh flowers in a vase or just use a fork.

★   ★   ★

From the moment our *project wedding* commenced, images of the Simon's Rock campus in the fall danced in our heads. This was where and when we first met, but it also held specific meaning for Justin. Since he grew up in Texas, his memory of the east coast fall leaves welcomed him to college, symbolizing new life, even as they died. We imagined a ceremony at the campus chapel where he used to practice the piano. We imagined Philip Glass (his music, not necessarily him, though that would have been cool, too). Warm, familiar faces freely wandering the campus at night, exploring the maze of shrubs, touring our old haunts. Everyone mingling, double-easy. Perhaps it would be a Day of the Dead wedding? Skeletons and flowers? Ghosts? Leaves of red, yellow, and orange, floating through the air. At the end, everyone easily finds their way back to the historic Red Lion Inn . . . in Stockbridge . . . which was a whole town away . . . uh oh.

Vinyl record scratches to a halt.

How would they get there? What's more, since it is an early college for younger students, we wouldn't be able to serve alcohol on the campus . . .

Here's the thing: reality will always take your dreams hostage, blocking your way, saying "Nope. You can't have that"—with arms folded tightly, head shaking, and mouth contorted as if its only goal is to piss you off. At that point, you'll have to negotiate with the old troll utilizing your creativity, what I call:

> ### Dream Hostage Negotiation (DHN)
>
> When reality kidnaps your dream—say to draw the yellow brick road with a piece of chalk—the trick is to not retreat or to have a tantrum, but instead to feel the blow of disappointment, and then adapt. To keep drawing yellow bricks on the pavement, if you will—perhaps in a new direction—until the world, transformed by your impact, has enough room for you to be in it. Your new road may not lead all the way to Oz, but it can take you to a place where dreams and reality can coexist.

Since you can count on reality to abduct your dreams at some point, you might as well maximize your dreaming potential before that happens. If you follow your desire all the way through, you'll find that it sometimes beats reality at its own game. And more often, through the process of DHN, you're likely to arrive at a completely yet deliciously unforeseen outcome.

Go ahead and risk missing the mark. You may end up hitting one better.

Take our very status as legal spouses for example. We were undeterred by the fact that our marriage would not be legally recognized—anywhere—due to the law in New York and Massachusetts in 2006. We. Were. Having. A. Wedding. All of our announcing, gathering of ideas, and stating of preferences stemmed from that place in our minds. So much conviction had we, that when we tried to announce it in the *New York Times*, we were met with the harsh rebuffing hand of "reality," which would only allow us to announce a "commitment ceremony" or such. And we declined. Now, just a few years later, our marriage is recognized to the fullest extent of the law. So you see, *facts* are not quite as important as your dreams—and your negotiating power to rescue them.

Make Room to Be Wrong

Unlike Joan of Arc, your vision isn't going to risk hundreds of lives if you follow it. Even if it doesn't entirely work. Even if you turn out to be wrong. Here's what acclaimed author Anne Lammot says about folks who let themselves be wrong: "[they] are going to do a whole lot better than you, and have a lot more fun while they're doing it." Being wrong opens the door to unforeseen possibilities.

Being wrong is the reason my husband and I are together in the first place. In 1999, when my younger brother, Mike, told me there was a cast member on *The Real World* who had gone to Simon's Rock, who was "really smart, funny, and gay," I got excited. You see, I had already put an "intention," into the universe—to reunite with Justin—months before. I had been watching Tom Stoppard's award-winning play *The Invention of Love* in London with my scholarly friend Dinah. I slept through most of it—Dinah never lets me forget—but awoke for a pivotal scene. The protagonist, a university student at this point in the play, expresses romantic love for his male best friend, and he's rejected. The language is penetrating. And it colonized my dreams. One year later, I performed the very scene at my acting MFA recital, with Justin in the audience—by then my boyfriend—hearing me say the line, "You're half my life."

It was indeed Justin on *The Real World*, of course. I hadn't watched the show since the 1992 season with AIDS activist Pedro Zamora—a standard of television the producers have yet to even approximate again. Justin's season in Hawaii was the first to get all naked-co-ed-hot-tub-party, which is all that remains of the franchise these days. (It should now be called *The Real Drunk Hot Tubbers of* [insert city].)

There was some movement in Hawaii in 1999 toward marriage equal-ity, which never worked out, but Justin tried to use the show to share these efforts. He helped organize a rally that was filmed, but never made the final cut for TV—never seen, recognized, or appreciated by American youth. Another dream taken hostage. I guess all those drunk naked hot tub scenes were more important; or at least, more "*real*."

Nevertheless, I watched his season, faithfully, every week. . . . He was much cooler, self-assured, and stylish than I remembered. But it was the whip-smart campy humor, and even more so the melancholic, no one-understands-me sort of vibe, that pulled me to him. I mean, to the television.

We *were* the two characters from the Stoppard play, he and I. But in a way, we were also both the protagonist—both having lived through palpable but often silent abjection—which made my desire to connect to him that much deeper. It's strangely erotic to see your vulnerability mirrored in someone else, especially as you recognize their unique strengths in the very same moment.

During one episode, a TV roommate asked, "Justin, why don't you talk to us more?" To which he replied, "Remember that school I went to, when I was sixteen? Well, there was this guy . . . His parents took him out of school . . ."

The women I was watching with erupted in shrieks and screams, and I joined them. At the end of the episode, I asked my girlfriends for advice, as it was clear to me that I was the guy Justin had referenced. "You should write him a letter," my friend Joy said.

And so I did.

He called me late one night. I was alone, watching him and his room-mates travel through India. Both on the phone and the TV, his voice was in two places at once. We were in two places at once; the world of twen-ty-two and the world of sixteen. We talked all night. And every night there after. I was so exhausted one morning after a late night gabfest, that I slept through a professional performance of *A Christmas Carol* in which I was playing both nephew Fred and a dancing gingerbread man. Totally missed the damn thing. I was clumsy, missing the mark every step of the way—in that play and that part of my life—but my desire led me to a gratifying life with Justin. As opposed to one as a dancing gingerbread man—which is a fine and righteous pursuit for somebody, somewhere, but clearly not for me. I shifted my life's narrative by *being*, more so than *doing*, but also by risking being wrong as I made a bid for my reality.

When our dreams lose the arm wrestle with reality we need to kick our Dream Hostage Negotiation into gear. And that means utilizing our creativity.

For instance, when we realized getting wed wouldn't work out on the Simon's Rock campus—no alcohol?—we made calls in that area. Any venue in the Berkshires that was worth all the fuss cost a pretty penny, and make that ten pretty pennies for foliage season. (Fortunately, years later, we were lucky enough to attend a "perfect" Stockbridge wedding taking place at both the Norman Rockwell Museum and the historic Chesterwood estate—just the sort of Berkshire wedding we couldn't afford ourselves.) So we got creative. We found a lovely little bed and breakfast with four decadent bedrooms, a Jane Austen–like sitting room—with piano and fireplace—and a banquet hall. We could have the entire thing there. The estate was surrounded by trees—bursting with color in October—and a river. Guests could explore the grounds, double-easy—like in our vision—and the Red Lion Inn was only a stone's throw away. No shuttle bus necessary. Also, the owners were new, they had never done a wedding before, and—most importantly—they didn't know what to charge. (I think now they have a better idea.)

Not exactly the Simon's Rock wedding in the clouds, but a close alternative that could exist in reality, one we never would have landed had we not allowed our imaginations to take flight. We went off the beaten path and found a location that was affordable, had the vibe we wanted, and exceeded our expectations. We booked for the following October and didn't look back.

★ ★ ★

Speaking of looking back, I haven't yet described the day I told Justin why I wrote him that pivotal letter that got us back in touch . . .

It was a sunny afternoon in Boston Common, about six months into our relationship. We were sitting on a bench. Justin turned around to look at something behind us. He pointed and said, "Doesn't that look like Ellen Degeneres?" I was incredulous; you see, Justin was going through this phase where he'd "spot" iconic lesbians with regularity. (I mean, he had seen Martina Navratilova only the week before, in a deli . . . in Providence . . . and Melissa Etheridge the week before that on a Bonanza bus.)

But this time he was right. It *was* Ellen! She was playing frisbee with Anne Heche and a film crew on the lawn behind us. They were as validating a famous queer couple as we had in 1999, or more crucially, that's what I dreamed them to be. (That was before we learned Anne was part alien.) What a perfect moment to discuss the trigger of our own romance.

I said something like, "Remember when you were, like . . . talking about me on TV?" *Pause.* "You know. About how you came on to me and how I left school . . ." *Double Pause.*

He replied, "I wasn't talking about you."

Oof. Narcissism interrupted.

My friend Joy—the one who told me to write the letter—puts it best. Joy officiated our wedding and during the ceremony she told our creation story. She explained that Justin was not talking about me on the show.

And also that he was.

7 Spotlights behind the Curtain: Queer Tips from Traditional Relatives

"Are you gonna wear a duct tape bridal gown?" I queried Justin's cousin Emily.

I'll have you know that Emily's mom, Aunt Corky, is the first to ever make a dress entirely out of duct tape! She designed it for Emily's prom back in the nineties. Emily's picture showed up in big magazines—like *Maxim*—and the trend went viral. The duct tape dress has become a phenomenon, a thing. It's now an ongoing contest and was even a design challenge on *Project Runway* in 2012. But to this day, Corky has taken no formal credit; they're private people. Which is why I asked provokingly about Emily's wedding attire—she was very-long engaged to her fiancé, but with no nuptials in sight. I wanted everyone involved to have the attention I felt they deserved. I wanted their queer truth—which had been obscured by normalcy/ "privacy"—to make the headlines.

> *You see, wherever there's queerness, there's truth. Wherever there's queerness, there's need.*

Many if not most of our modern weddings—be they gay, straight, or what have you—are *queer*, meaning they resist category or definition. I guarantee you are currently after such a nuptial yourself, one in which your truth outweighs tradition. That which is queer about you *needs* to deviate from the norm to exist, to live, to breathe—the way Emily needed a duct tape dress to feel like herself at prom.

Lyn and Jorge

My friend Lyn's wedding is a great example of queer = truth = need. Lyn was raised Jewish and only dated Jewish guys until she met Jorge—a non-practicing Catholic of Salvadoran descent. So, not Jewish. Conservative (and brittle) in his Judaism, Lyn's brother adamantly shared with Lyn prior to her wedding his strong belief that she should be married within the faith. To avoid further conflict, Lyn did not mention that a female rabbi would perform their ceremony, not wanting to hear more criticism. Her brother initially refused to attend. Meanwhile, Lyn's father—a natural born Jew cum Catholic deacon—had ruffled feathers that Jorge wasn't *more* Catholic. Her dad was also careful not to get too close to their chuppah during the service.

Lyn was aggrieved by all of this, for a time. Every choice she made induced holy wars. But when she became too tired to care, she reminded herself why she wanted a wedding in the first place. She loves Jorge. She wants to spend the rest of her life with him. And she wanted to celebrate that with the most important people in her life. Provokingly queer as her wedding seemed to some, that was not Lyn's intention. Her lovely wedding was simply the outcome of her truth and her need leading the way. And though it has taken time, her brother is now able to look at wedding photos and discuss the possibility of Lyn and Jorge having children together.

Your Reveal

So don't worry about being provocative as long as you're being you. The *Batman and Robin* wedding, or the *Black Swan, Steam Punk, Alien vs. Predator*, or *Star Wars* wedding—complete with processional to the Darth Vader March—can certainly all work, but only if the concept reveals you. *Not* if it shrouds you in extraneous camp. It can be tricky to tell the difference, especially when the normative police surround us in the form of our family and friends, and especially when the normative police are also us.

The Normative Police

The siren of the normative police goes off in a number of ways—Lyn's brother's crude approach, of course, but also by modes more subtle. My mother fearing we'd have an *Elton John Wedding* or people asking things like "You're *not* covering your tattoos?" or "You don't need to kiss at the altar, right? Since you're two guys?" Friends calling you *Bridezilla or Groomzilla* just because you want a shimmery dress or suit that makes you feel like a star. Family saying you're "too much," just because you're actually excited to get married or because you actually want to be seen in this light. It's so easy to be discouraged at these times, to closet your excitement and/or to wilt in shame.

> *Take some time to reflect on messages that restrain you from basking in the spotlight—especially when you're the one policing yourself.*
>
> Look long and hard at the ways you dream of showing off. Do these images give you chills? If so, maybe that's because the idea of celebrating everything you love in front of the people you love thrills you. Even if your choice of presentation seems provocative to some, provocation might not be your end goal. Even if you choose to tear down the walls of tradition—the way Lyn did in marrying a non-Jew and having a female rabbi—perhaps you've done this to create space for your truth to exist. Not merely to "make a scene."
>
> Moreover, maybe your traditional-seeming relatives have more queer wisdom to offer you than initially meets the eye.

For example, I once mistook Aunt Corky for being the normative police during a visit with her and her husband, Uncle John, shortly after our wedding. Corky didn't like one of the toasts at our reception, and she wanted us to know it. "I just didn't think it was necessary," she said, referring to the "political" toast given by our dear friend Sharon. Sharon's an intensely gregarious, fiercely articulate force—we sometimes call her *Hurricane Sharon*. She was kicking butt as an attorney for the ACLU LGBT project at the time of our nuptials, and with the fault lines of marriage shifting—legally and socially—we could think of no one better for the keepin'-it-real, advocacy portion of our illegal wedding than her. But Corky did not agree. "We were obviously all there to support you. Why did anyone need to go there?"

Her comments made me bristle at the time, but I short-sightedly, and innacurately, chalked them up to her being traditional.

Justin's mother, Sandy, had perhaps colored my view, suggesting that John (her brother) was considered to be "normal" by their WASPy parents, while Sandy felt like the black sheep. John and Corky had a healthy long marriage, a beautiful New England farmhouse—with a picket-fence—and two lovely daughters. While Sandy—though she had two lovely sons—was divorced and extremely unconventional in humor, in style, and in general. But this is just one perspective.

Look out for biased family narratives. They can create unnecessary obstacles between you and some of your relatives.

Sure, from the helicopter view, John and Corky may resemble the normal family from *Leave it to Beaver*, but if you zoom in on the lizard tattoo on Corky's ear, you'll see a fabulous queerness wiggling its way out. In fact, if you go to their house—which resembles a gorgeous, New England bed and breakfast—you may notice a magical light escaping from a door upstairs. That's Corky's craft room. Inside, you'll find hand-painted toys, chairs, clocks—and the occasional duct tape dress—all in her signature quirky style.

You know how Tim Burton has that iconic, other-worldly, black-and-white-striped, mystical, gothic aesthetic? Corky's is as distinct.

She once made Justin a chair painted with delicious candy colors and Miro-like shapes that seem to dance. She also sends us an inventive hand-made Christmas ornament every year: once, unforgettably, we received stuffed elves with our own faces silk-screened on, which we call our voodoo dolls. She is truly the most original, talented, and queer crafts person I have ever known.

But her preference is to remain unknown. Closeted, if you will. And I must learn to respect that. (At some point. Clearly I'm not there yet, as I'm obviously writing about her.) But this is just to say that even our very private, seemingly traditional relatives are not necessarily North Korean dictators. Their end goal may not be to shut us down. In fact, like Corky, they may have an abundance of creative queerness tucked away that can be of great use to us, if we know where to look.

Corky and John

As it turns out, Corky and John had a queer wedding of their own. (It was Black Sheep Sandy who had the big normal to-do on a fancy New Hampshire harbor. Remember what I said about weddings and irony, in chapter 1?) John and Corky, on the other hand, eloped. They were living in Kansas at the time, far from their families, and they just did it. Just them, some friends, and John's dog, Josh. Their terms. John gave Corky a Donald Duck ring at the time: a gesture that revealed their humor and queer sense of this ritual as a performance. They've had a variety of wedding rings over the years—ivory, jade, platinum—but John recently had the original ring reworked to commemorate their queer wedding: Donald now clutches a diamond.

And their queerness even went nuclear—as in family. As I write this, we have received an after-the-fact-announcement of cousin Emily's intimate, under-the-radar wedding. No duct tape dress, sadly. But true to herself, Emily went for bridal queer comfort: white tank top, denim shorts, and flip flops.

> ***Start lining up the usual traditionalists in your family and interrogate them.***
>
> You can weed through any normative suggestions you don't like, but meanwhile you might find inspiration in unexpected places.

For example, take my Aunt Rita, who upon getting hitched in the seventies, dove straight into the deep-end of suburban Long Island (literally, she was a swimming instructor). She was in her early twenties and this was her ticket out of the Bronx. As long as I've known her, she's been beautifully, blindingly blonde, brandishing nails with which you could cut a steak, and "tawking" like a Real Housewife of "Lawn Guyland." The glass slipper of suburban normal seemed to fit Rita's foot—until she got a divorce and suburbia became "Dawgville." And Cinderella of Lawn Guyland was viciously turned back into Rita from the Block.

The normal-polish wiped away, I can now see Rita freshly, wonderfully, queer. I imagine how she might have been prior to her traditional marriage. When she was a student at FIT and designed her own outfit for my parents' wedding in 1971, for instance. Wild hot pink hot-pants! (She has since corrected me: said hot-pants were actually, "salmon"). Not exactly what a status-conscious Long Island housewife would choose for a wedding. Totally queer. Who'd have thunk?

Had I asked Rita for a direct bit of conjugal advice, such as "Should our Moms give us away?" she might have wrinkled her nose disapprovingly—normatively, lazily—not having seen such a thing on "Lawn Guyland." But the trick would be to ask about the hot-pants. There, I'd find Rita's light, one that might have assisted our search for connubial truth.

As it turns out, Lyn's brother—the rabidly conservative Jew—also has a secret history of queerness—including wild nights in New

Orleans, and even a cross-dressing stint for Halloween, dressing as a campy, female nurse. Lyn has a picture. If only she could have accessed that version of him when planning her wedding.

We learn to better cope with the normative police in our lives, and to glean inspiration from them, when we understand where their regulating comments come from. They are not necessarily trying to be arbiters of tradition, nor do they necessarily have a phobia about people like you. What they may have is ambivalence about inhabiting the spotlight themselves.

Spotlight Ambivalence

Spotlight Ambivalence is mixed feelings about exposing one's creative truth when it challenges the norm. It causes folks to be reactive, and sometimes object when you take center stage.

But like Corky, Rita, and Lyn's brother, they may also be harboring a fabulous duct tape gown, hot "salmon" hot-pants, or a campy nurse's outfit behind the curtain. If we listen with an open mind, we might locate their queer truths, and become emboldened to showcase our own expressions of self.

I wish I understood Spotlight Ambivalence better when my Mom declared her fear of an Elton John Wedding. Or even way before that, when I was five. On the one hand, she let me be a witch for Halloween and got me a Miss Piggy puppet for Christmas. On the other, she was frequently uncomfortable—subtly, but with impact—when I drew attention to myself in gender non-conforming ways, e.g., "Do guys pluck their eyebrows?" and "Your S's are getting a little sibilant."

It's actually not uncommon for women and gay or gender non-conforming men to have mothers who exhibit this form of Spotlight Ambivalence. Our society tends to police or punish (or exploit) all things feminine. This places an unfair burden on many of us to shroud our desires for attention, for fear of earning the labels *flamboyant, drama queen, flaming, attention whore,* etc. Many of our mothers try to protect us from the harsh slap of society's hand by sending us messages—subtly or directly—to "tone it down." ("Do you really need that frilly dress?" "Don't be such a princess.") Yet many of the mothers like mine may have a closeted with of their own—albeit an ambivalent one—for us and for them to both dance in the spotlight.

For example, my mother's wish for me to have Miss Piggy to play with backstage co-existed with her fear of the cruelty that would be hurled at me if caught playing with Miss Piggy center stage. I get now that she wasn't inherently homophobic or especially effemiphobic. She was attention-phobic; afraid of attention that came from straying from the safety of the norm.

Of course when straight, white, masculine, men assume the spotlight—as they regularly do in ways that we expect: power, aggression, etc.—we often don't even notice. (My three brothers were spared much of my mother's subtle, normative regulation.) We don't perceive them to be asking for special attention since we've allowed them to dominate the spotlight from the start.

I understand now that whenever Mom complained about Serena Williams's short shorts or Angelina Jolie's . . . well, everything about Angelina Jolie, or my adolescent sibilant "S" (pre-drama school, mind you), it was her Spotlight Ambivalence talking. When she criticized her sister, my Aunt Connie, not just for her multiple marriages, but also for playing the sexy leading roles in *Chicago, Cabaret, Hello Dolly, Sweet Charity, Funny Girl, Gypsy* and countless others—lest we forget, she was hexed by Liz Taylor—it was Mom's Spotlight Ambivalence at play.

I wish Spotlight Ambivalence did not have so strong a hold on my mom; for her sake and for mine. I remember her rendition of "Dream a Little Dream" far surpassing the one bywMama Cass. She'd sing that when she put me to bed at night. But again, queerness comes out of need, and at those times, she needed to put me to sleep. As a tribute to this, she and I danced to that very song, in the spotlight, at my wedding.

> **The greatest Spotlight Ambivalence to wrestle with, though, is your own.**
>
> It can so easily be triggered and shut down your desire for due recognition at lightning speed.

A trigger word of mine, for example, is *indecent*. Our friend Lyle often uses it when people take the spotlight—which he perceives to be gratuitous behavior. He becomes a virulent, shrill character when he says it: "That's indecent!" One day, after becoming frustrated at one of Lyle's outbursts, I drew a cartoon of this character: a stuck-up, Victorian little girl with pink taffeta hoop-skirt and Shirley Temple curls pulled tight. I call her Lil' Priss. This image helps me laugh him off.

But at the same time, I've learned to realize it's likely his decorous, Southern-born mama crying *indecency* through him—as generations of Lil' Prisses cried through her. (Just as my reactive, rebellious, outspoken, Italian mother is writing through me now—we are in many ways who we came from.) And to be fair, Lyle has worked to negotiate his identity as a gay man with his conservative roots—e.g., he now bravely directs his indictments of *indecency* at perpetrators of homophobia. I try to keep that in mind whenever he rains on my parades. But I also hold out hope for Lil' Priss to one day let down her hair, shake it out, loosen that corset, and be the center of her own queer parade—just as you should willfully take the spotlight at your wedding.

> **As we've already established, it's a performance after all, like it or not. One in which the two of you are the center. If you're going through with it, you've got to want to be there. And if you don't, find a way.**

Consider what movie star Nicole Kidman says about acting: "I do whatever it takes to get to the place." Only . . . think of her saying that in her Aussie accent, it's way more fun. Use the time you have to get to the place. You'll want to find a way to feel good about being in that spotlight. Again, you can be as big or small as you want, so long as your intention is specific. And you want to be there! The only real crime in walking the aisle sporting a Lady Gaga meat-dress, for example, is conveying that you'd rather not be noticed.

And why shouldn't you be noticed? Traditional couples have taken this spotlight for centuries, and they avoid derision because they are expected to take it. Is it really so shameful to ask for the same attention? Just because your love story may not be the most popular ever told? The worst that could happen is you have extraordinary fun, while someone else does not. As actress Uta Hagen once said, "We must overcome the notion that we must be regular. It robs you of the chance to be extraordinary and leads you to the mediocre." There's no shame in asking to be viewed as extraordinary, especially when you've got passion to share.

Yes, you may have to hear a little something from Lyn's brother, my Mom, Corky, Rita, or Lyle, but you'll be able to put all that in context. Just offer a gracious smile—one that says, "Oh, let's not play that game." Toast to everyone's queerness—inside or out. And sip some champagne.

But we must also allow folks to celebrate their queer truths on their own terms, with or without an audience. Despite my wish to drag Aunt Corky into the spotlight—so the universe will praise her for inventing the duct tape dress!—it is hers to use however she likes. (Pardon my hypocrisy as I spotlight her here. We're all works in progress). Try to keep your focus on doing whatever's best for *you* and your event.

★　★　★

Justin and I decided to enter the spotlight from the beginning by creating a wedding brand image. This symbolized our quirky flavor as a pair. We used it on everything from save the dates to programs and place settings. After laughing, bickering, sketching, and some red wine, we constructed a queered up version of the American gothic painting with two male farmers: us.

Some of the normative police in our lives warned us not to use it, suggesting it was too silly (too queer?). But to us it felt right. We had just seen and were moved by *Brokeback Mountain*, which contained the most honest sexual love between men ever before seen on mainstream screens—ironically, two American cowboys. We were inspired to play with classic male iconography. The image was earnest, high-concept, and playful. Like us. And, for the record, we did this before The Advocate's 2008 *American Gaythic* cover, with a similar image of Ellen and Portia.

Years later, though, it occurred to me that our inspiration may have derived from a less expected source. While looking through old family photos, we stumbled upon a shot of Aunt Corky and Uncle John's discrete elopement of 1972: a sepia photo taken at a beautiful, rustic zoo—very American Gothic. She was in a gingham dress, he wore a casual suit. She looked spunky/radiant in a pixie cut—like Ellen Burstyn or some other actress of the time. He looked crazy in mutton chops, like Donald Sutherland or some other actor of the time.

Their eyes were shimmering with queer truth as they enjoyed their own form of the spotlight.

8   Engage!
Let the Drama Begin

"Omigod, she's so drama!"

A guy jeered this at me at a dinner party while I performed the "How I met Justin" story. Not unsolicited, by the way: it was on said guy's demand. My first reaction, of course, was "I hate you." But in fact, I was "so drama"—though not necessarily in the vainglorious way he meant.

Engagement = Drama

Quick theater history lesson: theater became what we call dramatic—i.e., acted out, as opposed to narrated—in Ancient Greece when Thespis stepped out of the chorus to give a monologue. (Hence the term *thespian*.) So in making your love story public, you are technically being "dramatic." But them's just semantics—not something for which you should be too self-conscious or derided, particularly when performing that moment we call getting engaged.

> *The act of engagement is the first dramatic performance in your wedding process. You take a bold, fearful step out of the safety of your dreams onto the critical stage of reality. You engage with your lover and with your people.*

Such an act has lost some of its thrill as we have grown accustomed to online lives in which we convert our dreams to social reality in the click of a button. We regularly hit UPLOAD or SEND without a second thought or an ounce of shame.

Where's the risk in sharing anymore? Beyond our own proclivities for oversharing, the government, Google, the Scientologists, the

Mormons, and the Nigerian scam artist all seem to know our favorite "friends," shopping sites, and porn. The opportunities to reveal something with stakes, with dread, with the thrill of the unknown, or the pleasure of surprise are nearly nonexistent. Our Internet lives preclude the anticipation of waiting for the next episode of our favorite shows and eliminate any real emotional cost when it comes to dating. We're online, but do we put ourselves on the line? Do we tell stories about ourselves that risk something? Do we make public declarations, or share self narratives that demand personal investment and cost? Are we engaged in the drama of our lives?

The Proposal

We do, of course, still maintain that popular bit of wedding drama called the proposal. But as of late, it's lost most of its function and its shimmer. You'll note that I've waited this long to even bring it up.

The proposal—traditionally of a guy getting down on a knee and offering a rock to a gal—has become a little *meh*, mainly due to its historical implications, which of course trace back to women as property. Adaptation continues to have its way with this ritual—slowly—as women now also propose, but there's still something not entirely gratifying for all involved. Do traditional proposals occur with voracious regularity? You betcha. But they seem to carry on in that depressing, "there's just nothing else to watch on TV but *Law & Order* reruns," sort of way. It's like when you're craving a climactic weekend dessert—say, chocolate crème brûlée with specks of gold—but all of you've got is Ring Dings. So you eat them. And then you feel worse. But there's no alternative, no turning back, and the sugar high drops so low that you finish the damn box!

Maybe the proposal has given us the sugar blues because we've figured out the trick of its magic. We know all too well that this surprise-evoking enactment provides an instant rush of hope: that our romantic lives will be more promising than the last couple of fools to sign up for endless disappointment. You know what does the same trick? A hit of crack. (And you don't want to get on that sinking cruise ship.) We understand that the proposal rush is not so long lasting, but we haven't come up with an alternative. So we either follow the same old normative steps—like lemmings scurrying off a cliff—or dismiss such traditions altogether, preferring a more "honest," mundane marital process than one that is false or based on sexist pretexts. One that throws out the drama with the sugar . . . and the crack.

Something's missing here, and I wonder if it's a willingness to commit to our own dramas, our own unique modes of storytelling. We all too often skim over the dramatic potential of our lives by sleepwalking through normative expectations. In so doing, we dismiss the rich significance of creative play.

> *We can revive the proposal if we think of it as a performance.*
>
> And performances, surprises, and dramas keep our lives and our marriages exciting, thriving, and healing. (We could all take a page from Aunt Corky and Uncle John here: consider the fun they had performing "engagement" and "wedding" using a Donald Duck ring.)

The storytelling of our lives is dynamic. Not fixed. Not predetermined or predestined. Not a set rhythm. No, those are the things people refer to when they say marriage is death. It doesn't have to be. You can engage in your story, your drama, and your lives together.

As Peter Brook says, ideal storytelling should involve a heightened, mythic reality coupled with the mundane. This, he says, can be healing. Not permanently. But, he continues, the temporary healings of drama can "constantly redress the balance of our lives."

In other words, get down on a knee and offer a shimmery rock if you must, but by Goddess, have fun doing it. Surprise yourself and your partner in a way that keeps you alive, awake, and laughing. You'll want to draw on this throughout your many years together. For example, on Justin's thirty-fourth birthday, he awoke to a cake of himself as a king, sitting atop a mountain of multicolored cupcakes, which was based on a weird dream he had shared with me when we were twenty-two. It was a great surprise, which we both appreciated.

> *So yes, we can enjoy the myth of our proposal dramas, but you'll maximize the potential of yours if you get ahead of it.*
>
> Balance the mythic surprise with mundane realness. Again, within limits, boundaries, and groundedness, the drama in your lives can fly free. You'll enjoy the feeling of being carried away without abandoning reason altogether, without belly-flopping into endless disappointment.

Lucy

My friend Lucy got lucky. The man she loves and whom she wants to be with proposed to her when she was twenty-four. But she says:

"Marriage was so off my radar it didn't even register that he was proposing when he had a ring box on the table. It was after he started a speech, and I noticed how anxious he was, that I realized, 'Oh, shit. This is happening.'"

The number balls luckily aligned for Lucy in this lottery she had unwittingly entered. And that certainly made for a surprise of mythic proportions. But what if the numbers were off? What if she said yes purely out of custom, or just for the thrill of it, or because it was the easiest thing to say in that moment? What if she discovered later that, with some distance and preparation, she'd have made a different choice? Shall we reflect on that last shot of *The Graduate* one more time?

> ### *Celebrate this moment.*
>
> Be in the present with your motivating, mythic fantasies of the future. Take your first step out of the chorus and onto the stage to tell your story. These are all worth doing right now. But the thrill of the surprise will be more thrilling if you're both on the same page; if you both share an understanding of your proposal drama, and if you accept it as a performance.

As you might have guessed, our planning was underway before any proposal was performed. Had it been fun for either of us to take that one shot at kneeling and proclaiming—with assertive assurance—while the other blushed passively—with unassuming grace—it would have happened. The stock gestures, which neither one of us found to be particularly off-putting, were not the reason neither of us knelt down. It's more that neither of us likes to cut and print on the first take. We're both the type to try out all the endings in a Choose Your Own Adventure story rather than try our luck with just one. So we invented Proposal Week.

The idea was that we would have one week in which to surprise the other with a creative proposal. During that time, we could also psyche the other out with a proposal-like drama as many times, and in as many ways, as we liked.

> ### *Invent a proposal drama of your own.*
>
> It can be one event, or many; take place at home, at the beach, or on Mars; involve rings, or custom made belts, or no props at all. And you can cast yourself in the role of *proposer, proposed-to,* or both.

We kicked off Proposal Week with calls to each other's mothers. These were intended to enliven the celebration, not to lazily oblige a tired old tradition or to negotiate with the moms over a transfer of property. The drama of these calls proved their worth. Both of them already knew the mundane fact of the wedding, as each had already agreed to give us money. What the formal calls provided was an opportunity to engage our future in-laws in a playful, mythic reality.

It allowed me to engage Sandy afresh; a bid for a new way of relating. Instead of exploiting my *engulfedness*—as she was wont to do, calling me "adorable one!" and eliciting my awkward inner child—she spoke to me with great respect, sharing relief that her son had found someone who challenged him.

It gave my mom the chance to recognize Justin as separate and distinct from me—instead of exploiting his *abandonedness,* which she often did by overlooking him and citing his greatest quality to be, simply, making her "baby" happy.

> *These rituals don't have to be stale. They can have spontaneity, joy, and meaning.*
>
> So don't worry if yours does not play out in the choreographed way you intended or expected. Think more of a modern dance that changes every night, staying alive and fresh. During your proposal dramas you'll want to be present, and in the moment; taking in all the delicious awkwardness, laughter, embarrassment, disappointment, poignancy, and pure love that can charge between us in a sincere moment of exchange.

Also consider that the pivotal drama you have contrived to forge may have already occurred in a form less formal.

For example, in 2000 when I told my mother—with ceremony—that Justin and I were "serious" and planning to move in together, she replied, seemingly bored, "Oh. Ya goin' to Vermont?" She was referring—too casually—to the historic same-sex civil unions that had been written into law that year! But I think the response I expected had already come my way in 1999, when I called her from an NYC hotel. Justin had stepped out to film some random game show for MTV—his fifteen minutes of fame had only just begun. This was the first time we had been together after our six-year hiatus after weeks of all-night phone calls. When he left the room, I dialed my mom reflexively, out of some primal need. I said, "Mom, I'm in love." I don't remember her words exactly, but I remember her tone—her "Dream a Little Dream" tone. I could feel the dramatic weight of the moment impacting us both. I held onto it, and it has proven to be more meaningful than any highly planned, traditional ritual could be.

Being Surprised While Seeing It Coming

Proposal Week progressed on Cape Cod. It was mid-October, so the air had that fresh, fall nip we both love, and it kept us on edge as we awaited the other's next move. It was also Women's Week in Provincetown, which emphasized for me the legacy of gender inequality in the act of proposing. The October chill does add to the Cape's New England charm, but I thought it ironic that the ladies are literally left out in the cold. (Will someone please propose a warmer week for these women?)

We took turns planning activities. Each time we went to a museum or a restaurant, a tiny babushka doll in the likeness of an owl would suddenly appear. Inside, I'd find a small card, each corresponding to a year we were together, complete with original prose and illustrations—and a string attached.

For him, I arranged a trip to Martha's Vineyard, which is a ghost town during the fall. We took a ride on the antique carousel, just us two, taking turns playfully trying to grab the brass ring. At a subpar restaurant (his seafood allergies make it hard to eat fancy on islands), I puffed myself up to make a speech. He gently touched my hand and said—with the dire delicacy of an old-school starlet—"Not now, not like this." (His decisive *abandoned* looking out for—what he perceived to be—my wishy-washy *engulfed*.) On the ferry back, I took him up on deck in the moonlight to make another deceptive declaration, but not before he uttered, "Are you sure?" The night I proposed to him for real, at an upscale restaurant in Provincetown, I overcompensated my performance with too much subtlety. He looked at the waiter, with whom I had arranged to bring two glasses of champagne, and said, "Huh? We didn't order these." So you see, you can have your surprise and know it's coming too.

Later that night I was visited by one last mini owl and also a bouquet of six roses, one for each of the years we had been together. The purpose of the strings now apparent: he had tied each card to a flower. There was also a surprise bottle of Veuve Clicquot, which accompanied the Korbel we had purchased earlier that day. (The local stores have slim pickin's on the Cape in October.). Together, we enjoyed the mythic along with the—devastatingly—mundane.

Neither of us offered nor received a ring; it just wasn't crucial to tell our story. That's the only reason to use such a prop—to help narrate who you are as a couple. I don't think either one of us needed it to convey, "Mmmhmm, I'm his, he's mine, back off!" I've always been told that I reek of takenness anyway; what with all those stories I tell at dinner parties being "so drama!"

So, nope, no rings for us. . . though I did try one on in Provincetown in one of those new agey stores. A mood ring. It was blue before I picked it up, and the priestess behind the desk said that meant "love." I smiled and slipped it on. Suddenly it turned amber. She goes, "Oh. That means insecurity." I thought it looked better off.

Your Engagement Story

Justin's roses told more about us than any ring, and so did the friendships we had cultivated in our six years together. When we weren't gaming each other during Proposal Week we were reflecting on the relational world of our own creation. A slideshow of images flipped through my mind. This was our story.

A story heightened by our friend Sharon—that's Hurricane Sharon to you—appearing on ABC's *20/20* one night that week and presenting a groundbreaking case for the ACLU. (She would go on to win in 2009, the historic outcome being that employees of transgender are protected under the law based on sex discrimination.) We were so proud to have her in our lives at that moment. Proud also to have my dear friend Aileen, with whom I had been texting all that week in preparation for a play we were producing together. Justin had written the play—a fantasy about the first child made from the genetic material of two men—called *StellYY* (get it, with the two Y's?). Aileen also played StellYY, the hope-inspiring title character. Friendship, storytelling, and creative visions of the future formed the band that held us together.

When we got home, I made a short video incorporating still and moving pictures of how we met, how we've grown, and with whom we've grown.

> *A celebratory slideshow can be an affordable, yet meaningful alternative to a ring.*
>
> Skim through photos and video footage of the people in your lives right now. The ones you can't wait to engage in your engagement. Tell a story using your chosen images; one that celebrates where you've been and anticipates where you're headed. Then take the emotional risk of sharing it.

Our video climaxed on our American Gaythic wedding brand image, and provided a date that we told everyone to save. I took a breath, preparing to step out of the chorus and onto the stage. Willfully.

Then I hit SEND.

Part 3

Setting the Stage

9 Liberating Limitations: Make Choices to Contain Your Vision

"You can have this whole corner for your event," said the party planner at a swanky NYC hotel.

The corner was all of five hundred square feet. But it was in the penthouse and surrounded by glass, revealing snowy city views. It made for a buoyant—yet tight—engagement party, the pleasure of which I credit to its non-negotiable confines. We could float without floating away, or breaking the bank.

★   ★   ★

So you're thinking, "What's the point of an engagement party anyway?" I know. It sounds extraneous. Something you would only do out of a mindless allegiance to etiquette. The sort of affair you might like to crash and glitter-bomb and wake everyone up, crowing, "What the fuck are you wasting your time and money for?!" (I've never actually had an outburst like that at an engagement party myself, in case you're wondering . . . This is pure keyboard courage.)

Which reminds me . . .

> *The written word is the mightiest place for your frustration, anger, and aggression throughout (most) of this process.*
>
> If necessary, please privately journal rather than burst out or punch walls (or people). But just as you practice containing yourself, you'll also want to contain your conjugal events. And an

engagement party, however large or small, can be a great first step toward that end.

You can think of it as a dry run for the big day, an opportunity to test your wings as a theatrical producer. You'll need to create a budget, set a location, structure the evening, choose a guest list, and somehow survive each other while doing it. Only with much lower stakes than the real deal.

Choices

Most importantly, an engagement party is the first opportunity you both have to convert your nebulous vision into a tangible event. You're now stepping out of the cozy warmth of your vision into the harsh chill of practicality, and all of that dreamy prep work will evaporate if you don't contain it. And you do that by making choices.

Strong, willful choices.

Even if they're not quite right at first.

As my former acting teacher Annie said, "Just because you start a scene badly, doesn't mean you have to continue badly." Stay present and you'll find your next move. In fact, it's better if our choices don't yield the precise result we expect. The dread of missing the mark keeps us alert and engaged with the people around us. And that is the real point of all this wedding stuff, right?

Give yourselves enough time between an engagement celebration and wedding week.

I recommend at least four or five months, if not more. We had ours in February (on Valentine's Day!), which left plenty, but not

> too much, time before our October wedding. Time to fail and fail better. Time to reflect on which choices worked (toasting our guests) and which did not (toasting our guests; neither of us knew what to say…). Time to improve our choices before the big day.

Without choosing clear boundaries from this point onward—regardless of what they are—your wedding simply won't take flight. That is, unless someone else reluctantly jumpstarts it for you. And that will come at a price.

A friend of ours was asked to DJ a wedding, which he ended up planning minutes before curtain when they informed him they hadn't really done any planning themselves. He frantically chose a playlist, and suggested some events—e.g., toasts, dances—and that they say some vows. His jaw still aches from the fake smiles he deployed while watching what ensued, which included the processional song—chosen by the bride at the eleventh hour—cutting short, leaving everyone with only the sound of the outdoor breeze, while she was half a mile from the grassy altar, on a hill, her veil blowing every which way. Fortunately, the couple was at least grateful for his help.

Another friend of ours, Tabitha, is still scarred from an unplanned wedding she attended. Upon arrival, she was abruptly asked to set up eleven canopy tents, in ninety-degree heat, break them down, and also pay to get her hair done as part of the bridal party. Better yet, the unrehearsed ceremony ran over. Starving and annoyed, Tabitha stared at the only dinner that would be served: a last-minute, hastily purchased, tray of macaroni salad. It had been carelessly set down on a picnic table and was unwrapped, curdling in the sun. There was also no alcohol. Tabitha's resentment only grows with time.

> ### *Limitations are liberating.*
>
> Don't be deceived by thinking not planning will somehow yield relaxed, double-easy fun for everyone. You've got to carve out the canal before the water can flow through.

Same-sex couples are experts on limitations, having been denied the right to marry for so long, and none of us should allow their wisdom-by-default to be forgotten. In other words, freedom should not make us—any of us—lazy. I know I encouraged you to daydream boundlessly in the last section, but now I implore you to set some tight parameters.

I feel your pain. Setting things in stone was the hardest part for Justin and me (to this day, we have not once successfully chosen an on-demand movie to watch together from start to finish). So fortunately, the very first, most crucial choice was made for us: the budget.

I was going back to grad school that year, he was working part time at a law firm while being a writer (unpaid), and our mothers weren't *Real Housewives* with sugar daddies or trust funds. These were all arguably good things, but it meant that between the four of us we had a hard twenty thousand dollars to spend on a wedding, in the Berkshires, in mid-October. This meant sacrifices, but also the greater glory of knowing that every part of our celebration was willfully chosen. And if anything was not ultimately wanted (I do wish we had skipped that whole feeding each other cake bit), it was in our hands and no one else's.

The fixed budget forced us to choose a venue within our means, thereby limiting our guest list, but also freeing us to make careful choices. With limited resources, and space, we had to decide who was most critical to our universe at that time. Believe me, with free reign, both of us would have invited absolutely anyone who'd ever been kind to us or the least bit influential. Ranging from close family friends, to the acting teachers I've mentioned, to Justin's ex-boss-for-a-minute, the lawyer Mary Bonauto—who won the Vermont Civil Unions case of 1999, and was instrumental in every major same-sex marriage victory ever since, including "Down with DOMA" in 2013. Had we a fantasy fortune, the guest list is where I would have splurged, the way some might do on an extravagant entrance via zip line, accompanied by colored smoke and a laser show. We also didn't allow guests without long-term/serious partners to bring a date, which of course incited folks—like our friend, Lil' Priss—to cry, "Indecent!" But without these tough limitations, the core vision of our event would not have had a life.

There will be regrets.

Oh, yes.

When I think back to our big day—who was there, who wasn't, who we no longer speak to, who had not yet entered our lives—I cringe. (Frankly, I sometimes wish certain faces would evaporate from the pictures, the way eliminated contestants do on reality shows.) But you learn from this as you move forward. And without committing to your choices in the present, without making some mistakes, without missing what life has taken away or has not yet offered, there's no way to know for sure who and what you want to keep close.

Besides, contrary to populist storytelling, your wedding is not your one shot at claiming an identity—as an individual or a couple. It's a step—a strong, committed, yet playful step—in the dance you'll eventually learn to do. And do better. There will be countless opportunities to perform this dance, again and again: as you represent friends and family at their weddings; as you celebrate milestone birthdays; children; gender reveal parties—pre-birth and again at sixteen, when they decide for themselves; graduations; and, of course, as you read poems or give speeches at funerals. You don't have to get the audience just right this time. There's a whole lot of theater ahead of you—happy, sad, and everything in between.

But we expect your wedding to be happy. (For the most part.) Without a quest for joy, we'd have no motivation. So let's get back to choices.

Your choices will carve out the canals allowing your performances to easily flow through them.

Now's the time to sharpen focus on your motivating images, to distill your nebulous ideas into workable structures.

Like the ceremony, for instance. Justin and I had both been taken to Christian churches as children, and both retained an interest not necessarily in the content of the services, but in the theater. We wanted a communal experience of contemplation, of splendor, and transcendence, similar to our memories of church—without all the homophobia or misogyny, of course. As inspiration, this meant a crowd focused on dramatized stories of sacrifice and hope; it meant organ-like music, a common purpose, the will to be healed and to be changed, and a chorus in unison. As choice, this simply translated to: Song, Text, Song, Text, Song, Text, Song.

From there, all we had to do was pick songs and text. Ones that held personal meaning, but would also simulate the righteous reverie of a spiritual service. Everyone would have a visceral recognition of the event they were a part of, only with content that acknowledged stories like ours. (And the truth is, even the most demonstrable churchgoers at our ceremony wondered if some of our selections were actually from the Bible.)

Don't skip the simple, but essential step of making a choice.

A vague motivating image without choice results in a vague performance. Even more dire, though, is the fact that—as with most things in life—if you defer making a choice, someone else will do it for you. How many weddings have you attended at which the house music has been passively handed to the uninspired DJ? How awkward is it to wonder if your friend—the highly successful, independent bride (who might also tower over the groom in both age and physical size)—actually chose to be referred to publicly as "Adam's rib."

B

Our friend B, for example, chose all the elements that made up the second of two traditional Hindu wedding ceremonies she and her husband had in India; this one was mostly for friends. The first one was performed only for family in the small village where her parents were from, and all five hundred family members in attendance had dictated how it should go. After hearing five hundred versions of what she was supposed to do—bow here but not there, drink unpasteurized milk, don't drink unpasteurized milk—B was burnt out. Like an actor showing up for rehearsals without choosing how to play her part, she suffered the slings and arrows of everyone's direction. But B took back her power, her freedom, and energy by reclaiming her right to choose.

Emily and Brandon

Justin's cousin Emily and her husband, Brandon, are also a great example of the necessity of choice, even for the smallest of weddings. Their proposal was consistent with the slow-going, easy-natured way their relationship had evolved—they had been together for eight years when Brandon proposed. They called people immediately after and everyone started to ask when the wedding was, what colors they chose, where was it going to be, etc. Emily immediately pulled back on the reins, thinking it was already starting to get out of control. Then, after hearing from Brandon's parents that they were expected to get married in a church, near their house, and that they were supposed to invite all the relatives to "thank them" for helping shape them into the people that they were, the wedding was deferred. Indefinitely.

After four years of waiting for the nuptials, Brandon's side of the family had an especially bad year due to several deaths. "Everyone needed a little down time and an excuse to get together and not have a funeral be central to the gathering, so his immediate family decided to come to Vermont for a visit," says Emily. They realized this might be just the perfect time to get married.

They told their families and they were thrilled. Within a week, they found a Justice of the Peace, a ring, and the courage to tell everyone exactly what they wanted: a low-key afternoon with only their immediate families spending time together—along with their Noah's Ark of pets (Emily's a vet, after all). The limitation of having only a week forced Emily and Brandon to decide what they actually wanted for that day, and they got it.

> *One crucial choice will be to decide who's in charge of what.*
>
> You'll want to draw a line in the sand, dividing up responsibilities—keeping in mind that it's quicksand on which you're drawing.

Justin claimed the ceremony while I took the reception. Though I ended up doing most of both anyway—I'm high-strung and overly ambitious. (Remember my yellow brick road project?) I also had years of experience catering big NYC events, on top of years working in the theater, so my domination of the event planning was inevitable. But at least there were designated roles to refer back to when disagreements or confusion arose.

You'll also need to have go-to positions for different tasks throughout the course of your marriage, so this will be good practice. That doesn't mean said positions can't change, or be fluid, but they need to be assigned to get things started. (Know what I mean?)

Other boundaries you may want to consider include how to discuss your planning with others. Be careful not to carelessly surrender your emotional process too soon. I made this mistake at our engagement party.

While talking to my Uncle Dan, I was taken off guard for a moment and clumsily discussed some complicated questions I had about including my three brothers in the wedding. Rather than offering the unconditional support I expected in my state of overwhelmed narcissism, Dan curtly shut me down with, "Just tell people you're choosing Mike as your best man because he discovered Justin on TV, and leave it at that." As much as I hated feeling scolded, I had to accept that it was my messy exposition that forced Dan to set this boundary for me.

This is not a lesson in "proper" etiquette so much as a question of how to protect your emotional process—from others but also from hurting others. Try to encapsulate any choices based on complicated feelings into an easily digestible form before sharing them with your audience.

Journal about it privately if you must vent, but then again, you'll also want to mind what you do with said journal.

I made yet another mistake of carrying mine bunglingly in a merse, which I left at a party several weeks later. At which Uncle Dan was present! On our way home that night, as Justin and I walked toward the subway, a cab pulled up to the curb. Inside was Dan, who handed me the murse with one hand, and the journal with the other. "I believe this is yours," he said, staring icily. I sheepishly thanked him and reclaimed my things, hoping to high heavens there was nothing about him in the journal. I opened to page one. The first line? "Talking to my uncle the other night at our engagement party was no fun." Ugh. My face burns at the memory. So yeah, I for one failed quite a few times before I got this whole "boundaries" thing down.

This process is emotionally complicated and taxing, so you'll need to vent. That being the case, I advise you to get ahead of it. Carve out private space to disentangle your feelings. Blow them out in a way that is safely contained—e.g., in a journal (that you keep locked in a safe), with a therapist, with trusted friends, during a meditative run through the park, or a walk along the beach. Or perhaps to a wedding planner, if you can afford one.

> ### *Remember that you're not alone in this.*
>
> You can decide what roles are necessary for this piece of theater, and you have the power to cast them.

Looking around our engagement party, this task was a no-brainer: after all, there was a stage manager, professional singers, a pianist, and a charming, multitalented emcee present—who was buddies with a great DJ. Which reminds me . . .

> You'll want a stage manager, professional singers, a pianist, and a charming, multitalented emcee—who is buddies with a great DJ. Start looking around your immediate group of friends and make some choices. You can keep this production team on an email loop throughout the pregnant months ahead, and if you choose talent who've played these parts before, they'll likely be more than happy to help birth the event.

Our engagement party taught us one more crucial thing: to choose our cake, have our cake, and call it a day.

The first cake to pop in our minds was carrot—a fall flavor, decorated with falling fall leaves. But then we thought: "What about red velvet?" "Don't you love chocolate mousse?" "What will be most pleasing to our guests?" So I made all three, served them at the engagement party, and had everyone vote. Let them choose cake! And so they did. And the winner was . . . chocolate mousse! I remember nodding, grimacing, and then kind of responding like that annoying computerized voice you sometimes get on the phone in lieu of customer service, "Mmm . . . I didn't get that . . . did you say, carrot? Mmmn . . . sorry . . . I still didn't get that. It sounds like you said . . . carrot. Okay, I'll put you through to . . . carrot." We went with carrot.

As Justin says, "It's not wedding by focus group."

Just get a grip. Make some choices. And make them now.

10 Deliberation Station: Space to Work It Out

"I'll need two hundred stamps for these invitations," said my boss as he dropped an enormous pink box on my desk.

Sometimes the pink elephant in the room is literally pink, and elephantine, and in your face. "No Americana!" he ordered. "Cara hates Americana. Something pretty. Flowers?" Cara was his wife. I wasn't working for his wife. Working for his wife wasn't discussed during my interview for this temp admin job or thereafter. Until this day. Which would be my last.

Fortunately, I made good use of the cushy office during the three months prior to plan *my* wedding. Section two of this book was all about giving yourselves space for creative play. Now you need space to work.

★   ★   ★

A literal space—like the one my temp job provided—is of course handy, but by *space*, I also refer to the area of communication, negotiation, and compromise between you and your fiancé: the space in which you will determine together how to arrive at decisions that must get nailed down at this phase.

Working in a pretentious office—for a guy who had nothing better to do than show off his massive wealth—had its advantages to be sure.

Organization, for one. One of my responsibilities was to keep track of his budget and daily spending. On a spreadsheet I would enter how much he spent on cupcakes for his wife, flowers for his wife, the limo that took his wife to yoga—three blocks from their Central Park home—and the occasional random treat he'd want me to special-order for his wife from a random shop on the random island where they had taken their most recent uber-random, uber-luxe vacation. After itemizing his daily expenses, I was then to cross check them with his intended spending limit for that day—which was always less than he spent. He'd sometimes groan, exhale tensely, then say, "Ah well. You should be so lucky, right?" I wasn't.

But I also was, in that I actually spent most of each day organizing our wedding budget on the same system. I can tell you now, with pride, that by the end of the affair, we slid into home plate just under our twenty-thousand-dollar cap.

Not that you need fancy software to do such a thing.

> *You can use a spreadsheet on your Google Drive and share it with your spouse-to-be and production team . . .*
>
> . . . and cross your fingers you'll have better luck getting them to open it than I did. But this document is the main blueprint, the floor plan, the bones of your entire wedding project, and the more organized it is, the more freely all the other parts of your connubial system will move.

The real trick is to somehow agree on what those bones are made of, and how much you should spend on each. You'll want to rely on some of that emotional mirroring you've been practicing since I enlightened you to the whole *engulfed/abandoned* phenomenon.

Who's Your Audience?

For us, the most difficult decisions obviously had to do with the guest list. Not only did I want to invite everyone who'd ever smiled at me, but my family also outweighs Justin's by about ten tons—in volume and, well, volume. Even after our compromises, our reception was undeniably seized by the raucous Irish/Italian pirate ship of my family, while the whispery WASPs of his floated by on a dinghy—almost imperceptibly. (Need I remind you which of us is engulfed and which is abandoned?) But we had limited space and all things needed to be equal. (What's the point of a same-sex wedding without equality, right?)

This meant making hard choices—the kind that our presidents (and future presidents…) always talk about being confronted with. The kind that piss a lot of people off. Although, I have to say, one of the great joys of non-traditional weddings is that you're never quite sure if relatives are disappointed, relieved, or indifferent to being left off the list, since—in many cases—your event defies their expectations anyway. You have more freedom than Prince William and Kate, or my ex-temp-boss and Cara, to edit your list. This wasn't actually that difficult for me, as I simply didn't invite anyone I hadn't been in touch with for more than a decade or whose unmistakable homophobia left me with a palpable sting.

People who wear their prejudices, hatreds, or self-hatreds
on their sleeves make unanimous guest list cutting
that much easier.

One notable cut took place after a double date with my friend Ben and his then-boyfriend Chris. Justin and I were discussing a fantastic book—*Same-Sex Unions in Premodern Europe* by John Boswell—explaining, excitedly, that we would draw from it for our ceremonial text, when things suddenly went sour. Chris interrupted to counter explain that accounts of same-sex unions from that period were erroneous, since the Emperor Constantine . . . blah, blah, blah. A glance across the table is all it took for fiancé consensus. (Well, a little more than that actually. We had already discussed our previous double date with these two, during which Chris argued that our fore-sisters and brothers at the Stonewall Riots didn't deserve our pride etc., etc.) The next day, I called Ben (from the office, and the phone, from which I was expected to order a car for the boss's wife to take to Pilates . . . two blocks away) and asked him to kindly attend the wedding solo. Anyone with *Overtly Toxic Prejudice* (OTP) was easily removed from our list.

> ### *Overtly Toxic Prejudice*
>
> I must make a distinction here: OTP is not the same thing as Spotlight Ambivalence. Whereas Spotlight Ambivalence reveals the beholder's general discomfort with attention by projecting it onto you, OTP is just plain pernicious. Those down with OTP want to induce shame in others and you don't have time for any of that on your wedding day—a day not based on hiding in shame, but rather on revealing your pride and joy. As our friend Lilly says, it's a day "you go into eyes wide open." If anyone on your list presents an obstacle to that, weed them out. This is the easiest way to keep your list of invites fifty-fifty.

Although, in some ways, our efforts to slice the wedding pie chart symmetrically between us sounded better than it ultimately worked. For example, to keep things fair, we did not invite any of our parents' friends, as a rule. That was hard for me at first, as it meant leaving off a couple who had given loads of support to my mother after my dad's passing. Justin had to remind me of the disparities between our family sizes—and also that the male in said couple made occasional references to "the Mexicans," which we really couldn't risk happening at the wedding (OTP anyone?), as one of my friends of Mexican descent would be among our multi-racial guests. To quash any residual angst about this decision, Justin agreed not to invite family friends either. But some of his mother's friends, on the other hand—in addition to not being racist or ethnocentric—were really the equivalent of his family, and in retrospect their presence was deeply missed.

Symmetry also proved to be an uneven measurement for our wedding parties. Justin's propensity for straight lines and exact measurements—he bakes, I cook—led us to parties consisting of one brother (he only has one) and three lady pals each. It was a strong choice, and it arguably worked. To make it work, I asked two of my three brothers to be ushers and had my dear friend Allie sing solos at both the ceremony and reception—rather than be party to the "party." But if I were to have been truly true to myself, I would have insisted on trashing the term *parties* altogether, and instead had one big, uneven "Grooms' Ensemble." The pictures pretty much tell that story anyway.

Literal symmetry is a tempting solution to dilemmas of wedding equality, but it can be just a reductive stand-in for the feeling of equal representation.

Lyn and Jorge

Take Lyn and Jorge, for example. It was important for Lyn to be married by a rabbi and for their wedding to honor Jewish traditions, but Jorge had no comparable religious connection. He didn't mind Lyn celebrating her Judaism, but he initially felt left out of the ceremony. So he offered a solution. Since he would have eloped had Lyn agreed, he suggested a Justice of the Peace be present at the ceremony, in his corner, to balance things out. This, he quickly realized, was an unwieldy request, but at least it opened a dialogue between them about how they could both feel represented. They came to a settlement after finding a rabbi who spoke Spanish and could therefore translate the ceremony for his Salvadoran family.

Quick Tip: Many Jewish wedding traditions can actually be great equalizers.

For one thing, both sets of parents walk each spouse down the aisle—which helped Jorge feel additionally recognized—and easily translates for same-sex couples, as well. There's, of course, the

Horah during which hands are joined in a circle dance to honor the joining of tribes, but also the breaking of the glass can have various meanings. Wedding planner Danielle Aspromatis says, "I like having the officiant explain to the guests that on this day, they will break the glass in an effort to break down barriers between people of different religions, cultures, and beliefs."

Just as Lyn and Jorge resolved their dilemma of equal representation, try to aim for recognition before accommodation in resolving yours. In other words:

Recognizing your partner's emotional need through empathic dialogue will lead to a more equal solution—e.g., having the ceremony translated into Spanish—than reflexively accommodating them with perfect symmetry—e.g., having both a rabbi and a justice of the peace.

Time and Space

And you know, it takes some time to determine what is worth your insistence. As much as you need to set some things in stone now, give each other patience and slack to articulate your wedding must-haves—space to determine your unique preferences. This will serve you throughout your marriage and help keep the soil fertile for each of you to grow—albeit at the speed of grass growing, in some cases.

I for one only recently contributed to the interior design of our home—picking fabric for our curtains!—having lived with Justin's eclectic taste in a state of choice-less awareness for fourteen years. And also, only recently, Justin—in addition to encouraging me to pick the fabric for the curtains—made a subtle shift, which helped resolve a chronic dilemma of ours: ordering in.

Deliberating take-out options in our home usually goes something like this:

J: "What do you want?"
Me: "Indian."
J: (*Silence. Big brown eyes blink.*)
Me: "Sushi?"
J: (*Silence. Big brown eyes blink.*)
Me: "Thai? Mexican? Canadian? . . . What do you want?"

This usually continues until he says, "Pizza." But this last time, he caught himself and said, "You want Indian? Okay. Let's go with Indian." But that was after fourteen years!

Do try to give each other space to identify and advocate preferences, but at a certain point, you've just got to move on. When you seem to be running out of time, you'll want to rely on a choice-making system: allowing the more decisive one to take the lead. (I mean, if planning the wedding were like decorating our apartment, I'd still be at my desk, in that odious office, organizing our budget, unwed.) Just be sure to make a footnote about your go-to methods of resolution. This way you can eventually refer back to them as the two of you adapt and grow together.

Even though I was what you'd call the point person—and wedding planner Danielle says there is always a point person—Justin was the top judge giving ultimate yay or nay. Between my persistent offering of options and Justin's firm preferences, we developed a working machine.

$$$

The items we spent the most time negotiating were actually not expensive. It was quite easy to come up with reasonable price limits for the big things like location, food, rentals, and outfits. Since the wedding *why* was so specific for each of us, much of the deliberating—aside from guest list—came down to things like song and text selection, the order of events, what norms to keep, which ones to revise, and which to leave out.

Our lack of overspending even baffled some people, including this girl Trish who worked at the desk next to mine at the notorious temp job—aka, my wedding planning station. Trish, an aspiring writer, was equally unenthused with her assistant job. To remedy this, she decided to write an article on a *hot*, provocative, topic: same-sex marriage—which was legal only in Massachusetts back in those days of 2006. And whaddya know? She had a ripe interviewee only inches away. In the three months of knowing her, I never saw her so jubilant than the moment she put this all together. Her racy angle? Same-sex marriage is good for the economy since "the gays" 1) have money and 2) they want to spend it. Oops. In the three months of knowing her, I never saw her as let down—and bored!—as the moment she asked me about our wedding priorities. Sorry, Trish.

Jamie and Aaron

Having a limited budget provides a wealth of opportunity for wedding features that are spectacular, unforgettable, and one of a kind. For example, my friends Jamie and Aaron could not afford live musicians for their ceremony and instead relied on their talented cohort. Using love letters the bride and groom had exchanged, their musical friends composed a song and performed it during the processional. I can say objectively that this piece of music has a distinct, goose-bump-inducing beauty anyone would be fortunate to have performed in their honor. Jamie and Aaron would have missed this sublime experience had they been able to throw some cash at a swanky orchestra.

This isn't to say that you shouldn't spend money on things that are personally meaningful, even if they're blindingly normative. If we dive in eyes wide open, some norms may prove to be plain fun—walking the aisle, public kissing, dancing, eating cake—or at the very least, they might hold you/make you feel secure. As a mentor of mine says, "Some norms are comforting. I like that the local grocer knows my name." Just be alert to normative expectations becoming normative excess. For instance, just because it's Valentine's Day doesn't mean you have to spend a mint sending your spouse cupcakes, three dozen roses, and a special treat from a random shop on the random island where you took an uber-random, uber-luxe vacation.

Lily and Bart

Our friends Lily and Bart got married later than the norm (she in her late thirties, he was forty) and were therefore free of normative pressures and persuasions in their planning, but they did find security in at least one tradition. Since they had both lost their mothers, they wanted something resembling a blessing at their ceremony. Though neither of them currently practices any religion, Lily's memory of The Lord's Prayer at her childhood Christian church comforted her, so they arranged for this musical benediction during their service. Now they were lucky in that there wasn't much negotiating or arguing between them, as Bart was happy to entrust all of the picking and choosing to Lily, saying, "'Tell me where to show up and I'll be there." Lily says, "That's exactly what happened."

Listen to Your Gut

Some of the selections you'll push for—like The Lord's Prayer in Lily's case—will be based on a highly subjective feeling more than anything else, and that doesn't make them any less worthy of your advocacy. You'll want to notice how strongly your feelings—e.g., for a piece of music or text—take hold of you and explain this to your partner. In our case, a mutual love of Philip Glass made it easy to choose his piano piece "Opening" for our opening. Sinead O'Connor's "In This Heart"—a melancholic ballad that chillingly evokes love's ironies—was the only thing I could imagine walking down the aisle to. It held me tight ever since Justin sang it over the phone, at three a.m., when we first got back in touch.

Others won't come as easily, and you'll have to rely on the system you develop to arrive at decisions. Don't rush these ones. We had to embark on a search-and-destroy for the song accompanying our first dance, for example. Or at least I did; Justin just said no until he didn't. I still think we ended up with the right choice: "I'll Be Your Mirror" by The Velvet Underground; what with all the *engulfed* and *abandoned* needs we had to mirror back to one another respectively during this process, it was perfect. Plus, it was upbeat, not sentimental, and short—which was good since we did have a wee bit of Spotlight Ambivalence when it came to dancing slowly for show. It was worth taking the time to find this song, and we were able to make other choices we had immediate gut feelings about in the meantime.

★ ★ ★

And speaking of gut feelings, let's get back to my boss's big pink box and the "pretty" stamps I was ordered to buy. The invitations were for a big party to show off his new baby, and I can only guess that in requesting "no Americana!" he intended to show off their "taste" rather than their patriotism. Now, my wedding planning was in pretty good shape—I had made enough phone calls and used enough supplies from the office by then—so I was prepared to risk losing the job by acting on impulse versus normative expectation.

The post office didn't actually have a whole lot of options for stamps besides American flags. But it was Black History Month, and there was a shimmery stamp of actress Hattie McDaniel, who won the Oscar for *Gone With the Wind*. (She was the first African American to ever receive this honor, making her an icon of trailblazing queerness). In addition to sending the message to my boss, "I don't know nothing 'bout birthing no babies!"—one of Ms. Daniel's famous lines—I also thought about his instruction to pick stamps that were "pretty." My gut told me these were pretty; they held me in a way I couldn't exactly explain. So I did it. I purchased two hundred of them—with his credit card—and put them on his desk, along with the pink box. Surely he wouldn't have a problem with these stamps or my sense of what is pretty.

Sometimes you don't know you are the normative police until your siren goes off. My boss's did. Super loud. Red-faced, he stormed out of his office.

"What the hell, Mark?!"

I looked up from my workstation, coolly. "What? You asked for pretty stamps. I picked an Oscar winner. What's the problem?"

Trish and the other assistants gaped. My queer way of exposing the truth—however mortifying for everyone involved—was well worth it, even as I packed up my desk later that day, never to return.

My one regret? I didn't keep the stamps. We could have used them for our wedding invitations.

11 Contracts: Never Having to Say "Oh, Shit!"

"Hey, it's Zondra, your photographer. I will *not* attend your wedding . . . So I suggest you buy some disposable cameras, give them to your guests, and *those* will be your wedding photos."

It was two days before the wedding. We had just arrived at our destination B&B. And we got this voicemail.

"Oh, shit!"

We first met Zondra through our friend, Lyle, and liked her right away. She was an independent spirit with a dark, campy sense of humor and a talent for taking pictures—dark, sometimes campy pictures. Mostly dark, though. (She had a whole series on starving strippers and bloody pavement.) When I needed a photographer for a play I was producing—titled *Contracts*, which Justin wrote—I called Zondra. As a friend, she was willing to help us out at an affordable rate, which worked out great; even if she largely captured the actors in their most deadening angles.

Years later, after deliberating our wedding budget and needs, we asked Zondra to take our photos. As a friend, this would be her gift to us, but we would provide her room and a nominal fee, out of respect (she knew our limitations). We took Zondra to dinner one night to verbally contract for this, all the while wearing blinders to the fact that, by day, she took photos for the city morgue.

What went wrong? Our contract wasn't clear enough. And Justin never checked with me—or opened the budget doc I micromanaged intensely (see Appendix for example)—before telling her one day that we planned to pay her more than we did or could or discussed when we had that contractual dinner! Justin then had to disabuse her of this notion, which was initially fine with Zondra, but then . . . she left that voicemail. As I said, "Oh shit!"—how do you find a professional wedding photographer in the Berkshires, in mid-October, with two days' notice?

> *Contracting with the crew of your wedding production is arguably the most difficult task of all.*
>
> Obviously you want everyone to want to help, but if you're not made of money, you've got to cut corners. This risks making your vendors feel cheated, and your generous friends feel taken advantage of—neither of which will make them love to love you. But you've got to set a solid frame now to contain the performance, the expectations, and your finances along the way. This means getting everything in writing—even if it's just email—and being extremely explicit with anyone you ask for help. If you can't be explicit with a vendor or friend, find someone else.

For the most part, we fared okay with contracting, but not without speed bumps, such as the one Zondra presented, abruptly, at the eleventh hour.

Be Explicit

As I've previously mentioned, the set we found for our conjugal production—on Main Street in Stockbridge, no less—was the stuff of fairytales—not only in its beauty, but also in that to claim this happy end we had to contract with the owner, who resembled Wallace Shawn from *The Princess Bride*. "Inconceivable!" Yes, he both looked and acted like the impish riddler from that classic film.

In some cases, we were able to come to binding agreement—such as the below-market flat fee to use the entire house for the entire affair over the entire weekend; it was their first wedding, so we were offering them something in return.

But there were a few riddles we didn't solve early on, which led to more than a few "what's happening?" moments, such as moving furniture. Somehow Justin and his brother Chris were breaking down tables the day after we were married, at the imp's command.

And also there were all the little things that would have been *inconceivable* at the contracting phase, and therefore slipped under our radar. Like, who knew the imp was going to insist on leaving his enormous, multi-gadgeted massage/armchair on the dance floor? Chris finally wore him down on the issue and convinced him to move it—thankfully without having to put poison in his goblet. To prevent such fiascos, we could have gone over mutual expectations in a manner more thorough, detailed, and clear when we contracted.

Including addressing his Overtly Toxic Prejudice (OTP) for Indian people—whom he described as being "careless" and "dirty"—I wish we had contracted with the imp to check himself during the wedding, as Justin's oldest friend, B—a beautiful, highly (super highly) successful business woman—would be present and was also Indian. B likes to play as hard as she works—as Justin says, just as Clark Kent becomes Superman, B becomes Party Banshee.

When she decided to have some fun with Lyle during our reception—posing for hilarious, suggestive pics on the pool table in the parlor (and giving Lyle a vicarious spotlight to enjoy)—the imp decided to shut it down for the night, even though others had aggressively crowded the pool table for hours prior to this harmless incident without causing so much as an eyebrow raise from the imp. Surely, we couldn't have gotten him to sign in blood to the statement, "I'll hide my racism during your wedding," but I wish we had made more of our expectations and concerns explicit than we did.

I also wish there had been a clause in our contract about items accidentally left on the premises, like the top tier of our cake. The imp never returned our calls when we realized we had left it, and you don't need to be the Dread Pirate Roberts to solve the riddle of what he did with it.

Contracting initially seemed like a no brainer with our caterer, Patti. We chose her because she had a quirky blog, shimmery silver hair, and a delightful, queer way. When we first met her, she gave us a tray of sample foods to take away. We sat down on the Simon's Rock grass in the afternoon sun and enjoyed mashed root vegetables with swirls of spinach, smoked salmon and lemon dill cream sauce, and parmesan crisps. Patti had wacky stories about her nontraditional journey to becoming a chef; yoga retreats with her son in India—a refreshing contrast from the imp; and how Judge Judy officiated her daughter's wedding. Our chemistry was instant, and thick as crème fraîche–stuffed potato puffs with caviar garnish and a sprig of rosemary. But you know, when things get too clickety-click with a vendor, you gotta be careful.

I knew all about rentals—e.g., tables, cloth, silverware, etc.—from my days as an actor/caterer, so I was On It from the get-go. I did tons of Internet research—from my wedding planning station at the temp job—and calculated what we could afford, based on number of guests, what we'd need, and our limitations—down to the exact number and style of napkins. Patti tried to loosen my tight hold on the budget for rentals and staff by sharing entertaining stories about her daughter's wedding and how she just had to stop pinching pennies at a certain point and "let go"—meaning paying for the likes of Judge Judy, apparently. But I pushed back, popping some of the bubbly vibe between us to save money. It worked. And it didn't.

Patti absolutely delivered for us, magnificently, but I think her wings might have been clipped a bit by my uptightness, and she went home before the party was scheduled to end. This was fine—she had fulfilled her part of the contract—but she left her staff under the direction of the imp, who let them go early, as well. Cut to Justin and Chris breaking down tables the next day. This breakdown of communication escaped being spelled out in a contract, and Patti was disappointingly not willing to make it up to us in any way. This reduced our chemistry, not to cheese-whiz on a Triscuit per se, but to something less than the potato puff it once was.

The only other catering contract failure was on me, and by failure I unfortunately mean success, 'cause I got what I asked for. In my strident efforts to limit spending, I arranged for the post-wedding brunch coffee to be cut after only two hours of service. Patti followed these instructions to a T. And I'll never forget the crazy, unforgiving glare in my sister-in-law Summer's coffee-craving eyes after being told, smugly, by my mother-in-law, Sandy, "You snooze you lose." Or the pang of guilt it induced in me, having broken the nonverbal contract with my guests to soothe their hangovers!

> *Contracts that are verbally explicit protect us from needless feelings of guilt, disappointment, resentment, and aggravation.*
>
> By contrast, our relationships with family, friends, and lovers, provide for us a range of nonverbal, non-explicit contracts that leave us with such messy emotions on a regular basis.

Justin dramatized this beautifully in his play *Contracts*—the one for which Zondra took the macabre pictures. The play's theme was summed up in its tag line: "You promised." In it, I played a wheelchair-bound law student whose nonverbal contract with his controlling mother—the dean of the school—was to overcompensate for his disability by overachieving; as if this would one day make him walk. In a climactic scene, he screams at her—"Stop!"—and explains he is dropping out of school to pursue painting and a life of his own making without unspoken guidelines hovering overhead like dark clouds.

In all intimate relationships we work out the kinks of nonverbal contracts by failing each other better, by making bids for recognition, and by attempting to be emotional mirrors for each other. And sometimes that works . . .

And sometimes these nonverbal contracts are not all bad. For example, when I first read a sample of the play for Justin one afternoon on the lawn of the Harvard Law School campus—where he was writing it, still a student—I felt contracted to eventually bring it to life, without him even asking. Completely out of love, without any burden or ultimatum. So I did.

On the other hand, contracting for your wedding is a very, very different animal; one that must be fail-proof and explicitly verbal. More tell than show. You can help yourselves by establishing a contracting machine between the two of you; which can take the form of a good cop/bad cop scenario.

If you're like me—engulfed; tending to get all clickety-click with someone like Patti; finding it difficult to say no or to set a frame with people—you can be the good cop; make 'em love ya. If you're like Justin, on the other hand—abandoned; all-business with someone like Patti; no problem saying no or setting a clear frame with people—you can be the bad cop; let 'em know who's boss. This method can be highly effective if you clearly work it out and contract between the two of you. (We seemed to have a breakdown in this department when it came to Zondra). This way if you're like me, you can secretly be the Lady Macbeth, saying no behind the scenes, wielding your Google Docs spreadsheet like a bloody weapon.

After years and years together, you can help each other get better at playing the opposite role. Although I still feel the compulsion to delegate a lot of bad cop duties to Justin, he assures me I've actually gotten quite good at playing "bad" myself. I guess it helps to have that mirrored back now and again, even after all those years. Likewise, he has effectively adapted to the part of good cop; I sometimes overhear him talking like an empathic therapist to his friends . . . and also to our cats.

> ***Wedding contracts aren't all us versus them, though. Sometimes they're us versus us.***
>
> I'm talking about prenups and religious or spiritual marriage contracts. These obviously need to be considered case by case, but they generally work best as living, mutable documents based on a lot of dialogue between you.

Yasmine and her husband, David, for example, combed through their ketubah—a Jewish prenuptial agreement—to contemporize the language and tailor it to their needs, particularly in terms of offering protections to both of them as ketubahs traditionally only protect the wife.

If you're part of a religious or spiritual community, keep in mind that marital contracts of this sort are not always flexible, which can make you vulnerable to emotional damage. The uncompromising position on divorce in conservative Catholicism, for example, can be quite distressing to practicing Catholics who eventually decide it's best to end their marriages.

Dani and Jaime

What is considered a breach of contract in any spiritual community can be surprisingly un-community-like, counterintuitive, and injurious. Like Dani and Jaime, who met in an all-women goddess spirituality group and were married by their teacher—a professional priestess. Three months after their wedding, Jaime came out as transgender and reached out for support as he engaged in the process of building a male identity. Because the women's community they were a part of did not accept trans men or women, they were forced to leave—"abruptly and painfully"—and not before their mentor and wedding officiant said very hurtful things to them.

When a contract is secure, you'll know, because the other parties will repeat back the terms to you with confidence and possibly even a smile.

This was my experience with my dear friend Aileen. Aileen sings like a bird—literally like a bird; she barely opens her mouth sometimes and lovely little birdy sounds sort of trill their way out. She also worked for an organization that brought dance-ed to public schools, and they had all the tech supplies you could want to put on a top-notch show.

So I took her and our multi-talented musician/artist/friend Deb out to lunch to explicitly ask for too many things: 1) Would Aileen sing our aisle-walking song? 2) Would she and Deb borrow the tech equipment from the dance org, drive it to the Berkshires, and set it all up? 3) Would they work with all the other musicians to orchestrate all live singing throughout the night? 4) Would the ineffably magnetic Deb be our emcee? and 5) Would Deb's good friend, DJ Concerned, be willing to help us out? (PS: DJ Concerned is SOOOO concerned. Truly. We had heard his funk, soul, reggae, Latin, Brazilian, disco, bhangra, afrobeat, hip-hop, electro vibrations before and fell in love.)

And would they do all of this for us as a gift, if we got their rooms? This was a *lot* to ask of anyone. But I went for it. Explicitly. And not only did they reply with a beaming "Yes!" but they repeated the terms back to me with great specificity and care.

We also went over everyone's needs and expectations repeatedly until the final hour. Yes, I'm blessed to know such radiant talents, and doubly blessed that they love Justin and me, but the outrageously generous contributions they made worked out because the contract between us was clear, explicit, and secure.

I've seen what the insecure version of this contract looks like, having attended a morning wedding at which the main performer—a drag queen billed as something like "The Illustrious Miss Understood"—never arrived. At one point, we noticed a two-year-old being wheeled into the venue—was *this* "The Illustrious Miss Understood"? It wasn't. As we exited, someone was entering whom I suspect was Miss Understood—as she was all tousled sequins and wig and said—"Aw, man. I missed it…" As one of the grooms says, "Asking a drag queen to arrive at eleven a.m. *anywhere* is asking a lot."

The trick is really to have a sense of the contract's security. If it feels like too much pressure, then you're probably trying to fit an overdetermined foot into a tiny glass slipper.

For example, if I'm to be honest, from the beginning of our contract with Zondra, it was not entirely clear just how committed she was to being our wedding photographer. Nor were we convinced from the core that she was truly the best fit—what with her penchant for images of death and suffering; she was a morgue photographer, lest you forget. When I told my friend Joy that Zondra would be the photographer, her jaw dropped. "Don't worry," she said, "I'll bring my camera."

We also might have noticed that at my friend Julie's wedding—in the French countryside, several months before ours—we discovered a far better fit for us than Zondra: Julie's cousin Ruthie—a magnanimous, Joni Mitchell look-alike—who took Julie's wedding pictures. We not only clicked with her and the shimmery, joyful places her eyes were drawn, but Ruthie, an L.A. native, had always wanted very much to see the New England fall foliage.

As much as I should have been apoplectic that Zondra bailed just before curtain—which, BTW, was for a gig of her own, and not really due to Justin's misinformation—I was actually relieved. This was an opportunity to form a contract that made more sense. I immediately called Julie, who called Ruthie, and within seconds we booked her a flight for the following day.

From this place of renewed strength, I was able to write a generous email to Zondra, apologizing for having inadvertently insulted her with our shoddy communication and inviting her to attend the wedding as a guest. She hasn't responded to that email to this day.

On the other hand, by mid-wedding day, Ruthie and the vibrant reds, yellows, and oranges surrounding our Inn were given an auspicious introduction. As she floated around the grounds snapping pics in what seemed to be an ethereal dance, Ruthie enjoyed the east coast fall. And in return, we continue to enjoy what she captured in her frame.

12 Open Invitations: Help Them Help You

"The baby that doesn't cry doesn't suck."

A waiter said this to me at a wedding in the Hamptons. I wasn't a guest. I was a waiter, and quietly, but crankily, in need of a dinner break. He was from Peru and his translation was a bit off; I think the phrase more commonly goes "The baby that doesn't cry doesn't get the milk" or "doesn't get fed." But I prefer his rendition. We don't read minds—most of us don't—so we have to cry for help when we want to "suck." But "suck" can have another meaning, and in crying for help, we also risk being the one who "totally sucks." In planning your wedding you need to take that risk.

> *If you single-handedly take on the whole load you'll get crushed.*
>
> To survive, you've got to ask folks to share in the weight. The clearer your needs are spelled out, the easier it will be for them to help, even if you inadvertently elicit some scorn in the process. The better you cry, the better you'll suck.

Learning to "Cry"

Delegating is tricky. To do so with purpose, without alienating or completely surrendering to someone else's control, requires discipline. It takes time and thought to translate your visions into codified requests. And if you don't believe me, I implore you to do a marathon of the reality show *Bridezillas*. Those girls are crying, but in all the wrong ways, and they toh-tally suck! (And with some of the guys

I know, *Groomzillas* could also be a show, but our culture unfortunately prefers to hate on greedy gals.)

What's not working for the *Bridezillas* is the lack of craft in their "cries" for help. We want to think of "cry" here the way babies or pets do it; the kind that would be a civilized request if only they could speak; e.g., "Please sir, can I have some more?"

> The *Bridezillas* expectations are impossible to meet only because they don't take the time to translate the impossible, twin tower cake of their dreams into a step-by-step recipe. You won't have this problem if you distill your vague wants down to crisp questions or instructions. Your people—the sane ones at least—will then be only too eager to help.

I have a hard time handing over the controls, or the yellow chalk of my childhood—"What if their yellow brick road is different than mine?" I literally had this problem on the playground in kindergarten while trying to produce my version of *The Wizard of Oz* by passing out "scripts" of construction paper with crayon scribble. Needless to say, the "actors" were uncooperative. Yes, I did cry, but not in a way that would help my cast better understand their text.

And yet, I went ahead and failed again, at my ninth birthday party, which I had intended to be an elaborate, live-action game of *Clue*. Each invitation contained a character assignment. Naturally, I was driven to tears when Miss Scarlet didn't kill the maid (played by my Miss Piggy puppet) with the wrench (a plastic stethoscope) in the closet via a secret passage (we actually had one) like I imagined. Fortunately, Colonel Mustard was a sensitive, problem-solver and he suggested we instead play hide-and-seek. As the irony gods would have it, this was more fun than live-action *Clue* and much closer to what I originally had in mind anyway.

Don't worry, I've continued to fail in translating my visions. And better. Countless times, I've handed writing to people—as an adult—only to get a can't-be-bothered "Huh?" in return. (Including versions of this book . . .) This happens in art, in theater, and in weddings. It's painful, but it's also part of the process. Don't let it shut you down.

> *Nothing is created, hatched, or born without pain, but the point here is that you have an ensemble to assist you, if you ask.*
>
> The theatrical event of your wedding is symbolic of your people supporting you through a painful transition. Entrusting them with some responsibility is part of this ritual. And you can help them help you better by writing their parts as clearly as possible.

You'll have to do better than scribble on construction paper. (If I had simply told the Wicked Witch in my playground production to "just run around and cackle," I might have gotten what I wanted.)

> *Remind yourself that people want to help.*
>
> Start from that premise. And that includes your other half—the one who isn't currently reading this book or planning as hard as you. Whenever Justin would say, "Turn the computer off and come to bed," I would sometimes get crazy-eyed, as though he were trying to sabotage the process. That's because I was too tightly holding the reins: too afraid to ask for help, too afraid I'd be misunderstood, or too afraid that if I didn't do it myself, it wouldn't get done, and I would fail, fail, fail! I pushed him away to protect my wedding fantasies from fatal engulfment. He was patient with me and eventually talked me off the ledge, reminding me not only that he was on my side, but that the big day was

about both of us. In protecting myself, I was also abandoning him. If I needed him to take over something—like the color printing of our American Gaythic image for our invitations (which he could do at the law firm where he worked!)—all I needed to do was get over myself and clearly ask.

You needn't wait to get crazy before you ask. Trust that they've got your back; all they need is clear instructions.

Help Awaits Your Command

If only I was so wise at the time. I had failed so well at reaching out that my friend Joy finally barged in, texting, "I'm coming over to help!" This was before anyone was allowed near our apartment—a.k.a. the wedding lab—that year.

The truth is we needed help cutting and pasting our invitations so we could get them out in a timely fashion, but I would not ask. We did them ourselves with fancy layered paper and our American Gaythic image, but putting them together required time, a glue gun, and several sets of hands. Oh, and letting go of my pride. I think it helped that I had acted with Joy several times. Actors understand process—trying, failing, failing again, and staying present with each other until something finally works. Wedding prep is better when approached this way as opposed to feverishly striving for perfection on one's own. I reluctantly, but graciously, accepted Joy's offer. And her invasion awakened me to my own need for help.

The point of prep work is not to generate more work.

No, the goal is to reduce labor—to pass it off and to make room for play. This means that in designing a wedding website (which, by the way, you can do by adding pages to a pre-existing website—if you have one—rather than paying a service), you're not creating an ongoing, full-time job for yourself. You're simply providing your helpers and guests easy access to your event—by way of organized information, dates, directions, and maps. You're inviting them to be part of it.

Be TMI

Don't be afraid of insulting your helpers' or guests' intelligence by offering too much information in emails, on your website, or in your wedding invitations. The more they know, the more they can help. We learned this lesson the hard way. Now, Justin and I consider ourselves to be reasonably intelligent, yet due to our ignorance, we got booted from a flight to India before his oldest friend B's wedding even though we had booked our tickets a year in advance. Apparently most people know that purchasing a ticket doesn't necessarily mean you have a seat and that you need to nag the airline until you do. But there are seemingly smart folks—like us—who don't read the fine print. There's no shame in adding this sort of info to your website, if only to ensure your guests get to India for your wedding.

> *Registering for gifts is another specific way you can help them help you.*

So don't waste precious time and energy with all that, "I just don't need anything" crap. You will become the tediously inscrutable enigma no one knows how to please, and in short, you will really *suck*—even as you attempt to avoid that very thing. Don't mess with the ironies in the wedding fire. Just pick some gifts.

If you're like us and pots, blenders, and espresso machines will cramp your city-kitchen style—and turn you into pathological hoarders instead of gleeful, yuppy homemakers—seek alternatives. We cherry-picked a few novel items (a mug here, a Le Creuset pan there), but mostly requested cash for our honeymoon, which was a smorgasbord of travel through Iceland, Denmark, and Sweden. I added a REGISTRY page to our website with luminous pictures and a button that said DONATE."

> Speaking of *donate*, if you truly don't want anything for yourselves, many people ask their guests to donate to their favorite charity, which is a meaningful and pro-social way to help them help.

Or you can skip tradition altogether and just tell them "presence" is "presents."

There are all kinds of gift-giving opportunities—ones that can actually be useful as opposed to mind-numbingly by rote. Justin's longtime friend Evelina, for example, did not think she'd ever be the girl who got *the dress*. Neither she nor her family could imagine the "aha" moment when it came to her bridal attire, fearing she'd be fussy, overanalyze her responses, and get in her own way. But when she tried on a gown that made her smile—beam, actually—her parents were quick to acknowledge this moment of unadulterated joy and bought it, even though they were in a tough spot financially. Evelina says, "I just thought at that moment, I am so lucky they would do this for me . . . and [they] never said a word about it, were happy in fact to do it."

On the flip side, it goes without saying that excessive requests do not help you or them. Going too far in the direction of asking/"crying" will obviously make it hard for anyone to want to come near you.

(The three-thousand-dollar three-thousand-thread count sheets may have to be something for which you save on your own.) You want your requests to invite people into your wedding space, not scare them off.

One way of conceptualizing this invitation is to think of your wedding as a play; one in which you write great parts for everyone else, but write yourself out of the script. At the final performance, we want to think of you two as being like royalty back in the day: watching theatrical events from their thrones, while the players played in their honor. And this will happen, if the players know exactly what you want. When you assign clear roles to people, everyone's happy.

Bill and Michael

Our friends Bill and Michael took that idea to the max! Their wedding was essentially a concert/variety show at an NYC winery/restaurant/concert venue. Expressions of love were showered on the grooms in the forms of live song, poetry readings, monologues, improvisation, and a virtual Candyland of desserts, all prepared by guests, upon request.

Both grooms have careers in entertainment—Bill's a phenomenal actor/mime and Michael a notable costume designer—so most of the performance slots were filled by pros. Two of my favorite folk singers—Suzzy Roche and her daughter, Lucy Wainwright Roche—were among them; and the actress Laura Linney interpreted a love poem—though not before saying, "Hi. I'm Laura Linney," precisely the way she introduces Masterpiece Classics, adding an extra tickle of queerness to the event.

What made this occasion so special, though, was the inclusion of performances by the non-performers. Bill's sisters from rural Montana enthusiastically staged and read text he had chosen, Michael's father and uncles sang a ditty they did for him as a child, and Michael's Mom exchanged a rotten orange with Bill onstage—a supremely-random and continuous practical joke they share. Everyone played a part. Not to mention all those cakes! We, for one, had a blast making a pink one—Michael's favorite color—topped with Bill as a black-and-white mime and Michael holding a pink strand of "measuring" Bubble Tape. It provided a great chance to mirror back our version of them.

Giving out roles makes things easier for you and for them.

For example, one thing I've not yet addressed as we discuss this period of invitation is all the ways our mothers tried to get in on the planning process. In other words, they had lists of people to invite— folks they mostly hadn't seen in thirty years. Neither of them was trying to hear us say no, even as we explained, and over-explained, and triple-axle-explained, our budget limitations. I should have encour- aged them to plan big birthday parties and galvanize their troops for that occasion. One need not wait for a child's wedding to celebrate with distant family and friends—especially at this post-tradition, post-etiquette, queer time we're in—but giving them both roles they enjoyed did the trick.

We tasked them with designing and constructing the table center- pieces, tapping crafty talents they both enjoyed using. This way they could dream themselves into the wedding, head a project—free of our micromanagement—and be involved in a way that helped rather than hindered. With my mom in New York and Sandy in Texas, they wouldn't even have to be roommates in the process (which, as you may recall, did not go over so well for them in Italy).

As you put roles, tasks, and responsibilities into other hands, you can begin to bodysurf on your crowd of support and a sense of wedding play can reemerge. The fun fantasies you had bolted up in a private safe in the name of work can be released.

During my dark weeks buried by spreadsheets, phone calls, and choices, I would sneak into the white light of my favorite fashion store, Costume Nationale. I couldn't afford anything full price, but I loved looking, touching, and trying on—I just love a good fit. One jacket that made me beam on contact—perhaps the way Evelina did in her dress. It was blue velvet, which would have been a queer outlier in our pre-conceived wedding palette of fall colors—though that really shouldn't have stopped me, and probably wouldn't have if the thing were only about five thousand dollars less. But the point is that the night Joy came over to help, a weight was lifted, and in sharing my jacket fantasy with her, I was once again able to freely play the game of wedding anticipation.

Joy didn't buy the jacket for me—the way Evelina's parents bought the dress—and that wasn't what I needed. It was enough to share my excitement, held by her helping hands. As she and Justin folded and glued, Joy mirrored back my moment with the jacket, singing in a queer, off-key baritone, "He wore bluuuuue velveeeeet . . ."

I leaned into the couch, chuckling, relieved. The invitations were now in other hands.

Part 4

Play with the Players, Party with the Parties

13 Casting Is Directing: Give Them Roles, But Let Them Play

"I am on a lonely road and I am traveling . . . Looking for the key to set me free . . ."

A sweet birdy voice chirped this from behind a door. It was the morning before our wedding and my attention was momentarily diverted from panic; Justin will tell you how not fun I am when overwhelmed. We crept toward the splendorous trilling, slid open the door, and peeked at our friends Aileen and Deb singing Joni Mitchell's "All I Want." We had commissioned a few live numbers from them for the reception, and though this wasn't one of them, what an effervescent surprise it was. They didn't do it that night, but this private, unsolicited performance—however weirdly voyeuristic—quelled my anxiety.

> *Keep your friends close, and your attendants closer.*
>
> Prepare these carefully chosen actors for your wedding play, but also let them interpret the roles you've given them. Once inhabited, their parts will develop a life of their own. They will buoy you through the rough seas of your nuptials and perhaps other tempestuous life transitions down the (sometimes lonely) road.

Directing

But first, you need to give them direction so they can prepare. I'm not the only one to witness that excruciating deer-in-the-headlights moment when a besty thinks they can . . . but oooh . . . they really can't give a toast on the fly. I once saw an unprepared best man struck completely dumb at the mic, followed by a very long, very silent walk of shame back to his seat—in front of two hundred guests.

I was that toaster at my friend Julie's wedding in France.

The day of the rehearsal dinner, her sister asked me to speak, and if I were George Clooney, I'm sure I would have charmed the enormous crowd with spontaneous clever words and a suave smile. But I'm not. Instead, I shared a clumsy story about falling in love with Julie's unabashed messy hair when we met in drama school—where, by contrast to Julie, many students overly cared about appearances. And it bombed. (My toast, not Julie's hair.) I mean, I'm sure I conveyed my genuine love for her, in my own queer way, but I'm also sure she would have preferred more polished words at that heightened moment. Given the opportunity to prepare, I might have achieved this.

> You might also give your chosen toasters some guidelines as to the kind of words you want to hear. Roasty? Poetic? Free style? Those with limited public speaking experience may not realize that their general feelings about you will not—I repeat: Will Not—translate without a specific focus or rehearsal. No one wants to hear, "Um . . . we've been through a lot . . . over the years . . . and um . . . yeah . . ." No one wants to *be* that unprepared fumbler either.

Though even when they choose a focus, without your guidelines, their toast could go horribly wrong. At a wedding that mixed both Jewish and Vietnamese heritage, I had the distinct discomfort of hearing an off-color mother of the groom's toast translated from Vietnamese into English. The translator was proper, polite, British, and tried to be as diplomatic as possible (think Maggie Smith as a hostage negotiator here): "The groom's mother would like to tell the bride's family that though they are . . . *[throat clear]* Jewish . . . and though America . . . oh dear . . . *[double throat clear]* bombed her home country all those years ago . . . she will try . . . *[triple-axle throat clear]* Yes, try, to welcome them to her family." Some angry booing took place amongst the confounded crowd, transporting us to a cage fight or an episode of *Jerry Springer*.

Casting

Of course, 90 percent of your job as director depends on casting. Now more than ever, issues of gender and wedding parties are generally discussed with a careful open mind. This is due to the growth of same-sex weddings with mixed gender parties, but also opposite-sex weddings which have increasing numbers of bridesmen and groomsgals. Unless your wedding is intended to be an historical reenactment, there is absolutely no valid reason to arrange the attendants based on gender. Remember, your wedding is a piece of theater, and the staging choices you make tell your audience a story. Your story. It will be more fulfilling if you're in charge of how it's told, rather than leaving it up to "tradition." You and the reps you've carefully chosen—male or female—are going to be more comfortable standing together on the same side, and if not, you might have chosen the wrong reps.

Justin and I each chose four toasters, with whom we were very specifically connected, so they were fore-armed with relevant stories. My youngest brother Mike, for example, was the one who found Justin for me on the telly; my cousin Lindsay and I shared in fantastic princess-play as children and in romantic dreams for our futures; Aileen—of the birdy Joni Mitchell trilling—was currently creating theater with Justin and me; and Julie . . . was just waiting to pay me back with an embarrassing story of her own. On Justin's side, we had his brother Chris, an emotional rock for him growing up; his childhood friend B, with whom he shared in precocious ambitions; his college overachievement-twin Evelina; and of course Hurricane Sharon, who shared in his passion for social justice.

These players knew why they were chosen. With time to prepare, they were able to dream themselves into their parts, empowered to love us up with purpose, humor, and grace.

Once the roles have been cast and the actors given direction, you can discuss what they'll wear. The thought of a "theme color" brings to mind the dresses and ties of teal, wine, grape, hot pink, and grass green that American weddings have been known for. And to go in that direction would have ended in death by vomit for me. So we looked to our original vision of flurrying fall leaves and decided to let the "costumes" bring that to life. We asked the ladies to dress in an autumn leaf color of their choosing; so they wouldn't necessarily have to buy something new. Our aisle billowed with gowns of red, brown, orange, and a wild tiger-print blouse worn by Hurricane Sharon. We told the guys to wear brown suits, though if I could do it over, I think I would have given them the option to wear any fall leaf colored outfit of their choice as well.

Costume Design

This may not be as simple as all gals in the same dress, all guys in the same suit. If for example one side of the aisle has all gents while the other has four ladies and one gent, does it make sense for the outlying guy to coordinate with his cohort ladies, or with the gents across the way? Or for them all to coordinate together? There will be a number of variables to consider before making a choice that feels most true—for you and for your cast.

When I was a bridesman for my friend Winnie, we collaborated on an outfit for me that fit with her party—which was all ladies in a variety of lavender gowns—as opposed to her husband's—which was all men in grey seersucker suits. Since tasteful lavender suits are not easily found, we got creative. The maid of honor and I chose to wear pale grey—me in a suit, with lavender tie and socks; she in a dress. Winnie then had us bookend the line of lavender ladies, making her party line cohesive and distinct. We made it work. Nothing was compromised in terms of relational storytelling or visual aesthetic.

Party attire was less complicated at my friend Allie's wedding—at which I was also a bridesman—since the colors were black and white. Gals in black dresses, guys in black suits (*Reservoir Dogs*–style), white shirts, black ties. And Allie in the middle, with a black satin sash round the waist of her winsome white dress and black patent leather heels to boot. Super symmetry—and without me having to stand inappropriately with her husband's friends.

Envisioning your wedding through a queer lens allows you to adapt tradition in the service of your truth. Give direction that reflects that best.

I was recently told about a wedding between a white girl from bohemian parents and an Indian boy from conservative parents. Their compromise was to have a traditional Hindu ceremony followed by a more free-form "Americanized" reception. The bride dressed in a traditional red sari for the ceremony (she changed into Western whites for the party), and her bridesmaids followed suit in pinky-purple. She also included a close male friend as a bridesman, who wore a white jubba—a long cotton tunic—to match the groom. The thinking was that though they were adapting tradition by including a bridesman, they felt they wouldn't go "too far" by keeping male and female colors separate. The result was beautiful, adaptive, and worked for everyone involved.

But I wonder about this choice. Since the bridesman was on the bride's side of the aisle, might not a pinky-purple jubba made him more cohesive with the bridal tribe? After all, traditional Hindu weddings don't even have bridesmaids and groomsmen to begin with—focusing mostly on the bride, groom, and their families. Why not follow the choice to adapt tradition all the way through? Our friend B, who is Hindu, says, "I don't think anyone would be offended by a colored jubba. Indian weddings are colorful anyway. And the good news about Indian weddings is that they're very flexible." No one felt compromised at this particular wedding, and so I'm inventing problems for them here, but it can only help to be mindful of the adaptive choices you make and how far you're willing to go with them.

In theater—yes, including weddings—bold choices without commitment are often worse than committed choices that are simple and safe.

For example, I was cast as one of the "lady" lovers in a contemporized production of *Love's Labor's Lost* years ago; the director is well known to be passionate about unsung stories. This Shakespeare comedy is setup like a classic wedding party, featuring romances between four royal ladies and four royal gents. The director's subversive choice was for me to play my "lady" as a man—who is paired off with one of the gents. Simple. No need to apologize or explain the choice to the audience. Fantastic.

Except that she wanted to open the show with a dance number that resembled a hip-hop video. And she decided it wasn't possible for my "lady-like" male to exist in that world. So I was cut from the opening number—the only cast member not onstage—which left me feeling degraded, especially as several guys in the cast made stupid homophobic jokes about it. The misguided premise of the director's choice undermined her original intention, which was obviously to transcend homophobia.

If you're going to make a choice to challenge tradition, don't halfway-house it. You may end up exacerbating the very problem you're hoping to explode.

Keep this in mind as you give direction to your wedding parties. For example, if you have a bridesman in an otherwise traditional, gender binary wedding party, craft a flight plan for processional and recessional that gives everyone smooth moves. Maybe all of the bride's attendants—including bridesman—can offer their arms to the grooms-men so that the entire tradition is subverted, taking undue focus off the bridesman as the odd man out. If you give enough clear, committed direction, you'll allow your party people to fully express themselves to you, each in their own way, without being distracting.

Now you might not have an official "party," and that's just fine. I'm sure you have an ensemble of some sort—even if it's just a few guys in white T-shirts and jeans pouring Lambrusco into plastic cups at your non-fussy marriage blessing. I attended such a wedding and it was delightful. Whoever your ensemble is, you'll want to similarly give them clear parameters, and within that, allow them the freedom to creatively problem-solve on their own.

As I have said, our "parties" were really just part of a larger ensemble. In addition to those folks who read text and gave toasts were our musicians: including my opera-trained-friend Allie, for whom I was a bridesman years later; our friend Brandon on piano; Aileen, a triple threat with verse, song, and toast; and Deb, who did everything from emcee, sing, and play guitar, to managing our crew. These four got together months before the wedding to rehearse the ceremony songs. All we did was give them sheet music while they took time to interpret the songs their own way. They collaborated on harmony, rhythms, and styling, culminating in a heartfelt gift to us. Within boundaries, they found the freedom to dream themselves into the wedding—giving us the opportunity to recognize them while they recognized us.

It's their day, too. It's their chance to creatively express themselves to you.

I've mentioned my friend Julie's wedding in the French country-side, where we all stayed for a week before the wedding. During that time, those of us who weren't helping to prepare fresh duck confit or bottle burgundy from the local winery picked wild flowers for the tables or assisted Julie's friend Claire—a notable pastry chef—with the delectable cake. Julie had directed Claire on the flavor and size, but I'll never forget the inspired moment when Claire spontaneously cracked open a random apricot pit, crushed up the kernels inside, and added them to the icing, giving it a queerly delicious tang. These are the moments that bring the wedding roles to life.

And the healing bit of theater they create plays for you again and again. Not only on your memory screen, but sometimes live.

One such encore occurred for me, poignantly, a few years ago.

I had been hit by an asteroid belt of transitions all at once: 1) A new full-time job at a mental health clinic; 2) A part-time psychotherapy job I had quit, due to the boss inexplicably deciding to stop paying me, while I searched for an office to which I could shepherd my clients (starting my own practice by default); and 3) Familial arguments about inheritance and my husband's protection if I were to die—the kind of stuff that drives people to murder in Shakespeare and Dickens, and in real life sends us into despair, if not relational disrepair.

During one particularly grueling day—after helping clients through hallucinations, suicide threats, and child abuse allegations—I listened to some voice mails. The first: angry, from my new controlling supervisor at the clinic. The second: angry, from the boss who stopped paying me. The third and fourth: angry, from my older brother and mother, respectively. The fifth: angry, from my family's financial planner.

But there was one more message. It was Aileen. She just called to say she was thinking of me during this difficult time. Within a second I was set free from my anxiety. She spoke in the same sweet, birdy voice she sang Joni Mitchell—unsolicited and in her own, playful way—on my wedding day.

14 Give Your Parties a Shower: Exploding Pre-Wedding Rituals

"Hey guys, d'ya have any cawk—tales?"

That's The Cocktails Girl. She's not real. She's a character I made up and play when I want my husband to laugh. And also when I want to have cocktails. And party. And not entirely own it. So I get creative and play her instead.

The Cocktails Girl is based on some of the twenty/thirty-something, dolled-up gals that carouse Manhattan late at night, *wasted*. I loathe them when they steal my cab on late rainy nights, using their crass, out-of-control feminine wiles gone wild. (One might argue that those who participate in LGBT pride equally contribute to such loud, crass performativity . . . but that happens one day a year.) I also loathe the male counterparts to these ladies, when they make needlessly loud aggressive animal noises, and when they threateningly call me, and other people, "Bitch!" or "Faggot!"

But aside from the horribly offensive vulgarity, I love their enthusiasm when seeking heightened, performative fun. It's of a brand I'm often too risk-averse to embrace—due to my own Spotlight Ambivalence, I suppose. This performative fun often shows up at bachelor(ette) parties and showers, and though I'm turned off by the stereotypical behaviors on the surface—howling at strippers; howling at non-strippers, while wearing penis crowns; howling at all!—The Cocktails Girls and their male equivalents are up to something I think can interest us all: a ritualistic, pre-wedding good time.

Need showers and bachelor(ette) parties be reductive, "naughty," vulgar, destructive, and over the top—ala *The Hangover*? No. They need not. So let's peek underneath the howling, and the penis crowns, to see what these rituals are essentially all about. That might free us up to enjoy them with our own spin.

Your Big Chance to Get Wasted?

The most short-sighted and stupid—though the most popular—answer to "Why have a bachelor(ette) party?" is that such parties are "just an excuse to get wasted." I say this answer is stupid only because it begs the return questions, "Why do you need an excuse?" and "Is getting wasted really the ultimate forbidden fruit?" This is an asleep-at-the-wheel way to view these events—and you'll have a much more pleasant ride if you're awake. (Not that you shouldn't get wasted, but is that all there is?)

Along the same lines of "an excuse to get wasted," I discovered this fascinating take on the bachelor(ette) party during a random online search (which I give to you in all its glorious, authentic poetry; complete with crudeness and misspellings):

"The bachelor party is not for the bachelor your stupid selfish asshole.

It's for all his single friends do get completely out of control with hookers and blow and have it be justified.

You are the gateway.

If you want to sit in the corner like a bitch and text your fiancé from the strip club, go for it.

We're gonna be nose deep in a butthole."

While this non-"selfish" (generous?) justification for partying with your party might strike someone's fanny . . . I mean fancy . . . it can't hurt to consider if it strikes yours. If accommodating your friends' feelings of entitlement to act out nihilistic sexual urges—because you have something they don't—sounds like a good time to you, by all means, dig in. But. To me this sounds like an end in itself . . .

Your Last Chance to Have Sex?

The next most popular response to the aforementioned question is, "This is the last night either of you have to celebrate your singlehood!" So, here's what I have to say about that: "Whaaat?"

Nowadays most fiancé(e)s live together before marriage and, guess what, they've had sex, too . . . Not that you should be ashamed if you haven't; you should be proud of any choice you've made that feels right for you. But, in most cases, couples have had, um, a LOT of sex with each other before their weddings. (Gone are the days of aunts asking brides, "Are you nervous about tonight?" as my mother's aunt asked her at my parents' wedding.) And in many, many cases, couples have had a decent amount of sex (hopefully safe sex) with other people before dating each other; and some also agree to have (safe) sex with other people while in a committed relationship. Most couples have had a lot of time to work out issues related to sex, cohabitation, and compromises before a wedding is even proposed. (Especially if they read Part 1 of this book.) So the idea of this night being a literal last chance at "singlehood" is largely an old wives' (or husbands') tale.

> *I disagree with Shakespeare's Clown in* **Twelfth Night,** *who sings, "Journey's end when lover's meet."*
>
> I don't think your wedding is the end, or the beginning for that matter. It's a stop on your train—a pivotal one. One that you get to do a lot of conscious creative preparation for in its process and execution, including rallying your peeps, which is really all bachelor(ette) parties are about.

If all you want is to rock out in the belief that your sexual freedom will literally, imminently, be extinguished, then you don't need my help. Anyone can tell you how to book a night at a "doll house" or exploit a guy with no health insurance to suit up like a fireman, plumber, or UPS delivery person, then strip down as he grinds against you with his package.

The Myth of Sexual Death in Marriage

I have to say, these traditions of the one-last-chance-to-indulge variety are antiquated. They derive from more puritanical times when that which was repressed dominated the psyche and was permissibly indulged in one explosive night of fun. (A fantasy of rapacious indulgence that has been part of male experience since the age of Zeus—remember all those myths about him raping peasant women, and then turning them into cows, or spiders, or just obliterating them with a lightning bolt—like it never happened? *What happens in Ancient Greece stays in Ancient Greece . . .*)

Bachelorette parties, on the other hand, didn't begin until the sexual revolution of the 1960s, and the first bachelorette party guidebook wasn't published until the mid-nineties. In the name of gender equality, the gals were after the same Zeus-like indulgence as the guys. All of them seeking one rebellious night of wild pleasure, reacting to old-school (1950s-style) social norms in which all non-spousal, sensual, erotic, relating was thought of in extremes, either unheard of or scandalous.

Although, today we're not quite as anxious and disorganized about our erotic feelings, and so this night of negligent purging doesn't really serve the same purpose. A lot of gay men, for example, frequently attend parties where they all dance together with their shirts off, enjoying each other's bodies without (necessarily) having sex, and without having to conceal such behaviors in shame. Couples of all kinds take tango and ballroom classes together where they swap partners, without (necessarily) exchanging keys, or feeling anyone's been unfaithful. Performers, such as actors, dancers, and acrobats, explore touching, kissing, and physically relating without having sex with each other (necessarily), or feeling the compulsion to run to a spiritual counselor and confess.

We are less threatened by erotic feelings now than ever before. Such feelings can be present in our social interactions without anxiety or fear. We have more socially acceptable options to work out our latent "naughty" sides than we once did (though some politicians might disagree). So paying for "one last grind" may not actually be the most freeing, fun, or even titillating way to enjoy this erotic, transformative, pre-wedding time with your friends.

Erotic Rituals

I suggest that getting wasted, grinding, and going nose-deep in buttholes are all merely ritualistic gestures; symbols of your independence transforming into interdependence. Sure, there is always destruction in a transformative process, but that doesn't mean you're celebrating "The End" of sex at this time. Perhaps you can think of your bachelor(ette) party as a ritualistic dance dramatizing the end of a certain kind of sex and a certain kind of self. You are moving beyond sex that is associated with "singlehood," total independence, and omnipotent fantasy. After all, the big advantage of being a bachelor(ette) is that, in hooking up with strangers—whom you'll never call again—you get to maintain a fantasy of yourself as an omnipotent sexual being without challenge or compromise (like Zeus). Marriage puts a cog in that wheel, to be sure.

But it also affords you a new mode of transportation. One that, with time, mutual empathy, trying, failing—failing again, and failing better—will make vulnerable pleasures available to you. These can only be experienced with experience. You will find yourself in the push and pull of a tango as you negotiate sexual fantasies with your partner; as you choreograph a fresh, new dance. One you can enjoy together, as an interdependent couple, in reality, as opposed to a fantasy of omnipotence—sitting atop Mount Olympus, alone. The symbolic bachelor(ette) party gestures can be seen as a fun ritual to send you on this journey rather than a literal attempt to indulge in "one last time."

The antics of The Cocktails Girls and—well, I guess we can call them The Butthole Guys—aren't as crass when we view them as non-literal, symbolic, performative gestures. An episode of *The Ellen DeGeneres Show* comes to mind here, in which she crashes a bachelorette party in Vegas. Dressed as her androgynous self, in white sneakers and comfortable pants, Ellen's wardrobe alone deconstructs the performative nature of the Cocktails Girls who are stereotypically outfitted in short skirts, big hair, glitter, and heels. She engages the gaggle of gals in standard "naughty" activities, but her queer presence increases the group's capacity to watch themselves playing their parts, from the outside. This only seems to heighten their sense of fun, and not just because they're in the presence of a celebrity. They are in touch with themselves as performers in this ritual and can therefore enjoy their creative potentials.

Creative Energy

As I've said, creativity is what we use to navigate between dreams and reality throughout our lives and therefore in our marriages. This time of transition is a fantastic opportunity to garner tribal support for your creativity. Along these lines, we can think of the Eastern practice of Tantra as underlying our wedding party parties. Tantra teaches the creative, erotic potential when opposite forces collide: e.g., mind and body, divine and earthly, singlehood and couplehood. The downside of tantric philosophy of course is that in promoting the idea of "opposites attract," the scriptures—depending on who interprets them—can get old-school-hetero-heavy as far as male/female sexual connections. Therein lies an unfortunate overlap between this otherwise progressive philosophy and religious conservatives who over-idealize the procreative potentials of traditional marriage. Obviously not all couples (same or opposite sex) *can* procreate, so in our pre-wedding parties we serve ourselves better by preparing for marriage with a ritualistic fluttering of our *creative* wings, as opposed to our *procreative* ones.

Creative energy of course includes procreation, but also just creation: dancing, painting, writing, theater, cake decorating. (All of which Justin and I have collaborated on since we started dating; and as I mentioned earlier, my Aunt Connie and her husband continue to collaborate together into their mid-sixties.) But maintaining your marriage alone requires creativity in and of itself. This creative energy within you is what your circle of friends are rallying around at this party time.

Take a moment to consider the meaning of your bachelor(ette) revelry and you'll expand your options of what to do. A night at the strip club is fine, but it might be more fun to be subversive: to take a strip-tease class or a workshop in burlesque dance, with a mixed gender group and then have a paintball tournament in the woods with the same group, dressed in "butch" camo fatigues? Or engage in a thrilling activity that has always frightened or eluded you—like rock climbing or bungee jumping—buffered by the fellowship of your peeps. There's always room to work some nightclub action in there as well, and yes, getting wasted if you so choose. But why not maximize the creative potential here?

Just as in theater, bachelor(ette) rituals are easier, more organic, and more fun when they have specific intent.

For example, though Justin and I had a blast partaking in Hurricane Sharon's bachelorette party—eating good food, dancing—I was somehow more impacted by the dramatic ritual we spontaneously performed on her behalf years before.

We had rented a house in Provincetown one summer with Sharon and Aileen, who were both single at the time. One night we all showed up at a "girl club"—to dance and to support Sharon in her quest for love. I can't remember how it began, but somehow we were circling a box in the center of the dance floor. The other revelers instinctively backed away; something was happening. We each slapped the box, one by one, as if to endow it with some sacred purpose. Sharon found her way on top and the three of us kept circling her on her high Sapphic perch, in a ritualistic dance. And though she didn't get lucky that night, I'd like to think this tantric exercise somehow prepared her for her marriage, years later. I also have a suspicion that Aileen stealthily initiated this dance, and that stirring up creative, erotic energy, intentionally on Sharon's behalf, conjured the current romantic love in her own life.

Even if you choose to do something unimaginative, literal, reductive, vulgar, and boring for your pre-wedding party, I wish most of all for you to be riotous with your friends while also feeling supported by them. If you choose to have separate parties—not everyone does—use the opportunity to celebrate your individuality in the company of your most trusted companions. They may want to surprise you with thrills, but make sure to give them strong hints for ways you'd like to play.

> ### Oh yeah, and then there's the whole idea of a shower.
>
> Well, if you need things for the home, and have more storage space than I do, sure, have one. But doing it just because "that's what the girls do" is just a dull reason to make everyone spend more money than they have. On the other hand, whether you're a girl or a boy, using a shower, or some such afternoon gathering, can be very functional if designed to be low-key and used as a launching pad for whatever evening of debauchery awaits.

When you distill the underlying meaning of these rituals, you consolidate your efforts, save everyone money, and maximize creative fun.

Remember this as you consider what to ask of your friends. Getting them to shell out too much money for travel, drinks, or spa treatments (or demanding the over-thirty-somethings to stay out past four a.m.) could turn an overly nurturing friend into one who suddenly understands the feeling of postpartum depression! (It's happened to me.)

I had the good fortune as a bridesman to plan shower/bachelorette parties for two different brides—Allie and Winnie—on two different occasions, using the same fabulous Soho hotel suite. (I only reinvent the wheel when something's not working.) Both ladies had indicated that great food, bar hopping, and the opportunity for lying around with their crew—in style—were priorities. So the respective bridesmaids and I surprised each of them with the suite. It provided a luxurious home base in which to visit, play performative games, and return to after a night out.

For Winnie, we concocted a lavender flavored cocktail—lavender was her theme color—and I made a lavender cake, decorated with a *Midsummer Night's Dream* concept: an edible Winnie waking from an erotic dream, in a forest of shimmery candy green, and lascivious woodland sprites surrounding her and ready to party.

We had blindfolded her at another location and escorted her to the suite. When she showed up at the suite, after her blindfold was removed, she said she imagined we were leading her to my apartment, so I could make her dinner—to celebrate her in a place she felt at home. Her response makes me think that the core of these celebrations is a little deeper than noses in buttholes.

For Allie, we sipped champagne, had our own private dance party, and got to know each other via embarrassing questions. Which brings me to the main advantage of having a central location for your party: it allows everyone to break the ice, bond, and become a new tribe. The trust your various friends develop will pay off when you rely on them—and they rely on each other—during the most high-stress, high-stakes moments before the wedding curtain rises. Also, this inclusive fellowship will surround you during future transitions, and in turn give the tribe a sense of belongingness at all of your big events. Their connectedness to each other will move along with you as you grow—a gift both to you and to them.

To summarize: use your bachelor(ette) party to celebrate your erotic, creative potential within a tribe of your own making—one that makes you feel like you.

If I had to do our pre-wedding party over, I might spend a day with my friends taking a cake decorating class; maybe bring that game of live action *Clue* I dreamed of as a kid to life, once and for all; take a dance class out of my comfort zone (*Magic Mike*–style striptease? Hip hop?) and then try out our new moves at a club. Maybe I'll do all that down the road, if we ever renew our vows.

What we actually did was get a Thai massage together. And then get wasted with good friends. While I played the Cocktails Girl.

'Til Wedding Do Us Part?
When Truths Collide

> **J:**   "You did ____ to me."
> **Me:** "No I didn't."
> **J:**   "Yes you did."
> **Me:** "Did not. You're crazy."

J is for Justin, but also for Julie. And for Janice, a former friend who exited my life as Justin reentered it. Weddings—and romantic love in general—present ruptures across a wide swath of relationships. With the gains come corresponding losses of recognition, of identities, and of friendship. Some of these ruptures can be repaired through the safety of empathic communication, while many others simply cannot.

Crazy-making Conflict

When Justin and I faced off—bitterly, furiously—two months before our wedding, and only hours before a Californiacation, neither of us considered the cliché of pre-wedding jitters. Maybe we believed our situation to be so unique that it could not possibly be shared or understood. I recognize now that tectonic relational shifting is a thing. It causes inevitable fear and pain. It begs us to choose between a relationship or being right.

He was wrong. That was all there was to it. What he accused me of doing did not actually happen. This made me so crazy that I called both of our mothers that night for validation—a mistake I never repeated and do not recommend. My mother said, "Yeah, he's wrong. You wanna come home?" And his said, "It doesn't matter what happened. Fight fair," which really meant, "I'm not on your side." My mother truly meant well, and though his would prove to be the rightest of all, at the time neither helped. There was no justice.

Forlorn moments like this are when people say, "I'll never trust another living soul again," and then become one of those prickly, never-vulnerable types (sort of like in sci-fi movies when a downtrodden character morphs into an invincible swamp thing). I was aware of my potential to join these ranks in my cab to the airport the next morning—alone, with five a.m., post-quarrel nausea.

Fortunately, we had planned to fly separately to San Francisco, where I would meet up with my dear friend Julie. The original plan was to find a grooms' suit before Justin arrived, but the real focus was to have a meaningful play date with Julie before adulthood got more complicated—she had just gotten married months prior. I'm forever grateful she was there with me when I landed—I mean, toppled down.

No attachment felt secure at that moment. Without Justin and me in agreement on an objective truth, I found myself floating in some insane limbo. If only someone would catch me and then go beat up Justin for making this happen.

Julie did neither. Which was a little frustrating, until I realized how loving she was being by patiently listening to me agonize. She parroted Justin's mother, Sandy, only more lovingly, saying, "It doesn't matter what really happened." And she was right. As I complained, listened, and reflected, I realized Justin and I both wanted the same thing: to get through this. The obstacle was the disagreement, the thing: he said it happened, and I said didn't. I won't tell you what *it* was because, as in the wise words of Sandy and Julie, "it doesn't matter."

I will say we agree that it was not illegal, nor did it include a firearm (sadly that statement is not redundant). If it had involved anything of the kind, moving forward would not have been likely—there are limits to the things for which we allow multiple interpretations.

As I tried on suits—helplessly following Julie's fashion-forward lead—I wondered why I was bothering to play dress up at all. Was this all a lie? Was I going to suit up in this costume to perform a potent, connubial, myth, only to mask my hollow, ineffectual, little self? This is that *Runaway Bride* (or Runaway Groom) situation, and I get it. You run from the altar and hide under a blanket, believing you don't have what it takes to both lose yourself in a relationship and still feel that you exist.

The morning before Justin arrived, I went for a run through San Fran's foggy, perilously steep streets. I paused at the Golden Gate Bridge to catch my breath and to see something larger than myself.

You're Both Right, You're Both Wrong

I realized that it was all true. Even if it wasn't. I may not have "attacked him" exactly how he had accused, but my outburst during our argument likely had a threatening edge. I recalled that my father had a similar edge when he lost his temper. My father's parents had it worse, and their Irish ancestors worse yet. This I could own, apologize for, and then make an effort toward future change.

If only Justin could equally appreciate the trigger: that when I fail to garner empathy for hurt feelings, the engulfment around me constricts. Then I react—perhaps threateningly—to wake him up before I suffocate. As with any escalating conflict, the game then changes from hurt to anger, from aching to accusation. Which leads us to the part when I invalidate and then abandon him—not just his accusations, but him.

Which isn't to say it would have been useful for either one of us to merely give in to the other's idea of the objective truth—that would have only made one of us the dictator. Many couples resolve situations in this very way because it's not as scary as being alone. But I hoped for a resolution with less precarious tension and more safety—less like a super-taut high wire from which we would constantly fear certain death, and more like a balance beam, closer to the ground. Or better yet, a bridge, appearing and expanding out of a fog.

When Justin arrived in San Francisco, he was no longer the enemy, even if his story was not the same as mine. I called out for him willfully from the gut—seeing him anew, and choosing him all over again.

We still haven't agreed as to what really happened during that fateful argument, and time has proven that it truly doesn't matter. We did agree, however, to fail better at mirroring each other's feelings. We also agreed to do this before becoming reactive in the future.

As we talked and walked the ups and downs of the San Francisco streets, we found stability in recognizing each other. This crucial rupture and repair saved more than a wedding; it increased our capacities to survive, appreciate, and even enjoy one another's subjective experience.

> ### *Navigating relationships is much ado about subjectivity.*
>
> Often when we think we've agreed on an "objective truth" we're really just opting not to challenge the oppressor—he with the most aggressively insistent narrative. That's how systems of power work. Have you ever been to Singapore? Pretty, tidy, not a fly in sight. Ideal? Perfect place to relax and have same-sex sex? It may seem that way, until you realize there are people hired to swat you out of sight, just like the flies—you could go to jail for years if you're caught. Objective narratives always seem like a good idea, until they write you out of existence.

Lawyers are often deceived by the notion of objective truth. (Hmm, Justin's a lawyer . . .) Lawyers do great and righteous work when they help the disenfranchised to narrate subjective experience in a clear and relatable way. But many of them insist this is all objective "fact"—facts that become laws, and laws that hopefully afford us all more equality and freedom.

A brief flip through American history shows how the "truth"
on which our laws are based is always subject to change—
including your current right to get married.

I once made a lawyer very upset at a dinner party making this point. She was motivated by the belief that finding "the truth" was possible. We all have to be motivated by something, I suppose, and I'm sure that way of thinking enhances her performance in the theater of court.

But it does nothing for us in the dance of intimate relationships. There, we have to make room for everyone's subjective story. Unless it puts us in harm's way, in which case we may need to seek professional intervention or say goodbye. Only you can make that call for yourself.

This is not only true with lovers, though romantic love always steals focus—like a photo-bomber—during any conversation about "relationships." There are many significant attachments in our lives and in our weddings. The betrotheds—and sometimes the parents—are the top-billing super stars, but the Oscars for best supporting actors often belong to friends.

Good friendships are of the most crucial kinds of love to have, to hold, and to hold closer by way of risking conflict. For instance, if I hadn't fought with Justin before flying to San Francisco, I just as easily could have fought with Julie after landing. I wasn't consciously angry with her at the time. How could I be? She was saving me from emotional free fall and increasing my will to play, but there was a smoldering resentment that didn't burst into flame until years later, when our lives—i.e., careers and families—intensified. What could have made me so angry?

I wasn't invited to her bridal shower!

Alright, sue me for being overly sensitive. And I know you're thinking, "What guy cares about a bridal shower?" but as Julie would tell you herself, "This one does." Before you dismiss me, though, at least examine exhibit A: I didn't know she even had a shower until some chick told me at Julie's wedding, saying, "We didn't think you'd want to be there. . . . You'd be the only guy."

I didn't reply with, "That's why you should have asked, beeyatch!"— which was good, because it was Julie's day to be queen, not mine. But I should have shared my feelings with Julie soon after rather than holding them in, expecting them to subside, because the heat only intensified when I wasn't invited to her baby shower two years later. Her friend's words still haunted me, "We didn't think you'd want to be there . . ." The word *We* was the most annoying of all. *We, We, We.* There's *We* and then there's *You. You* are not *We.*

Growing Apart Conflicts

The word *We* is the crux of all *Growing Apart Conflicts* (GAC), no matter who you are. Consider your single friends who get nauseated when you incessantly use *We* to refer to you and your *luvah* as one collective unit. Every time you say, "We love that new series," all they hear is "*We* looove having each other, and snuggling, and being on top of the world . . . without *YOU.*"

Consider also every time your friend who married for money and social status says, "*We* had lunch with Michelle Obama" ever so casually to emphasize the inevitability of his good fortune relative to *Yours.* Or when friends use *We* to refer to themselves and their babies when explaining "*We* have to indulge his adorably fascinating baby-ness, all day, while *You* watch us" or "*We* can never make time for *You*—ever—because *We* are now parents, and therefore the most important people in the world."

When *We* excludes *You,* the rupture begins.

And the awesomely frustrating conundrum here is that it works both ways.

When I confronted Julie—six years too late—I did so fueled by being right. My anger was completely justified, as triggered by her

We-ing her way out of a mini catch-up-cation—just the two of us—like the one in San Francisco. The *We-ness* of she and her baby; of she and her family of origin—who had a Von Trapp sort of tightness, always vacationing together in the hills—of she and her new friends, with money, and kids . . . It seemed like everyone else was clearly conspiring to shut me out, rudely and viciously, in the cold. And now, she was doing exactly the same.

When she reminded me that she had initiated all our contact in the past decade—calling me at least twice a month in that time—I couldn't disagree. When she reminded me of the efforts she made to visit me, with baby in tow—even for a weekend on Fire Island, where there's nothing for babies to do but get cursed by evil queens—while I rarely reciprocated, I could say nothing but, "Oops." When she reminded me of all the projects, and trips, and career advancements Justin and I—a.k.a. *We*—had the freedom to engage in, while she juggled raising a kid with a developing career of her own, I realized I wasn't as right as I thought.

This is what I call a *Beaches* fight. By which I refer to the 1988 film *Beaches* starring Bette Midler and Barbara Hershey as lifetime pals whose friendship ruptures and repairs—all to a sentimental Bette Midler soundtrack. A *Beaches* fight is a full articulation of emotional needs, followed by mutual, empathic mirroring. By testing each other's ability to tolerate our own versions of the truth, Julie and I created a bridge—one that our friendship currently balances on and one that is stronger than ever.

> **You see, when friends become family, they are no longer polite.**
>
> They attack and/or reject us, driving us to fight or flight. To salvage, adapt, and grow the relationship at this point, we need to engage in a *Beaches* fight. However, we rarely choose to go there, fearing what we'll get hit with in return and that we lack the

> effective tools for change. So instead we live with resentment or say goodbye, and sometimes that can't be helped.

As we reflect on these shifts, rifts, and losses, we become so much better in our roles during big life transitions.

★   ★   ★

This occurred to me recently, after visiting Julie just before she had her second baby. She called to apologize after the visit was over, concerned that the *We* of she and her son, and her dog, and her soon to be baby, had left me bored, stranded, and shut out. After all, this visit was such a far cry from our party time in San Francisco, when we were "young."

I told her the truth—a more expansive truth than I would have been capable of prior to our *Beaches* fight. I was happy to have this time with her, and I appreciated every effort she made to entertain me—e.g., making me pancakes while carrying a gargantuan boulder in her belly.

On the surface, this visit with Julie might suggest the dullness of life fading with time. But when I think back on our time in San Francisco, the real event there was not about being young and free as a bird. It was Julie's willingness to be with me, as a mirror and a support, during a fearful time of transition.

16   Oops, I'm a Celebrity: Prepare to See While Being Seen

"Just be yourself."

Don't trust anyone who tells you that. Because no matter who you are, the moment you're being watched—by a crowd, unprepared—you will not know who "yourself" is.

Take it from Justin's former *Real World* cast mate, Kaia. After seeing herself captured on TV—a highly specific version of herself; solipsistic, mostly nude, with coconut shell bra, and random Eastern décolletage—she began to doubt who she was. This break from reality became so severe that at one point after the show had aired on TV, she flipped through old photos of herself, pointed and said, "That's not me." She was not prepared to be watched and, as a result, her sense of self became stunted.

Asking for a whole lot of attention is a tricky thing. A lack of mental preparation can cause deer-in-the-headlights syndrome, or as in the case of Justin's castmate, a break from reality, rendering you *not really there*. Too much preparation can turn you into a monstrously demanding bride or groomzilla, rendering you *all too there*. Either way, you get caught in a dilemma that I call "Oops, I'm a celebrity."

> ### *"Oops, I'm a celebrity."*
>
> This occurs when your sense of self gets trapped in a moment of panic and narrows to a fixed, brittle object that is watched, overly watched, and watched some more. You become trapped in a hall of mirrors with only one image of yourself staring back

> with no freedom to move, mix it up, engage, or transform your environment.

It's like when you get that big ERROR message on an Excel spreadsheet because the formula you entered is endlessly self-referencing.

Here are a few examples:

1) Me—shell-shocked upon entering my ceremony, having thought "I don't need to prepare. I'll just be me. This isn't a performance." Oops. I was wrong. So sheepishly unprepared was I to receive the attention that my Aunt Rita from Lawn Guyland got all weirded out, saying, "Oh my Gawd, ya seemed sow nervous. What happened? Aren't you an actah?"

2) A groom I know—gobsmacked when it came time to say his vows, while we all watched, suffering together the slings and arrows of a blank mind under pressure.

3) A bride I know—armed with a perfect, lacey-meringue gown and regal veil—glaring from the altar like a furious goblin in response to a wailing toddler, as though she couldn't see us all there, watching her.

> Guess what? Not preparing to be watched is just as narcissistic as over-preparing. Both choices keep you trapped inside yourself and distant from your guests. You might as well film your wedding privately in advance and then invite everyone to a screening while you hide behind a curtain.

Now that's something we're all prepared to do, right? After all, we have mini-screenings of our lives on social media daily—sharing everything from brushing the pet to plucking our nose hairs. Maybe weddings will head in this direction, too. Filmed and screened, with top-notch production values: cinematography, editing, and CGI—just think, you could have a digitized Lady Gaga as your officiant. Your guest list could be unlimited, as you would merely need to click UPLOAD and POST to send your "wedding" into viral infinity.

But that would defeat the entire purpose, no? If traditional weddings provide anything worth preserving, it's the raw fact of them being live theater; a thrilling, perhaps fearful, exchange between actors and audience. And it's no wonder that frightens us. We of the oversharing "posts" are less prepared than ever to face people live, which makes it all the more crucial we prepare for our entrance.

Though, ironic as it may be, by preparing yourself to perform—as opposed to just being "yourself"—the more humble and generous you'll seem to your guests. And you'll have a hell of a lot more fun that way, too.

> ### *But how do you prepare to be watched, effectively—by all of them, all at once?*
>
> How do you find the right balance: without being *not there* or *too there,* but just comfortably present?
>   I suggest we find this balance when we let "them" in.
>   Who?
>   Them: our fears, insecurities, flaws, and most important of all, our people. When we let *them* into our consciousness, we have more room to expand our sense of self than when we remain frozen in a frame.

This is easier for some than others. Justin, for example, entered our wedding stage with a more poised, generous presence than me and with less internal conflict. He was less interested in how his flaws might be perceived and more so in truly showing up. He watched the faces as he walked down the aisle; listened to the singing and the reading;

and absorbed the toasts, the energy, and the chitchat throughout the evening. He wasn't just "himself," he was also them.

So, to escape the "Oops, I'm a celebrity" trap, you've got to loosen your grip on the role of "watched" and become "watcher," as well. Bring your people into sight, into mind, into yourself.

Lindsay and Paul

That's how my cousin Lindsay survived the bridal hot-seat. Lindsay is Aunt Connie's daughter, but unlike her mom, she wasn't bitten by the acting bug, nor hexed by Liz Taylor—Lindsay doesn't like to be watched. As she floated down the endless lawn of aisle, in front of two hundred-plus guests, Lindsay panicked. Like Sandra Bullock's astronaut-in-crisis in the movie *Gravity,* she found herself in limbo, gasping for air, thinking, "Tell me what to do, tell me what to do . . . " Until she saw her husband Paul's eyes and let him in. Suddenly, she was grounded. She could then let the rest of them in as well.

If she hadn't told me, I would never have known Lindsay was lost in space for that moment. To me, she seemed calm and radiant throughout her wedding, thoroughly enjoying her guests.

Look Around You

Give yourself advance time to reflect on *them*: all of the people you've chosen to co-create, support, and witness your event. Watch them, recognize them, and hold them in mind. Take in their humor, kindness, talent, quirkiness, strength—all of the shimmery qualities that draws you to them and that heighten, challenge, and inspire who you are. (After all, they are who you are. Whenever I get a compliment, it's usually for a quality I've stolen from a dear friend.)

This preparation will help shatter the treacherous looking glass as you enter your wedding and allow you the freedom to see, not just be seen.

During our last phase of planning, I found making a slideshow of our chosen people to help me get over myself. I only wish I had allowed more of that spirit to walk with me on the big day, as I processed, painfully, from privacy to public view—startled, as if I'd been caught backstage.

The hours I spent making the slideshow, on the other hand, were lively and joyful. That process brought to mind the relationships we had forged, maintained, and most importantly, chosen. There was no rule book for weddings like ours, and since we were on a budget, everyone on our short list was there by our choice. No one was invited out of guilt or obligation. The slides told that story.

I set each frame with a picture of me on the left and Justin on the right. The concept was our lives growing together, side by side, from babyhood (when friends and smiles were not a choice) up through the present (when everything around us was chosen: friends, smiles, selves). I was completely engrossed and impassioned as I made it.

Remember before when I said we'd all rather upload photos than face a crowd? Yeah, that obviously applies to me. As my Aunt Rita pointed out, I am an actor; but that just means I like to pretend to be someone else when I face a crowd—which is not unlike uploading pictures of yourself in the light in which you want to be seen. And about that . . . I should tell you that I programmed the slideshow to speed up during all awkward adolescent pics. Oops. Guess I was trying to control my image. Like a celebrity.

Oh, and we should also talk about the picture of me in drag that triggered a big ERROR message for Justin and me, which was followed by some soul searching.

The Insidious Power of *Normal*

It was a picture of me at eighteen, striking a pose in a shimmery mini-skirt, boots, makeup, and barretts. I put it next to a photo of Justin and his teen friends masquerading as the cast of *Beverly Hills 90210*. Both of us playfully nodding to camp, in parallel. Or so I thought. Justin winced when he saw it, like I had squirted lemon in his eye. He asked me to rethink using it, as if somehow the sight of me in drag would stain the entire show. Red hot shame instantly rushed to my face.

Oops, I'm a celebrity . . . in drag. *Outed!* Cut and print. So much for impressing everyone with my impressive normality.

In my head, I knew that my first instinct to use the photo was rightest, queerest, and therefore truest. I also knew that with the wedding two months away, Justin and I were both reflexively, anxiously—irrationally!—reaching for perfection. But there was a crack of doubt through which my mother's Spotlight Ambivalence crept in, and I became flooded with her fear of The Elton John Wedding. Who was I? Who did I want them to think I was? Why was I trying so hard to control their perception of me?

We step into an "Oops I'm a celebrity" dilemma like this when we think of ourselves as an encapsulated image. Naturally, we prefer this image to keep our perceived flaws at bay: those qualities—much like other people—that might challenge us and keep us on our toes. But those same perceived flaws free us up to have a more fluid sense of self.

Self, Interrupted

Movie star Winona Ryder generously volunteered (sacrificed?) herself for possibly the best demonstration of "Oops, I'm a celebrity" of all time:

Gen Xer that I am, Winona's iconic performances in the 1990s were *everything*. Always playing an adolescent uncomfortable in her own skin—not quite settled in her beauty, sexuality, mind, or talent—but who railed against this fragile sense of self with angst. This was the celebrated spirit of Generation X. What we didn't realize at the time was that our wide-eyed leading lady wasn't leading us anywhere. Remember her graduation speech in *Reality Bites*?: "Fellow graduates, the answer is . . . I don't know . . ." She really didn't. Instead, she was trapped in a premature, narrowly defined self-image—one that became stunted in our gaze.

Looking back on the poster for the 1999 film *Girl, Interrupted,* Winona's alarmed, wider-than-ever eyes—telegraphing both "I've been caught" and "I need help"—may have revealed more about "herself" than her character in the film. She eventually enacted getting "caught" in real life, which led to getting "help" when she was arrested for an inscrutable bit of shoplifting. Career, interrupted. We brides and grooms unwittingly telegraph similar signals to our guests when we're "caught" on the altar, unprepared for attention.

But we need not be unprepared for their gaze. We need not wait to get "caught"—e.g., shocked, speechless, apoplectic, drunk, or zombied out on pills—before we let them in.

See While Being Seen

I can't say for sure, but I suspect Winona is better off now. Her time away from being watched has certainly freed her to watch, not just be watched. And I imagine we'll see more fluid and various versions of her, both in art and in life. Much like Justin's *Real World* castmate, Kaia.

Having lost sight of herself upon seeing herself—too aware of her own nakedness, like Eve having tasted the apple—Kaia broke free of being watched. She achieved this by covering herself both literally (by putting on some clothes) and figuratively (by stepping away from the public eye). And also by watching other people. She became a lawyer and now involves herself admirably in global human rights efforts, social justice, and work with children—vocations that have expanded her sense of self by letting other people in. She's much happier now, free from her limiting celebrity image. She also now goes by her given name, Margaret.

Similarly, the groom I mentioned earlier, who forgot his vows, rescued himself—and us—during his frozen silence. Rather than helplessly succumbing to the pressure of being watched by saying something cliché, or just cracking, he finally looked at his soon to be husband, leaned in close, and whispered. I'm not sure what he said, but it seemed organic, simple, and honest; the kind of moment Sofia Coppola captures in her films, again and again. He then looked at a few of us in the eyes and smiled. Free.

Likewise, the bride I mentioned? With the furious goblin glare? Yeah, she recovered, too—once cocktails had been served and she could shake and stir things up with her friends. In my memory, she was her most radiant and free self that night while presenting a special birthday cake for her childhood best friend who had flown in from Israel that very day.

Russ and Frank

Now, some folks cut off this entire "Oops, I'm a celebrity" thing at the knees by letting *them* all the way in. For example, a guy I know, Russ, avoided the pressures of being watched at his Burning Man wedding by marrying not only his husband Frank, but all of their polyamorous guests, as well—albeit, symbolically. An interesting fact about Russ and Frank: they have an open relationship that neither has acted on. But by simply having the agreed upon freedom and possibility of "letting them in," their marriage remains spontaneous, alive, and free.

★   ★   ★

Obviously it's far easier to recognize how this phenomenon impacts people other than us. For instance, more clearly than my own dilemma I could see my mother, trapped in self-referential grief during our reception. I recall seeing her off in a corner with my older brother, looking forlorn, stuck on the absence of my deceased father; oops, I still have pictures of these celebrity mourners. But when my friend Deb led my mom out onto the dance floor, she came back to life with the simple touch of another living force and by simply letting Deb in.

Don't worry, I got over my celebrity self, as well. I found a way out of my head and into the wedding by watching my friends perform, by asking them questions (mind-blowing solutions here, really), by taking a genuine interest in *them*.

Oh, and by letting in my perceived imperfections.

There's something so grounding, shoulder-dropping, and freeing when you invite your perceived ugliness into your body. (Cinderella's stepsisters could have used this advice: remember how unhappily unfree they were after chopping off their feet to fit into the silver slipper?)

So yeah, I left my cross-dressing picture in the slideshow. It now seems completely stupid that I ever gave that a second thought, what with today's rousing variety of cross-dressing children and teens. And besides, I'm hardly gender conforming when dressed as a man, so . . .

During the show, there were giggles when my drag pic came out. My uncle's boyfriend catcalled, "Werq!" And then the slides moved, and the audience with them. Their reactions flowing from tickled to touched as they recognized various versions of the present company on screen, including themselves.

Part 5

Project Alter: Making Things Work, Letting Things Go, and the Wisdom to Know Which Is Best

17 Control the Narrative: Don't Blame, Just Reframe

"Are you ready for your big party?" Justin's grandmother asked during a phone call. She was referring to our imminent nuptials. She had been using the word *party* repeatedly to describe our event.

Justin was flummoxed and crestfallen, even though his grandmother's move was familiar to him.

For as long as he could remember, her WASPy charge sent him, his mom Sandy, and brother Chris, into a frenzy. Before the grandparents would come for a visit, they'd all gussy up the furniture to give Sandy's home the impenetrably sterile appearance of a New England yacht club. This was still never enough to stop granny from declaring something out of place—as though she were the Queen of Hearts in *Alice in Wonderland* crying, "Off with its head!"—as she marched from room to room in her red LL Bean sweater, pressed khakis, and scepter with the Fox News logo on it. (Ok, I made up the scepter, but I imagined her holding one when I witnessed this ritual.).

Sometimes Justin would scuffle with her a little—on his mom's behalf—but he'd soon give up. All of them were ultimately aware they were temporarily under grandma's rule—her narrative, her idea of normal.

Yet, even after years of her unrelenting normative regulation, he could not be prepared for the sting that came with her asserting the word *party* instead of *wedding*. He did not—could not—respond. They finished up their phone call, and he hung up, leaving reality as she thus spake it.

At this stage in your planning, it's easy to get beaten down by someone else's narrative. You're tired, there's too much on your mind, and it may seem best to—as my brothers used to quote *Star Wars*—"let the wookie win." But this of course depends on how much *the wookie's* version of reality impacts you: how powerful, hurtful, insulting, degrading, and/or alienating it is.

> Surely you didn't spend the past months preparing to go public with your love, only to let someone else rewrite your press release at the eleventh hour. Being invalidated wasn't part of your plan—especially by someone you love dearly. But only you can decide if it's better to try and turn the tide or to wait it out.

Pushing Back

Justin thought he could wait it out. Why should one word disrupt him from resting in his truth? But his unresolved hurt feelings took on a life of their own, and emerged, as such feelings always do.

One day his mom called him with some concerns of her own: she wanted her parents to sit next to her during the ceremony, and I had told her no. I had a methodical plan in mind, you see: everyone speaking, reading, or singing during the ceremony would sit up front, and everyone else would sit behind them. Sandy was reading, his grandparents were not. It made sense. But considering the discrepancy in our family sizes (mine's ten times larger than his) and that more of my family had ceremonial roles, Sandy justifiably felt invalidated. I was altering her narrative by publicly seating her without family. Making her feel degraded and disconnected.

Well this seems easily solved, right? A little musical chairs never hurt anyone. Except Justin was hurt. And the thought of his grandparents sitting up front without dignifying the event with the word *wedding*, made him feel degraded and disconnected from them.

After sharing this with Sandy, she took the dilemma on herself, writing an email to her mother on Justin's behalf:

Justin was upset and humiliated by you continuing to call their wedding a "party" and he wants to let you know how that makes him feel. Just FYI here below are some benefits that apply to married couples that will be denied Justin and Mark.

Sandy had included a long bulleted list of marital benefits that she had copied and pasted from the National Gay and Lesbian Task Force website. She continued:

They are not getting married because of any of them. They are getting married for the best reason of all. Because they love each other.

This message was compelling in and of itself, but Sandy took it further; reframing the concept of marital "traditions" and hoping to broaden her mother's mind and heart.

Also FYI, the word "marry" comes from the Latin term for "a husband" (*maritus*), which comes from the Latin word for "a man" (*mas, maris*). The notion of "marriage" therefore doesn't seem to refer to "wives."

Here Sandy intriguingly illuminated for her mother that to invalidate our wedding based on "tradition," she would have to invalidate her own, as women were historically viewed as non-entities with regard to marriage.

But Sandy did not stop there. Having scoured the internet for documents of religiously sanctioned same-sex weddings, she copied, pasted, and reframed history (and her story), including accounts of men united in pre-modern Europe—e.g. "The Office of Same Sex Union" (tenth and eleventh centuries), the "Ordering for Uniting Two Men" (eleventh and twelfth centuries), the "Order for Solemnisation of Same

Sex Union" (thirteenth century)—and also a Serbian Slavonic "Office of the Same Sex Union," uniting two men or two women (fourteenth century). After controlling the narrative thus, Sandy concluded with:

Just some things to think about . . .

Sandy's email provided a marvelous education about a history obscured, but it also revealed her own obscured story. By advocating for Justin, she was advocating for herself. She had deferred hurt feelings of her own, not being entirely seen by her mother, and here was an opportunity to make a bid for recognition. Vicariously.

This chain reaction of feelings—of historical perspective, and the symbolic power of words—seemed to be snowballing with no end in sight. As loving as Sandy intended to be in writing her mother, and though her points were strong, the rift was not likely to be healed this way. If only Justin had nipped it in the bud with his grandmother on that fateful phone call.

But easier said than done.

Without a reserve of self-assuredness, insight, and sensitivity—and who has that when talking to family?—our attempts to set the record straight can easily devolve into unintentional war. Justin didn't want war. He wanted his grandmother to recognize him. So he wisely took some time before getting back to her.

Wearing Your Story on Your Sleeves

Fortunately this all took place during the time we were shopping for suits. With the big day around the bend, it's a good idea to get into your body whenever possible—so as to dilute the emotional intensity and clear your mind. And trying on clothes is a great way to do that.

> *Your choice of attire is a significant way to control your wedding narrative.*
>
> Your costume reveals you. It is ideally an expression of imagination that also makes you at home in your own skin—no matter how simple or flashy, traditional or queer.

Several people asserted the opinion that we should wear matching black tuxes. You know, to reference the traditional cake topper and say to the world, "See, we're normal in every way, but one." Lobbying for one's normality has always made me feel a little nauseated. It suggests a desire to prove, rather than to express, and I've always preferred the latter. I recall one time, in our early twenties, for example, when our friend Lyle (who was closeted at the time) instructed us that the "ideal couple" was *never* to be affectionate in public. (He has since discovered that holding hands in public is "nice.") Justin and I weren't "the ideal couple" then, and we had no intention of appearing that way now.

So, no black tuxes for us. We each chose very different brown suits that our eyes were drawn to respectively. His was more formal—chocolate, with orange pin stripes; while mine was more fashiony—made from beige, shimmery, wool that wrinkled as per the style—quite queerly. Smiles instantly ensued when we each put them on. This is how you want to feel when inviting guests into your world, your couplehood, your home: comfortable in your skin, in your story, and eager to share yourself with them.

> *You're creating a system of belonging, and you want your storytelling to reflect that: both in the words you use and the clothes you wear.*

> In controlling the narrative of our weddings, we want to think about inclusion, rather than exclusion. Justin and I discussed this while trying on our costumes.

In the spirit of inclusion, together we reflected on his grandmother.

Rethinking the Enemy

Though I keep referring to them as WASPs, his grandmother was actually born to Cuban immigrants, while his grandfather grew up on a small Midwestern farm. Together they controlled the narrative of their identities and marriage, performing, and successfully achieving—through education and social prowess—a WASPyness that was considered to be The American Dream during the 1950s. In other words, grandma's normative regulation hardly came from malice, but rather from the will to maintain her earned status and to encourage her kin to achieve the same for themselves. Yes, this sometimes came at the cost of misattunement with her children and grandchildren, but that was hardly her intention.

To sense her intention, you'd have to spend Christmas with her. Those of us who were lucky enough to have this privilege got to enjoy the Cuban queerness behind her WASPy curtain and experience her heart. Each year, without fail, she would put on a Santa hat with a blinking light, which instantly made her smile. She'd then sing "Feliz Navidad," warmly and embracingly to her entire family—including me.

But she wouldn't be wearing the Santa hat at the wedding, and she would have only her words to express her love and respect for us.

Reframing the Narrative

Having processed his feelings, gathered his thoughts, and harnessed his intention, Justin wrote his grandmother this email:

Grandma,

I'm looking forward to seeing you, Grandpa, and the rest of the family this weekend! We think it's going to be a great time.

I decided that I had to write to you before this weekend comes. In our last conversation on the phone, you referred to our wedding as "your big party," and I was really hurt by that.

You have asked me more than once about why we are getting married if it does not confer an enforceable legal bond upon our relationship. You may or may not know what a complicated question that is: that if we just lived two hours northeast in Massachusetts, our wedding would be legally enforceable; that we can't get legally married as New York residents in Massachusetts only because the governor of Mass. recently chose to dig out a dusty law from 1913 and to selectively enforce it against same-sex couples; that just months ago we narrowly lost the right to legally marry in New York state; that only weeks after that we lost the right to travel to Washington state and legally marry there (by a vote of 5-to-4 in the Washington Supreme Court); that in weeks or months from now, we may get the good news that Mark and I and other same-sex couples can get married in Connecticut. And so on, and so on.

I wanted to provide you with all this legal detail because this is our life. Every time a court or legislature rules on our fundamental rights, our hearts go up into our throats. We cross our fingers and squeeze our eyes shut, hoping. Once, in Massachusetts, we erupted in joy. The other times, our hearts dropped to our feet. You know what this feels like? Ping pong. It feels like our life together—all the love and work that goes into making a home and a lifelong relationship—is a ping pong ball knocked back and forth by politicians and judges on any given day. It really makes us question the country we live in and what it means to be an American. But it also makes us ask: what is the meaning of a marriage? Of a wedding? Is it simply legal? Is it the legal status alone that makes a marriage real? That can't be true. Suppose that after you and Grandpa had been married for one year, or two years, or four years (the time that Mark and I have shared the same home together), suppose that a law was passed that said: "Men with the last names starting with B cannot marry women with last names starting with A. Such marriages are null and void and have no legal status." This would apply to you. Would that mean that you and Grandpa were no longer married, because the law said so? Or is the reality that a marriage is much much more than the significant (over 1,000) legal benefits and rights that can come with it? We believe a marriage consists of many things: publicly vowing your love and fidelity for the person you will share your life with; mutual support of all kinds, financial, emotional, intellectual; making a home and building a life with someone out of all the everyday materials; compromise and listening and many other things. We believe a wedding is the day when you pledge all of this before the community that loves you most. You are a part of that community, Grandma, and so is Grandpa and all the rest of our family. This weekend, everyone gathered together knows what they are gathering for: a wedding. They know this because they know us. Most of them are our friends, people of our generation for whom a wedding between two men is a less confusing thing than it probably is for you. I know that you sometimes struggle with how to understand my life and who I am. But I also have seen you and Grandpa get older the past few years. I have seen you grow more isolated in the way that aging will do to people, isolated from the world outside and even from each other. This is hard to see for those who love you, almost as hard as it must be to witness it happening in yourself. But I love you very much and I don't want you to feel isolated or confused or out of place this weekend. I want you to feel like you fit in, so I thought I owed it to you to try and personally explain the meaning of this weekend. And, at the bottom of it all, I want to feel understood by you, I want you to understand the meaning and beauty of my relationship to Mark. That's all anybody wants: to be understood. We are both so excited that you are alive and well and able to come share our wedding with us. My old friend Lyle's mom barely made it to his sister's wedding before dying of cancer last month. We know how lucky we are to have you with us and what a mistake it is to take anyone's attendance for granted at such an important event. I love you, and see you very soon.

Justin

The email contained no blame, no moral superiority, shaming, or excluding. It was a careful reframing of the narrative and the intention to include. And it was effective. His grandparents showed up and had a good time. No hurt feelings, no war.

I took a similar approach to conflicts of my own throughout the wedding. Whenever someone said, "You need to iron your suit," rather than fire back with, "No I don't. Fuck off!" I would just smile and say, "That's the design. I love it. How are you?"

18 . . . and Release: Having Your Mess and Surviving It Too

"That woman looks like a mess; we should go talk to her," said Justin, with a smile.

We were at an upscale wedding and it was getting stuffy. That is, until the middle-aged woman with wild hair and brightly colored kaftan swished by like fresh air. A drink was attached to her hand, as though she were a collectors' doll called *Messy Nessy. . .*

Why are we so entertained by mess?

Gay men in particular have always found messy gals—like the ones from the hit show *Ab Fab*; Megan Mullally on *Will and Grace*; Christine Baranski in everything she's ever done; and the overly tan, overly botoxed reality stars with high frequency meltdowns—to bring them joy. Many women also enjoy heightened girly-mess, though perhaps less of the medicated variety and more of the overly aggressive sort. (Two sides of the same coin?) Check out the Lifetime Network's buffet of shows with ladies screaming, tearing at each other's hair, or wielding over-the-top weapons—e.g., fire irons, pitch forks, antlers—against each other or would-be rapists.

> *Perhaps we identify with the amplified strife within these characters.*
>
> After all, many of us have endured crazy-making obstacles, injustices, and doubt in our own pursuits of recognition and respect.

It's fun to see your disavowed truth in someone else—"That's not me, that's her"—and also cathartic, especially when there's a campy distance between you and the bathos.

(Pop entertainment is even evolving, giving us a wider selection of messy characters to enjoy, including—wait for it—men.)

In contrast to these characters, however, we prefer ourselves to be mess-free and to have our weddings follow suit. With the finish line in sight, you're perfecting the seating chart, making sure the cake arrives on time, and hoping that all deep-seated issues between folks are checked at the door. And though it's well worth trying to get these things under control, you also want to make room for mess. Because when it arrives—and it will—there won't be a campy *Messy Nessy* doll—with Kaftan and big hair—to take all the credit.

The last chapter was on controlling your narrative: mindfully, reflectively, and inclusively. And you should always try that first when you hit a relational speed bump. But if that doesn't work, you'll need to let go.

Scream!

Maybe literally, maybe not. Maybe at a person, maybe not. Don't club anyone with a pair of antlers in the style of a Lifetime Movie Network thriller, but at this point you'll need to unleash overwhelming feelings. Otherwise they will erupt on your guests or eviscerate you during the wedding.

I know I advised you to contain yourself at the beginning of this journey. But you've worked so hard, and with the show about to go on, you'll want a big release now so you can play later.

We're our most sensitive right before we go onstage, before we reveal our greatest passions. And according to George Eliot: "Our passions do not live apart in locked chambers, but . . . mess together . . ." *Mess* meaning "to eat in a particular place" and *mess* meaning "mess." So, passions are messy. They resist containment and will not be controlled. But if we don't satisfy their appetites, they'll take control of us. In other words, you likely have intense feelings about many, many things right now—e.g., people you've never loved more, people you've never hated more—and you best get messy with these passions before they get messy with you.

> *Don't leave your mess to explode at a moment of its own choosing.*
>
> Now's the time to get an expensive massage; punch a punching bag; skydive; buy some over-priced, fluffy slippers; dance all night at an illegal party; or have an argument you would otherwise defer.

I just barely let mine go at the eleventh hour. It was the eve before driving up to Massachusetts for the wedding. I had midterms the next day—having started grad school a month prior—and I decided to call my mother.

Here's why I knew that was bound to be a mess: on our last call, she told me she might skip the rehearsal. "Your older brother's flying in that day," she said. "I can't spend time with my son?"

Where to begin? I was incensed, despondent, gobsmacked. Did I hear that correctly?

I waited. She didn't seem to hear herself. So I reluctantly went ahead and spoke the clumsy line I hoped to avoid: "Your *son* is getting married in a few days. And you agreed to do his centerpieces."

Such lines are hard to hear in films because they're superfluous; we hear them and think, "Ugh, too much. I get it." But she didn't get it. Even after I said it.

So I went on. I tried explaining how what she said made me feel: hurt, unimportant, invisible.

Silence. We hung up.

Again, I knew the next call would be a mess. But it was a mess I didn't want living inside me for the duration of the weekend. Maybe she'd come around this time—having had a few days to think. Maybe now she'd hear how much I needed her support, emotionally and practically. Maybe she'd agree to attend the rehearsal and to join Sandy in putting together the centerpieces, as promised . . .

I began the call safe, going over basics: We would stop at her house for dinner the next day, on our way to Stockbridge. *Great.* One of our guests had chosen not to drink at the wedding—he was going through a rough time—and another would refrain from drinking as well to show support. *Great.* Justin and I would likely celebrate with some champagne at the reception, but we'd be sitting at our own table, so it wouldn't be in anybody's face.

Uh oh. Let the royal mess begin.

"Oooooh," she said, in a "La-dee-dah" sarcastic tone. "So you can drink at your wedding but no one else can?" So . . . already we had gone from zero to psychotic. The empathy I was seeking on this call was eclipsed by volatile nonsense.

I tried explaining that what she said was unfair; that we were both sensitive right then; that our feelings had to coexist. But she only felt lectured and criticized, "Mark, I'm not your patient."

After a few rounds of this unwitty banter she suggested a solution: "Let's not talk."

As you can see, reframing the narrative, as Justin had effectively done with his grandmother, wasn't working here. Nor could we find a bridge between our truths—as I described having done with Justin and Julie in the last section. The only alternative to arguing she could imagine was to "not talk."

I got emotional; I raised my voice. "Mom I need your support right now. I have tests tomorrow. I'm getting married in three days!"

"But you don't see that I haven't been included in this wedding. I have family whom I would have liked to invite . . ."

Ugh! This was just another reaction; an aimless punch. We had been over all of those logistics. Sandy too wanted more family (or at least familiars) to attend. We were all making sacrifices to make this work. But my mom was working out a primitive anger she could not put into words.

This will happen.

As the finish line approaches, you will get sucked into baseless, heated arguments over practical details—e.g., uninvited relatives, the color of napkins, the type of vodka at the bar. Be aware that logistics may be the trigger for these combustions, but they're not the cause. The cause is, of course, those highly flammable, often irrational, intensely human feelings that possess us all. However you engage in these conflicts is up to you, but don't be fooled into extinguishing them with facts, logic, or sense.

I foolishly tried to conquer this wild fire between my mother and me with all I had—a little garden hose of logic. I wanted her to be excited about my wedding. That's all. To show that excitement by agreeing to arrive—on time—and help us set up, along with all the other major players. But she wasn't hearing me, and I wasn't hearing her.

"*No one* else is saying, 'I'll get there when I can!'" I said.

"I wanted to do the centerpieces. Why is Sandy doing them?" she said.

"We've been over this. . . . You are doing them *together*. Why must it be your way or the highway?! Why can't I have your support?!"

Screaming. More screaming. Then I hung up.

I had lost control, after weeks of nothing but control. Justin and I had our own boot camp going: early bedtime; daily exercise; a diet of chicken, broccoli, and lettuce; and drinking absolutely nothing but water. We wanted to be fit and glowing for our nuptials.

Oh well.

I downed a glass of scotch, bought myself some cigarettes (which I hadn't done in years) inhaled two; and then sucked down another glass of scotch. And another cigarette.

So much for that glowing skin.

I also had a warm bath with aromatherapy salts. Had I been more mindful of my emotional needs, I would have done that sooner. I would've also had some scotch, but I probably would have skipped the cigarettes.

**You can indulge your mess without being self-destructive,
if you get ahead of it.**

The screaming, however, possibly needed to happen. It felt awful. But having failed to reach my mother with my narrative ability—failing again, and none the better—I needed to release my frustration. The screaming taught me that I didn't want it to happen again. And also that there are limits to my relationship with my mother that I need to accept.

Time has proven this.

Flash forward to my older brother Angus's wedding: me, Justin, and my mom in a car, driving to the rehearsal.

"Can't we go faster?" she says. The song "Get Me to the Church on Time" from the musical *My Fair Lady* plays in my head. This was far from her madding cry of, "Can't I see my son?" days before my wedding . . . and at the same time not. It was, after all, the same son. She then proceeded to tell Justin and me about her visitation the night before from the ghosts of my father and my grandmother. They had smiled at her, in blessing of this "special occasion."

I felt the blow. But I didn't scream. Instead, I acknowledged my feelings with campy humor, "Who visited you the night before our wedding? Messy, boozy Aunt Titsy?" (It's true, she had an aunt named Titsy. Who was messy . . . and boozy.) She laughed. I laughed. But she didn't *really* get it. There are ways in which my feelings can never be recognized by her.

That is sad.

It is also true. For me and for her.

> ### *But with mourning comes the dawn.*
>
> We are no longer plagued by mess when we allow ourselves to move through it, to feel its impact, and to face the losses it brings. This sets us free.

When in messy conflict, my mother's suggestion to "not talk" should only be the final solution, after all other attempts to find a connection—any connection—fail. The great thing about moving through your mess is the freedom it affords you to create a new mode of survival. One that is more sustainable than projecting onto characters—like *Messy Nessy*—whom you laugh at from a distance. Instead you might laugh at, and with, yourself.

Rifts like the one I had with my mother can leave you floating—like a baby in space—but even in this state you might find a connection.

> ### *Limitations liberate us to discover and enjoy what we can actually have in relationships, in reality—with less confusion, doubt, or tension.*
>
> Like the stranded astronauts in the movie *Gravity*, for instance: lost in space, free floating, they tied themselves together with a thin cord. Here they found a sense of connection—however precarious—for the remainder of their time together.

The day after that messy phone call, we stopped at my mom's for dinner, as promised. Her voice was shot from the night before. (For my part, I was grateful to have had years of vocal training . . .) She had fixed a few of my favorite things—salmon, creamed spinach, turnips—and prepared them with great care. This is a way in which she has always been boundlessly loving and will always be. The loss of her voice coexisted with the abundant meal she had created.

The next day, she made it to the rehearsal, and together she and Sandy giddily assembled the centerpieces: of gold and burgundy ribbon; mini pumpkins and squash. But she was giddier yet after the rehearsal dinner and a couple glasses of wine.

We were in her room at the inn, just the two of us, laughing. She didn't say any words to which I could attach, but she had a palpable, can-you-believe-you're-getting-married-tomorrow? vibe, to which I tethered myself.

I had stopped in for aspirin; her industrial-sized, portable medicine cabinet (for her migraines . . .) was set up on the bureau. Her silver hair was a little wild, and she wore a big colorful kaftan-like scarf. She cackled. Yup, she was kind of a mess. So was I by that point.

And I wanted to talk to her.

19 Rehearse!
Land Before You Launch

"What do you need?"

Now this was a refreshing sound for sore ears. The rehearsal was about to begin, and her voice—at once soothing and all-business—eased my shoulders. Shimmery silver hair framed her luminous face; she had arrived to save the day.

This wasn't my mother; no, my mother was in the next room telling a stranger her favorite story: about an epic fight she once had with her mother-in-law. It wasn't Justin's mom either; no, Sandy was venting to Justin about her family having been told to arrive the next day, while some of mine was already there. The helpful voice belonged to my friend Joy.

Joy was the friend who watched Justin on *The Real World* with me and told me to write him a letter. She was also officiating the wedding and had taken it upon herself to run the rehearsal. We had gone to drama school together and she knew how to effectively stage a performance. Upon hearing her voice, I knew I could stop anxiously running the show for a moment and just be *in* it.

The role she played here—we'll call it the Rehearsal Master—is a crucial one. The rehearsal is your opportunity to take those first, wobbly steps onto the big stage. It's your chance to be horrified by what doesn't work—to fail, to be disappointed, frustrated, to fail better, and again. And also to get it right—to experience what it could be like to do the show precisely as planned. The rehearsal provides a safe zone within which trial, error, and having it your way can take place, and the *Rehearsal Master* creates that zone for you.

Your Rehearsal Master

Your *Rehearsal Master* could be your officiant, your wedding planner, or a designated friend (preferably one with stage experience and a voice that is at once soothing and all-business). Whoever it is, she needs to be committed, but also emotionally neutral. Anyone likely to be reactive will only be distracting—so, no moms, dads, or frenemies.

Once the wedding curtain rises, there's no telling what direction the wind will take you. But the rehearsal lets you land momentarily so you can get a grip, be held, and learn to believe that this is possible. Holding that in mind will keep you securely grounded and focused during the wedding, allowing you to play and to be spontaneous without feeling completely lost.

There are two kinds of rehearsing and they are equally important.

The first is *the moves*: the choreography, the flight plan, the things that cannot, should not, change. This includes practicing the pronunciation of names, memorizing ceremonial text, the order of who enters, when they enter, and how. This is not creative. It's the opposite of creative. I once overheard a pretentious British guy say, "Choreography undermines the creative process." I can't know what he meant for sure, but I think it was that sometimes you've just got to practice a performance technically, and without creative freedom, for the sake of clarity, cohesion, and safety.

You can appreciate the value of this: just consider how awful it is to hear an officiant mispronounce a bride or groom's name (or the family name of the one hundred relatives from Croatia . . .). Not cool.

Also not cool: having your parties enter to a cheesy pop song, doing cheesy dance moves, like those cheesy world-famous Youtube videos . . . unrehearsed. If you want those kinds of hijinks then—as Justin's well-bred Southern friend, Laurie says—"Gooooood!" But be sure to have them practice those damn steps. I beg of you not to make everyone suffer the stink of a half-assed attempt. It won't be fun for you either.

> *Safety must be considered, as well. This may mean taking a dry-run through the flight path while taking into account everyone's shoes.*

I was once in a wedding party in which I was paired with a fourteen-year-old girl who wore platform heels—that were about the height of a small child. We had to walk for a good forty feet arm-in-arm, and this included going up steps, which we then had to go down. During the ceremony, her parents scrutinized us intensely, step-by-step. Fortunately we had coordinated this high heel act so well that the flight was smooth and the landing was safe. Her mom spent the rest of the night introducing me to the whole family, as though I had rescued the girl from a burning plane. The uncles all had an intimidating *Godfather/Sopranos* sort of look. I'm glad we rehearsed.

The second type of rehearsing is *the potential moves*. These are the ones that could happen. This could include practical preparation—like accommodating late arrivals—but is more about preparing for emotional responses and how they might affect you.

For example, when we ran through our ceremony the first time, I was flooded with emotion. Hearing Aileen sing Sinead O'Connor's "In This Heart," to which Justin and I entered, accompanied by our respective moms, unexpectedly sent me to a dark place. (Not least due to entering as Aileen sang the word *grief*.) It hadn't occurred to me how sad the song is. I mean, I was smiling when Justin sang it to me on the phone way back when, but now I was in tears. Like the wedding itself, the song is as much about losing love as it is about gaining it.

I was not literally moving away from my mom to be with Justin, but performing this symbolic gesture—of creating a family unit of our own—in front of other people impacted me differently than I had imagined. It was raw, sad, and real.

Having experienced this layer of grief ahead of time, I was prepared to feel it again the next day without getting thrown off course or disconnecting from the guests. Maybe I'd even be able to smile the next time we ran through it. I didn't. But I had more freedom to do so, having the security of a rehearsal under my belt.

The most critical goal when rehearsing *potential moves* is trust. In going through the motions together, your team is developing a group sense of the event. This means that if something breaks from expectation during the show, you can look any one of them in the eye and together make it okay. This trust gives you permission to be present, free, even a little experimental, knowing you are securely attached to an ensemble that is committed to the structure and purpose of the event.

Trust

Along these lines, we can think of the wedding itself as a rehearsal for the rest of your lives together. Your community is there with you, going through the motions, the potential moves, so that when you need them they can say, "I've got your back."

My friend Winnie even included a declaration of this trust in the script she wrote for her officiant when she married her husband, Mason:

You are their wedding community.

You are the people who mean the most to them; those who have shared their lives, who have provided for them and protected them. You have nourished their spirits and helped them sort out their emotions.

You have watched them grow as individuals and as a couple. You have believed in them, encouraged them, and shared the most significant aspects of their life.

And, as their wedding community, it is fitting that you covenant with Winnie and Mason to pray for their marriage, encourage their friendship, and support them in times of need. If you so promise, say together: "We Will"

We did.

The contract of your vows can also be a rehearsal for *potential moves*. This can include acknowledgment of the safe zone you will provide for one another to grow, adapt, and evolve as individuals. My friend Dani says that when she married her bride Jamie, for example:

"It was important for us to acknowledge that we would be changing and growing as people in unpredictable ways, and we were inviting that to unfold, rather than trying to freeze ourselves as we were that day."

Since Jamie came out as transgender a few months later, and by now has completely transitioned to living as a male, "That turned out to be a fortunate attitude!" They had contracted and created a secure, safe zone, with their marriage, in which to experiment, expand, and create.

Wedding Rings

Rings can symbolize this safety zone, if you choose to have rings. Like the Rehearsal Master herself, the rings are visual reminders of the security you will give each other to fail and fail again. You

> can literally keep the rings on your body at all times, while that's probably too much to ask of the Rehearsal Master. And so you'll want to pick the right rings.

The metal, color, and design don't really matter. What matters is whether the ring will stay on your finger.

Justin's fell off and got lost a week after we were married.

Now, I don't tend to endow accidents with too much superstitious significance, but this one made me inexplicably uncomfortable. And was only made worse by the unsolicited palm reading we had soon after.

We were at a *Real World* reunion, and a former cast member named Montana decided to read our palms. As she scanned the lines on my hands (making note of my wedding band), she concluded that in relationships I need to have "filet mignon," and that once I have it, I never let it go. Whereas Justin (who was clearly not wearing a band) was like Bill Clinton—really, she said that very thing—and could go for filet if it comes along, but will easily settle for a cheeseburger. . . . Hmm. I couldn't tell if I was the Hillary filet or the Monica burger, but either way my anxiety was provoked, and I knew it wouldn't subside until we got Justin a more secure ring.

So we found one. That locks. Not like, a medieval contraption with a bolt and spiky ball attached, but an innovative band that remains secure if turned. This ring is not a prison sentence, but rather a playful safety measure, allowing him to live freely without (me) constantly, anxiously, checking to make sure it's still there.

Like the rehearsal, our vows and rings represent a foundation, a safe connection, and a secure rehearsal zone within which we can fly and fall and fly again, practicing our *potential moves* and also our potential tastes—whether those be for cheeseburger or filet mignon. These chosen boundaries yield freedom within. As our friend Lily says, to feel safe enough to let go within a marriage, "you've got to invest; to have skin in it." And that means to rehearse.

After the run-through, we gave the rings to Joy to hold, just as she had held us during the rehearsal. We were now securely attached to the ceremony, to the event, to the promise of what would occur. After the ceremony the following day, we would wear the rings as transitional objects to remind us of these symbolic gestures and to hold us as we experiment and grow in unpredictable ways—together and apart.

As we exited the drawing room where the ceremony would take place, my friend Julie said, "This is a marvelous piece of theater you created." I took it in, because it would never be the same again, and hearing it made me feel secure.

Then I let it go, open to whatever the next day would bring.

20 Unregistered Gifts: Plans . . . and What Happens Instead

"Why are you doing this?"

Said Patti, our caterer, a few hours before the wedding. What she meant was, "Why am I dealing with you, and not Justin: the not-crazy one, the one who can actually help me?" (Justin was helping another vendor right then.) But in this moment—the slide projector frozen, our crew's hotel reservation lost, the flowers all horribly wrong—the words she actually said resonated.

Why *was* I doing this?

This was not what we had planned; things were falling apart. I had gone to bed the night before willing to be all zen, to surrender to the universe, but now I had doubts. Not about Justin, but about this big production we had overweeningly fantasized and planned and which was now collapsing before our eyes.

I replied to Patti, "I don't know." And then my eyes went blank. I sometimes have what I call *Rain Man* moments, by which I refer to Dustin Hoffman's character with autism in the 1985 film *Rain Man*. This character struggled to adapt when things didn't go according to plan. At such times he would panic, short-circuit, and repeat things like, ". . . definitely . . . definitely wasn't supposed to be like this . . ." Yes, I was having a *Rain Man* moment.

If I could go back in time, I'd whisper something reassuring into my jittery ears. Something like, "When a plan abandons you, something else shows up, something wonderfully unforeseen." Though hearing such wisdom whilst facing the icy winds of failure, disappointment, or loss is rarely comforting. If only we trusted that by letting those winds carry us, we might be guided to unexpected gifts.

When the Practical Tips Are Not Enough

I had a hard time going with the flow that morning. Instead I staved off those cruel winds using the tips I've described in earlier chapters, which tempered the storm a bit. I let my cast **interpret their roles**: upon seeing me self-destruct, Deb, our emcee, immediately swept in to deal with Patti. When I couldn't fix the computer projector, I cried out in obvious distress, **helping them help me**: Evelina stepped up, pressed the F8 button on the computer keyboard, and that was that. And when the manager of the inn down the street insisted there was no reservation for my crew (for whom I had booked rooms three months prior) I very firmly—nay fiercely, nay ferociously—reminded her, verbatim, of our verbal **contract** (much like her lovely inn, she was an early twentieth-century relic, had not discovered email, and so had not sent an e-confirmation). That worked out as well.

As for the flowers, Justin had said "I don't!" The mums that arrived looked much cheaper than what we had seen online, and they were a bad fit with the exquisite fall centerpieces our moms had assembled. We had only a couple of hours to replace them with fresh ones from the nearest florist in Great Barrington, twenty minutes away. And since Justin was needed on site—being the not-crazy one between us, able to be calm and mentally present under pressure—he made a **clear choice** to send me and his mom, Sandy, on the hunt for floral October. Problem solved.

Yet still, something was not quite right.

Sure, we plugged up the holes in the dam with practical solutions, but I was still flooded with doubt. Why were we doing this? I wasn't supposed to be stressed out on this day; I shouldn't have been running around plugging up holes. I was supposed to be meditating, mindfully relaxing, preparing to translate our private vision into a contagious piece of theater. That was *why* we originally wanted to have this wedding: to enthusiastically share our story, to be recognized. But suddenly I didn't feel like sharing myself with anyone. I wanted to hide.

This was exacerbated by the thought of driving alone with Sandy. We had gotten along throughout the years but I was sometimes on guard with her one-on-one. She expected me to perform, to be on, to be fake, and if I didn't make the effort, she would feel rejected—and then complain to Justin, who would complain to me. Justin did finally interrupt that cycle. He confronted her about the dynamic—which was painfully productive for them both—and things certainly improved from that point forward.

But on this day, as I got in the car—my plans failing at every turn—I feared I would have to be fake. Fake! For the entire day.

. . . definitely . . . definitely wasn't supposed to be like this . . .

Then we hit the road. And something else happened. Something unexpected.

Unexpected Parenting

We laughed, for starters. Rather than suffering my *Rain Main* moment in silence, I briefed her on my *Rain Main* moments, and we laughed our way into the present.

Letting my guard down, and Sandy in, allowed her to release her expectations of me, her pushiness, and her demand that I perform on cue. Instead she listened, learned, and supportively mirrored back what she heard. We had found a way to be together. And as we navigated the windy autumnal streets, I realized that this version of Sandy, and of our relationship, had been available to me all along.

In times of transition, our fear takes the wheel and steers our focus toward the negative things, the weird things, the ones that make us feel insecure and out of control.

In my case, that would be the first weekend I met Sandy, at Justin's law school apartment, catching her lurking on the balcony outside his bedroom window one morning, watching us lay together while she smoked a cigarette. INVASIVE. Or when she left for the airport that day, gripping our hands, warning us, "Your love is very new. Be careful ..." AWKWARD. Or when she'd pinch my butt, make strange faces, and generally try to beat laughter out of me, and then cry to Justin when it didn't work. ENOUGH!

We fear losing our grip on the wheel at these times—afraid to discover where the windy road might take us, or where it has taken us already, while we drive defensively, eyes wide shut.

When I let my eyes open, I could see that the road had led me to Sandy's warm and welcoming home at a time when I needed it most. My father passed away only a year after Justin and I started dating, and my family's first Christmas without him was grim. It was like trying to do an outdoor play with a collapsed set, in the middle of winter, and with a cast on strike, no longer believing that the show must go on. Definitely ... definitely wasn't supposed to be like this . . . But the following year, I joined Justin at Sandy's home and learned that the show not only goes on, but that it's so much more than what you get in your local theater.

Sandy did not replace my ghosts of Christmas past—the comforting memories of my family ensemble, fully cast and raring to play. No. But she awakened me to new possibilities, new celebrations, new modes of survival. She loved Christmas, and I loved how she loved it. I loved her enthusiasm for theme trees: Christmas trees that she trimmed differently each year—e.g., Santas, snowmen, angels. She made these—sometimes beautiful, sometimes odd, but always novel—ornaments from old clothes pins, loose fabrics, crushed soda cans, and various other unexpected materials that were repurposed and given new life.

I learned to love Sandy's love of community. Her participation in the local church choir—utilizing that baritone Justin loved to mock—and the lunches she would host in her home for her students at a junior college. I loved how she held her own against Fred Phelps: the Christian warrior most famous for picketing Matthew Shepard's funeral in 1998.

Phelps was, of course, head of the Westboro Baptist Church and the creator of GodHatesFags.com and lived and loved to spread hate, having made a career of picketing events that had even the faintest of gay presences. In 2002, Sandy's college staged a production of *The Laramie Project*—a riveting play documenting Matthew Shepard's murder and its aftermath—and wouldn't you know, it didn't escape Phelps's gay-seeking laser eyes. He sounded the alarms on his oh-so-Christianly-named website, targeting Sandy's school, and . . . Sandy— having discovered she was adviser to the LGBT student group. He didn't stop there, though; he also called for protests at Sandy's church, which he called a "queer-friendly dog kennel and leper colony masquerading as a church." Now, the church hardly sponsored a float in the pride parades, but Sandy had convinced them to organize an AIDS service there and had also founded a chapter of PFLAG.

With encouragement from Justin, Sandy sought help from various LGBT civil rights groups that track Phelps. The organizers promised to counter-demonstrate should the nut actually show up. He didn't. But he wouldn't have been the only one holding a megaphone if he had.

Sandy's efforts inspired me to hold my own megaphone and to ask for help when I needed it at the same time.

Surely my own parents had inspired me to be on my own side. My mother had led the Gay Straight Alliance at a high school in Westchester where she was the psychologist. She also quit after being advised against leading such a group due to fussy, conservative parents in the district. But she showed her teeth in the form of righteous letters to the Board before she bolted. Years before that my father, the high school principal in our small town, taught us to guard our house against "egg-bombers" on Halloween night—outfitting us in black ninja camo from head to toe—and sacrificing our trick-or-treating for the greater glory of protecting our home.

> *There's much to be learned from our parents, our primary attachments, but it doesn't stop there. There's more parenting to be had in this life, if we let it happen.*

My mom taught me to commit to my dreams and to my anger if anyone tried to shut them down. My dad taught me to be disciplined, to lead, and to protect that which is mine (both of which are righteous qualities that have served me well). But my life has become all the more rich having also learned from Sandy to follow, to share, to allow space for vulnerability, and to adapt. To turn a crushed Coke can into Santa.

Now not every in-law-to-be is Sandy.

Toxic In-Laws

In marriage, many of us will become the recipients of families who are not only less nurturing, but far more toxic than our own. That doesn't mean we shouldn't let them in the car, but we might not trust them at the wheel. Here they may offer us a form of parenting by default, teaching us to set boundaries in relationships where we may have missed that lesson with our families of origin. From our new toxic in-law, we may learn to engage in conflict and to stand up for ourselves in ways we never needed to as a child. And we may also learn to survive this.

Exhibit A: My mother's favorite story of all time, in which she defended my father against his mother, who threw shoes at them (with a cigarette tightly in her teeth) upon discovering she couldn't invite anyone she pleased to their wedding.

> ### New Family
>
> No matter who or how they are, your new family members are valuable additions to your life. They will inspire you to reveal untapped facets of yourself—one way or another—and they will see facets of you that your family of origin forgot or failed to notice.

During that short drive to the florist, I was seen by Sandy like I had never been seen before. She saw my adaptiveness: having somehow survived as a gender nonconforming child in a small rural town, coming out, transferring schools (several times), surviving deaths, and piecing together a career out of a fragmented life as an actor and the passion to become a therapist. This adaptive person was a far cry from the crazy man Patti, the caterer, had mirrored back to me earlier that day. In that moment, I was mindful of the gift that was Sandy, and also of how ever so reluctant I had been to receive it. Until then.

Sandy would die abruptly of cancer only two years later. At her memorial service, I would recall our time in the car that day, while standing on the altar of her church, reading text she had selected. I would have a sense of belonging, facing the community she loved so much along with her sons. I would feel both empty with her loss, but also full having gained her; so grateful for her unexpected parenting.

When we returned to the wedding location, having completed our mission, Sandy turned to me and said, "You're a survivor."

I inhaled for the first time in days. "Where's Patti?" I thought. I knew *why I* was "doing this" more clearly now than ever.

We got out of the car and walked toward the wedding, the flame-colored leaves shimmering around us as they fell.

Part 6

Showtime

21 Picture Not Perfect, But Alive: Making Emotional Memories

My favorite wedding picture of all time is of Cynthia Nixon, and I took it.

Not of her wedding—I wasn't there. In this picture she's on the steps of the Capitol building in D.C., during the National Marriage Equality March of 2009 where she gave an indelible speech. She had organized a group from NYC to attend, and we were lucky enough to tag along.

I was completely enthralled by her brazen selflessness as she alone led us—while holding her little son's hand—from the bus, to the subway, to the streets, marching with revelry through the crowd, to her podium. Without a flinch. In *heels*. She then gave one of the most eloquent, passionate battle cries I've ever heard, connecting the denial of equal rights to hate crimes—referencing Matthew Shepard's mother, Judy, who had spoken just before her.

I captured the moment with my smartphone, framing Cynthia to the right and the back of her son's head to the left. He was watching his mom speak, sitting on the shoulders of her now wife, Christine—the glimpse of a rainbow flag billowing just above their heads.

The image, which is still on my phone, instantly recalls my emotional memory of that moment: emotions that define what a wedding is, better than I can in words.

Ironically there was a "real" wedding photo shoot at the same building at the same time. As our group headed back to the bus, we couldn't help but notice a straight couple, in traditional cake-topper attire, posing for conjugal pics on the Capitol's backside. The rally for marriage equality was still happening in front—still massively attended, still riotous. I believe Lady Gaga was speaking, and the newlyweds didn't even notice. Or care. Their strained smile teeth were memorable, but in all the wrong ways. You really can't make this stuff up.

Your wedding pictures are windows

Portals through which you can travel to rekindle the emotional essence and meaning of your event. They evoke the drama of what took place and the significance it holds in your life.

That being said, as with your entire wedding, you'll want to let the truth outweigh tradition. Let the staging—if there is staging—evoke rather than impress; let it reveal your awakening battle cry rather than your stultifying smile teeth.

As we've previously discussed, *truth* is a tricky word with a variety of meanings. There's truth in the ideal pictures you imagine, as well as in the mundane realness around you that exists beyond your control. I encourage you to shoot for something in between, for that glimmer of life that occurs as we reach away from reality toward our dreams. Like Cynthia Nixon reaching to the stars while connected to the groundlings.

Any attempt to seek perfection, or to copy some sort of standard in your photos, will be in vain. Those pics will ultimately be less gratifying to look at than ones that capture spontaneity, awkwardness, and unadulterated flickers of life; ones that transcend a mere replica of the elements—the hair, the teeth, the posture. Go for images that light a shimmering flame within and that take you back to a moment that was lived, rather than posed.

I know, I know, you're thinking, "Great. How do I do that?"

In two words, you don't. As with all of my ideas in this book, I offer you a concept, not necessarily a direction. Let it inspire you to play—to be mindful of what this day is about, this moment—and to do what feels right for you. And also, the following guidelines might help.

First of all, there are two kinds of wedding pics to consider: the staged and the candid.

> ### Staged Pics
>
> These are the ones that you plan, organize, and arrange. A lot of times they are done right after the ceremony. Tradition? I don't know, but you don't have to do that. I'm not saying don't—I've seen it work—but you don't have to. It disrupts the flow of events. It stops you from being at your wedding and forces you to pretend to be at your wedding—at an idea of your wedding. Unless your goal is to use your photos as bait for "likes" and :)s and <3s on Facebook, try to preserve memories of where you are instead of fabricating ones of where you should be.

A few years back, we attended a traditional wedding on Long Island at which we alone were the outliers, having been invited as the plus-two of the bride's sister, a bridesmaid. That's all to say that we were packed into a stretch limo after the cathedral ceremony, along with some rowdy coeds. While the other guests mingled at the reception hall—the next town over—we were pulling off the Long Island Expressway (L.I.E.)—like, right off of it—into the abandoned parking lot of a . . . convention center? Office building? (It reminded me of the opening scene of *Back to the Future* when Michael J. Fox first evaporates from the present.). To this day, I'm not sure what the building was, but there were tall fake plants in the lobby, which turned out to be the backdrop of choice for this couple's "magic moments."

Now, who knows? Maybe those fake corporate ferns take them back to a moment of shared meaningful bliss, and that's really all that matters. All I know is they would take me back to *Back to the Future*— to an abandoned parking lot where the natural flow of life and time has been interrupted.

One way to avoid staged pics that recall the L.I.E. is to do everything at the same location: ceremony, reception, photos.

More and more couples are doing this and not only because it's trendy or practical, but more significantly because it sets the stage for a cohesive, shared experience—of a time, a place, and an event. This experience will be revealed in your shimmery eyes and those with whom you stage your photos.

Also, consider taking your staged pics before the ceremony.

This way everyone involved is focused on one event at a time—nothing interrupted, nothing missed. Not unlike staged photos for live theater, which are done well before curtain-up on opening night.

Imagine watching a performance when suddenly the actors are whisked away, mid-scene, as the stage manager announces, "Oh don't mind them . . . they're just doing pictures. Sit tight, have a drink." Imagine the actors: extricated from the stage, driven to a random pier across town where they are ordered to do weird poses, before being chauffeured back to the theater to finish the scene. Not the most vital or coherent time at the theater, and we could expect no more from the pics.

When Staged Pics Work Best

Though staged pics can block the life from your wedding, they can also reveal it, larger than reality will allow. Take, for example, the great fun I had posing like classic American portraiture with my brothers all over the Jane Austen–like inn—e.g., on the stairs or next to the fireplace. The pics illuminate our shared sense of play and ineffable emotional closeness. They transcend the mundane reality of that time, namely that we were scattered all over the country, and hardly in contact the way we wanted to be, because of our busy lives.

Also one of my favorites—and Justin's least—is a staged pic of the two of us entering the front door of the inn, attempting to symbolize our significant life transition. The image captures us midway between this heightened pose; a little unsure, slightly embarrassed, but tickled with life as our eyes connect. It recalls for me the spirited vibe between us and amongst everyone during the shoot.

Playing versus Contorting

Trouble enters the frame of your staged pics when playfulness is interrupted. This might be your photog's doing—dictating that all the guys stand in a row in traditional, soldierly, crotch-grab pose, or that the girls look to one another with a wax-museum-fake "OMG this is so fun" pose.

You might also get in your own way. A friend of ours, for example, found herself re-taking and re-taking staged pics to make sure her ear wasn't poking through her hair. When she showed us the results—which she finds disappointing, because of the six hundred pics there are only "three hundred good ones"—I barely noticed the ear, and when I did, I actually thought it added an elfin charm to her gorgeous, happy face. As I told her, don't waste your time photoshopping perceived flaws. When you flip through your wedding album at the age of ninety-five, you'll look beautiful to yourself in all six hundred pics, ear or no ear. And your eye will likely be drawn to the imperfect ones; the ones that remind you of living as opposed to contorting/trying to be perfect.

Words Are Worth A Thousand Pics

If there's something to truly fear about staged pics, it's the emotional earthquakes that will reverberate—for the whole day, if not forever—when your choice of who to include is not communicated clearly. Now's a good time to review Section 3 to freshen up your **choices**, **boundaries**, and **contracts**. Decide who all will be shot—no more, no less—make sure they know, and don't make any last minute changes. Trust me.

We had decided to stage just a few pictures with only our immediate families and parties. We would make use of the various sitting rooms and outdoor benches, playfully arranging ourselves in various groupings like the cast of a TV series—e.g., *Friends, The Sopranos, Six Feet Under*. And then my cousin Lindsay asked me if her mom, my Aunt Connie, should join us for pictures. And because I'm an *Engulfed* and overidentify with people's feelings and was a bit jittery that day, I said, "Of course."

Here's what I was thinking: "This way I won't hurt her feelings. She can just hang out while we take the planned pictures, and then we'll snap a few with her and my mom when we're done."

Here's what I wasn't thinking: Sandy had told her family not to arrive until later in the day since they wouldn't be needed for staged pictures. Sandy was already feeling sensitive that my family was ten times the size of hers, and that she wasn't able to invite family friends. And if all of my extended family made it into the staged pics, and none of Justin's did, Sandy would be pissed. Pissed!

Here's what happened: My extended family all made it into the staged pics and none of Justin's did. . . .

To this day, I can't look at *The Sopranos*–style photo of us sitting around the luxurious dining table, flaunting our spectrum of fall leaf colors, without noticing the expression on Sandy's face suggesting she truly wants to shoot someone. And not just anyone. . . .

But at the same time, remember the first thing I told you in this book: everything true about weddings is also untrue. So, though I get self-loathing chills when I see those pictures of Sandy Soprano, they also remind me that failure is inevitable, that it's okay, and that we learn from it. They remind me to be awake when I make last-minute choices and that there are times when rigidly sticking to a plan is worthwhile.

Saying no to one person is ultimately far kinder than trying to accommodate everyone's feelings.

Those pictures are a record of my having lived and learned rather than an illusion of perfection—of having luckily, blissfully, floated through the day by the skin of my teeth.

Sandy did end up with a few family portraits after all. When her parents and brother's family arrived, our photographer, Ruthie, snapped several shots of them out on the lawn. And it rained—nay, poured!—the entire time on an otherwise gloriously sunny day. And so my guilt grows deeper when I flip through our album. But at the same time, the ridiculous irony makes me laugh; I mean, what are the odds? And _that_, my friends, is life. The better we can laugh at its ridiculous outcomes, the better we can survive. After all, it was these photos that caused us all to laugh through tears, and connect as a group, years later, when Justin's family and I scattered Sandy's ashes into the Maine River in the pouring rain on an otherwise gloriously sunny weekend.

Candid Pics

These days there's really no need to stress about staged pictures when the most personal, evocative photo memories will likely come from your _candid pics_ anyway. These are the HD images that everyone besides your photographer will be aggressively snapping on their phones. For your photographer's six hundred, your guests will yield six thousand and will be more likely to capture the nuances: e.g., the creasing smile lines when you see your spouse-to-be for the first time as you walk down the aisle; the glimmer of sadness as you kiss your mother; the millisecond of unadulterated joy as you hug your brother.

Another favorite wedding photo of mine is also one I took—and it too remains on my phone. It's of our friend Sharon walking down the aisle on her big day. Her eyes shimmering with love, hope, and anticipation as they first met with her bride Emily's, who was waiting for her at the altar.

Capturing Non-visual Memories

But the memory trail back to your wedding need not be paved with pictures alone. Consider the power of fragrances, of music, napkins and flowers and centerpieces that can be preserved in albums or collages. I surprised Justin the day before the wedding with a gift: a bottle of cologne neither of us had tried before. We both continue to wear it—often, to this day—and even now it leads our minds back to that weekend in a way that is pleasing for us both.

Not that you have to agree on everything. Find ways for each of you to recall the day—the joy, the significance, the life that was lived.

When I shared my thoughts on this chapter with Justin—on pictures, and memories, and flickers of life—my words didn't seem to resonate with him. But then I asked him to pick his favorite wedding photo. He chose a candid pic that his mother had taken of us, putting on our ties, side by side. Just performing a mundane task with our eyes aimed toward something larger than life.

22 The Moment Before: Be Apart to Be Together

You're about to go on. Do you:

    A) Stare at each other and hope for the best?

    B) Pop a Xanax, close your eyes, and hope for the best?

    C) Wait by your entrance, wide-eyed, poised for your aisle walk, and hope for the best?

    D) Take some conscious time, apart, with your respective friends— what I call *The Moment Before*.

Now I'm not really here to tell you what to do, but the answer is D.

> *By all means, do whatever feels right for you, but also know that every performance in life—e.g., plays, weddings, arguments, sex— is easier, livelier, and better with a moment before.*

Actors are encouraged to consciously choose a moment before prior to entering each scene. Take Shakespeare's Juliet, for example: the actor will seem more credible, alive, and at ease if she has imagined locking her bedroom door, brushing her hair, and checking her newly kissed face in the mirror before stepping onto the balcony. Otherwise she's just an actor entering a stage for the sole purpose of delivering a soliloquy to an audience without any specific conviction of where she's come from or where she's going. Without a moment before, she will be forced to jumpstart her acting engine as she enters the stage. She will attempt to generate some sort of arbitrary wistfulness for the sake of a "performance"—which will seem false, forced, and overdone. From this state of mental constipation—for actor and audience alike—there is really nowhere to go but toward further constipation.

However, if she imagines her moment before she can then step away from one specific place, moving toward another she has in mind. She will then be genuinely driven to engage an audience with ease along the way.

So too will you if you take a moment before entering your ceremony.

This idea is not unlike downhill skiing: you want to be centered, know where you're coming from, and have an idea of where you're headed before sliding down the slope. That doesn't mean you have to stick to your original target or that you even have a choice in the matter—say if you hit a patch of ice—but from a place of mental clarity, you can choose where to go next, e.g., pivot to the left, or the right, or come to a full stop.

However, entering the slope without a sense of where you—and you alone—are, where you'd like to go, and where you're actually going will result in panic, chaos, pummeling other people, and toppling downhill on your butt. You can always get up and try again, and that is a righteous way to be, but it's a smoother, more fun, and exhilarating ride if you take a "moment before."

To Each Her Own

Justin suggested we each take a moment before prior to the ceremony—it was actually about a half hour before. We had spent the whole day together thus far, but he sensed we would benefit from a little time apart with our respective support teams. And he was right.

I didn't want to at first. As an Engulfed, I prefer to be surrounded by Justin's emotional needs when the curtain rises, instead of my own (which is why I suppose I like acting (*it's the character, not me*). But as an Abandoned, Justin knows he needs his own space before engaging an audience—any audience. Growing up, he felt he had no choice but to rely on himself for emotional survival, and he now has this wisdom to show for it.

So he gathered with his closest friends in one room, and I with mine in another. And thank goodness. Otherwise I would have been a baby in space, floating around the Inn for those endless thirty minutes, getting in Justin's way, and getting frustrated when he proved unable to hold me steady. Our moment before allowed us to be held separately, by our people, and gave us a specific place from which to enter before meeting up on stage for the big show.

My friend Julie helped curb my palpable anxiety by encouraging me to do simple tasks like making the bed. This kept me from pacing and was quite meditative, engaging my mind-body connection, keeping me mentally present. Now that I was unfrazzled, she could actually talk to me—about simple things, like how her mom bought her a new dress for the occasion. And I was able to hear her, and even respond, with words that made sense. *It looks great on you.* I may have been taking the ski slope super slow—perpendicular to the mountain if you will—but I was centered, awake, and able to move with ease and without fear.

Aileen was there, too, and as she rehearsed her toast, I noticed she too was nervous. So I shared my new tools with her: we finished making the bed together. We talked. We laughed. We connected. And with each other's support we would all make an entrance, one by one—with a sense of origin, with purpose, and without toppling over each other.

This idea of separating into your mini-tribes for your moment before may resemble the old superstitious "rules" about brides and grooms being kept apart the day of, or even several days before, the wedding. But my intention here is very different. The tradition of the bride censored from the groom's gaze before the nups derives from the idea that she should be virginal and "pure" and unblemished before the groom *takes* her as *his own*. By contrast, I suggest that you are equals and that you need to gather your unique minds before show time.

> *You also might take this time before engaging in all big entanglements together in the future, be they public or private.*
>
> Like, for example, the arguments, fights, and debacles you two will have—which will only increase in size and stakes in the future. You will need to stay in the ring to work them through and taking a moment before will help.

This certainly means treating yourself to alone time—a brisk walk; a bath; sitting still by a body of shimmery water—while you parse through your thoughts and feelings. This way you get to know them before they are blocked, obliterated, or taken prisoner during the course of spousal verbal combat. But it may also mean taking time for those thoughts and feelings to be heard, nurtured, and challenged by your emotional support team.

Just as these folks help center you before your ceremonial entrance, they can prepare you to ski down the steep slopes of marital unrest. They can help you determine a clear sense of where you'd like to go and what you're up against without excessive blame or clinging to your poles defensively, or hopelessly screaming, without direction or design. This doesn't mean that your couple-clashes have to end up precisely as you intend, but with a clear and supported sense of where you've come from and where you'd like to go, compromises can be reached: you can pivot and turn to the right or left. You can hear each other.

> *Moments before with your friends prepare you for performances of verbal sparring with your spouse.*
>
> They also prepare you to be vulnerable without overdoing it, and to be confident that your unique mind and heart are valid. This support will give you the strength to consider your partner's point of view, as well.

The two of you are different. And that's a good thing. Moments before help you to celebrate your difference, rather than showing up onstage expecting to be exactly the same and slogging through a mentally constipated performance trying to make that happen.

Sex and Marriage

And let's talk about sex. The sexual challenges that arise in every long-term relationship cannot be worked out in the bedroom alone. Or even between the couple alone. Sometimes you'll need to read books on your specific challenges or practice certain things on your own—with the help of toys or porn or whatever does the trick for you and you alone. And most validating, liberating, and reawakening of all will be the friends you can trust to talk about this, particularly long-term coupled or married friends.

There is a pervasive shame that corrodes the sex life of every long-term couple. This shame bullies us into shrouding our inevitable obstacles to constant, active, spontaneously creative sex after years together in order to save face. But honoring your unique challenges, and garnering validation, empathy, and support—from books, from a therapist, but most significantly, from friends who share in this challenge—can help you not only to get over the hurdles, but to have better sex than ever before. It is the lack of mutual recognition, acceptance, validation, empathy, and therefore communication that causes so many couples to split. But giving yourself the opportunity to ask for help, to be supported, validated, and mirrored by friends—by people other than your spouse—will allow you to enter the stage for that epic performance known as sex with clarity, ease, and the ability to explore. To have fun, no matter how long you are together.

> ## *Visualize Where You're Headed*
>
> The moment before arms you to engage with your spouse vulnerably but without inadequacy, guilt, or the fear of losing yourself altogether. And it works better with a clearly verbalized decision to temporarily be apart so as to meet up again later at a pre-chosen destination.

Before our pre-ceremonial parting, we had found a small bench carved into the staircase at the inn next to a tiny window through which beams of white sunlight shone. A Kyssen Baenk, if you will—a term, we would learn during our honeymoon in Denmark, that translates to "kissing bench." We chose to stop at that bench immediately following the ceremony to collect ourselves: individually and together. Having the Kyssen Baenk in mind kept me present during the performance. I could look people in the eye—without panic, without fear of the unknown—as I knew exactly where I was headed. Having my sights on the bench motivated me, focused me, and prevented me from skidding down the aisle as we exited the stage . . . I mean, altar. I mean, drawing room . . . It's all the same thing really. It all depends on the meaning with which you choose to endow the space during your moment before.

I'll never forget the rush of excitement and relief when we finally sat down on that bench and were able to enjoy the finish line we had chosen together. We could take a moment to exhale. We knew that throughout our lives together, we could take time apart, rejoin, and have this moment all over again.

23 Presenting You

You enter. You walk. You arrive.

And how you make these moves will tell a story; one that holds both public and private significance. So, what's your story?

Ours was about two men who had been raised, loved, and supported in their marriage choice by their moms. We entered our ceremony on the arms of those moms; a no-brainer decision as they were the only parents in each our lives.

> *How you enter your ceremony depends on two things:*
>
> 1) What story you want them to take away, and
> 2) What story you want to take away for yourself.

Consider both when asking yourselves how to walk the aisle or if you even want an aisle, as well as when you're deciding how to be introduced (e.g., "Who gives this (wo)man away?") and when choosing images and gestures to symbolize your independent life—before it transforms, via ritual, into one that is interdependent. You may feel your lives are already interdependent, but trust me, something happens during your ceremony—an ineffable, mysterious, but palpable, transformation.

Winnie

My friend Winnie knew she wanted to walk the aisle alone. She says that even if her dad had attended her wedding, which he did not, she would not have chosen to be "given away" by him. She considered walking with her mother, which she felt appropriate as her mother had raised her, as a single parent. But this didn't feel quite right either, for two reasons.

First, though petite in stature, Winnie's mom is a world-famous choreographer with a tremendous personality. Winnie had always struggled to assert an identity as something other than her mother's appendage and wanted her declaration of marriage to be unequivocally her own. Second, and more importantly, Winnie's mom had effectively raised her to be an independent woman. She had lived on her own, traveled the world, and supported herself for more than a decade before her wedding, and planned to continue supporting herself after. So she decided to enter solo, and her mom did not question it. How could she? As Winnie says, "She's the one that raised me to be like me!"

However, when her great aunt learned Winnie would not be "given away" by her great uncle—with whom Winnie had a good relationship, but by no means a father/daughter one—the aunt galvanized a battalion to apply pressure. The lot of them threatened not to attend if she did not accommodate her great aunt's wish. Some of them showed, some did not, but even so, Winnie told her story, her way.

She ultimately decided to pick up her mom—who was seated in the front row—during her aisle-walk and together they approached the altar. Winnie had given the officiant a script that read, "Who *presents* this woman to be married to this man?" and her mother replied, "I do." This was the story of a self-possessed woman who chose to be married, who chose to enter her wedding alone, and who chose to acknowledge her mother's role in her life—by being *presented* by her at the altar. This is the narrative she wanted her guests to hold in mind and the one she wants to carry with her throughout her life.

But what if you don't have the luxury to tailor-make your entrance like Winnie did? What if the obstacle is not merely a matter of nagging relatives, but one you absolutely can't ignore? Namely, death.

Rachel

Our friend Rachel faced this conundrum whilst planning her wedding, as her mother and father had both passed away. Rachel told me she was bombarded with the question, "Who will give you away?"—sometimes out of love, often out of "rude curiosity." She decided to walk on the arm of her brother, her only sibling, saying that though the feminist within her didn't want to think about being "given away," this was what she felt most comfortable doing. But deciding how to stage this entrance was particularly challenging for her.

You see, Rachel's parents had advised her to beware of "giving herself" over to marriage. (This story was actually described in a 2013 *New York Times* "Vows" article titled "A Reluctant Bride Conquers Her Fears.") Her father had warned her, "career first, family second," and her mother had told her "not to marry her first boyfriend or to rely on a man for anything." After first meeting her now-husband, Marvin, in college, it would be twenty years, several breakups, and a lot of living, failing, and failing better, before Rachel would decide—willfully, and from the gut—that she wanted to marry him. In staging her ceremony, she wanted to both honor her parents—for raising her to be the independent thinker that she is—as well as to honor her very own tried and true mind and heart.

Having had the good fortune to attend their wedding, I can say that Rachel's entrance symbolized a woman choosing to begin her own family, with verve, and with the support of her family of origin—as represented by her brother. It was quite moving, and as per Rachel's intent, it honored multiple truths at the same time.

Your family of origin can be emblemized in a number of ways, even if your parents or immediate care takers are deceased.

Chris

My brother-in-law Chris's family of origin, for example, is two gay men—Justin and me—or at least that's how he portrayed us at his wedding. Chris and Justin's mother had passed away, and though their father was in attendance, he hadn't been an active part of their lives for many years and accordingly was not asked to play a part in the ceremony. So Chris had Justin and I read poems he had chosen (the only people asked to stand and represent him in this manner), providing us the privilege of being recognized as his immediate family/primary support.

> **_The symbolic gesture of being presented for marriage needn't be limited to your entrance alone._**
>
> Text can be used for this public enactment to great effect.

We chose a selection from the epic poem, "Gilgamesh"—the oldest piece of literature on Earth—and had our mothers read it. For the religious/spiritual types in our audience, the use of ancient words added gravity to the performance, which—as you can surmise from the text, below—was a mothers' blessing of a love like ours:

His Mom:

There was once a king, Gilgamesh, who had a dream. / He asked his mother, the Goddess Ninsum, the wise, the all-knowing, to interpret the dream:

My Mom:

I saw a bright star, it shot across the morning sky, it fell at my feet and lay before me like a huge boulder. / I tried to lift it, but it was too heavy. / I took it in my arms, I embraced and caressed it, the way a man caresses his wife. / Then I took it and laid it before you, mother. You told me that it was my double, my second self.

His Mom:

Then Ninsum said to her son: Dearest child, this bright star from heaven-it stands for a dear friend, a mighty hero. / You will take him in

your arms, embrace and caress him, the way a man caresses his wife. /
He will be your double, your second self, a man who is loyal, who will
stand at your side through the greatest dangers. /Soon you will meet
him, the companion of your heart. Your dream has said so.

My Mom:

Gilgamesh said: May the dream come true. May the true friend
appear, the true companion, who through every danger will stand at
my side.

It was a thrill to share this performance with our guests, and also to
receive it—a grand, highly specific, and unforgettable presentation
from our mothers.

Dani and Jamie

My friend Dani and her then-wife, now-husband, Jamie created
another version of being presented for their conjugal. They exploded
the tradition of an aisle by conceiving of their wedding as a spiral and
having all of their guests present them within it. Everyone formed the
shape based on where they stood: the outer arm was "community," the
next circle inward "friends," the next "family," and finally the two of
them at the center. From the outside in, their people presented them
with poetry, blessings, and candles.

Lindsay and Paul

Pictures can also be used to show your guests the people who present
you to your new life. My cousin Lindsay and her husband Paul's outdoor, midsummer night's dream of a wedding featured framed pictures
of their respective parentage along the sidelines of the aisle. Even though
Lindsay chose to enact being "given away" by both of her parents, we
could all experience another story, visually, at the same time: generations
of family providing a foundation for Paul and Lindsay, *presenting* them to
be married—whether they were there in the flesh or not.

And if you're getting married in the American south, you'll be encouraged to present *yourself*—literally—in the form of "wedding portraits": framed glamour shots of y'all in full costume. Many southern couples showcase these at their ceremonies and/or receptions. Winnie had been born and raised in the northeast, but got married in the south, where she learned about this phenomenon via friends who constantly nagged her about getting these done. She finally had to feign a scheduled date to get them off her back. She didn't want her wedding to resemble a funeral "with a picture on the casket," preferring to make choices for her ceremony that represented her life as opposed to her death.

How you are *presented* is as much for you as it is for them, so prepare to notice moments of personal significance—which may even take place offstage.

Lily and Bart

Our friend Lily did not have any parents *present* at her wedding at the Central Park Conservatory Garden, as her mother had passed away and her father was sick in the hospital. She agreed to be walked down the flowery aisle by an uncle, whom she hardly knew, because her family found this gesture to be meaningful while she was indifferent. But more impactful for Lily was the presentation she was given earlier in the day by her little niece.

Lily and her now-husband, Bart, had agreed to a brief meeting in the garden to see each other in their finery before the ceremony. Several of Lily's nieces and nephews accompanied her on this walk, which I imagine made her look like Disney's *Cinderella*, surrounded by plucky little creatures. When she saw Bart, they both wept and held each other. After giving the couple a moment, Cinderella's team of escorts encircled them with affection. And then Lily's tiniest niece,

Carrie, offered her a proportionately tiny handkerchief to dry her tears. Lily keeps it and the story of how she was *presented* to her husband to this day.

Karen and Jamie

Another thing is that you don't have to be *presented* by people. My friends Karen and Jaime, for example, were presented by the land they were raised on. Their officiant—the great dancer/choreographer/creative mind Jacques D'Amboise—asked them to gather samples of earth (of dirt) from the towns in which they each grew up. Jacques poured them together during the theatrical ceremony he created, symbolizing their places of origin mixing and creating new land from which new life could grow.

Tabitha and Jason

Your choice of processional music might also signify how you're being *presented*. Our friend Tabitha's husband Jason, for example, is obsessed with Johnny Cash: having read his biography several times, and seen Walk the Line several more, he owns a library of boxed sets and records, and even got to see him live after being sneaked into a concert through the back door.

Despite not being religious himself, Jason accommodated Tabitha's mother in agreeing to a Catholic wedding, complete with pre-wedding counseling; he was happy to keep the peace. But when he discovered they couldn't pick music other than approved church hymnals, he *drew* the line.

Fortunately, he asked his good friend Phil to play the organ at their ceremony. Phil gave Jason a very special wedding gift—much to everyone's surprise—by playing "Ring of Fire" instead of church hymnals as guests entered, and Jason got in place. It was still playing when Tabitha entered, walking the line (so to speak) with a huge grin on her face (while avoiding eye contact with her mother). The rest of the ceremony was scored by forgettable hymns, but Jason got to be *presented* in a way that felt authentic to him.

However you're *presented* at your ceremony, it's the recognition of people—both old and new—that will give you a vital sendoff to the next phase of your lives.

Justin recently said that making an entrance—especially for a ritual of great public meaning—is a lot nicer when you don't have to do it alone. And I agree. But not being alone does not necessarily mean having a parent escort you down an aisle. That image was part of my wedding story, to be sure. But the image of Winnie entering her wedding solo—stepping into the light, in full possession of her heart, her mind, and her choice—is one with which we can all identify.

> We will have to enter into big, meaningful moments again and again throughout our lives. And we will want to possess our hearts, our minds, and our choices to do so; there won't always be a ceremonial team to embolden us as we walk. But being presented at your wedding, on your own terms—ringed by a shimmery fire of recognition and support—will give you the confidence to enter the spotlight again.

Even when you can only rely on yourself.

24 Something New: "If Music Be the Food of Love Play On"—Shakespeare, *Twelfth Night*

And then it happens.

The moment you've been working for: the dramatic, public performance of one becoming two. You're here, at the harbor. Let go. And let the music ferry you to the next stop on your voyage.

> *Music* transits us to new places of deep emotional meaning more effectively than do words. Words are deceptive. We try to navigate life transitions with words, to make sense with them. And they do undoubtedly help. They set the stage. They frame it. But music connects us to the play and to each other. Music transports us to new worlds before we think to speak.

Justin chose a piece of music for the ceremony that didn't make sense to me. It was a very short, sweet piano solo by Chopin with no connection to our wedding as far as I was concerned—in terms of content, context, or function. Meanwhile *every* other piece of text or music we had chosen *did*: e.g., an essay by Rilke on love, a selection from Plato's *Symposium* on the origin of love, *Love's Old Sweet Song* . . .

When I asked him to make a case for the Chopin piece, he simply said that it made him feel good and invigorated. That it motivated him to live. "Okay," I thought, "but how is it going to fit into the program? What story will it tell? What sense will it make?"

This is the kind of debate artistic collaborators have all the time. Although, artists (at least good ones) have the wisdom to know that the most evocative performance will spring to life on stage left while they search-and-destroy for it on stage right. They know that the most evocative text is not exactly what you said or what (s)he said, but something else entirely; something that happens by accident along the way. They know that the most evocative outcome will be the most playful, the most alive. And they know that on the surface it may not immediately "make sense."

Couples who collaborate as artists—particularly performing artists—are at an advantage when it comes to weddings, as they pretty much have them all the time, showcasing their expressions of conflict and creative play, as individuals and as a pair. They fail—again and again—in the constant process of self-reinvention and discover flashes of new life as they go. For some of you, your wedding will be the only, or at least the biggest, piece of theater that you produce together as a couple. But you too can dip into this wellspring of experience again and again—planning parties, making career changes, or even negotiating everyday choices as individuals and as a pair.

> Creative collaboration reminds us to listen to the music, to sail through life transitions with a free mind, with pleasure, and a sense of play.

Acclaimed actress Olympia Dukakis, who has been married to acclaimed actor Louis Zorich for fifty years, has offered some sage wisdom on marriage and creative collaboration. She had a revelation while working with her husband on a production of *Long Day's Journey Into Night,* which they had performed together twice prior. "You'd think, *what is there to unearth?",* she said. But during one rehearsal, she became blocked. She complained to the director (who was her brother) that she did not know what to *do* since her husband was not making the *right* choices; and thus she could not do the scene *right*. Her brother replied that he too was at a loss, not knowing how to help when she clearly "wanted to control the stage." Hard as this was to hear, Olympia tried letting herself be impacted by her husband's choices, and she then said, "What I had rejected was exactly what I needed to see. I had to stop trying to win. I had to start playing again. Which is of course a great pleasure. Never mind that the best work comes from it, but it's a great pleasure."

Being open to her husband's sense of play—to his music, if you will—helped Olympia discover something new in a play she had decided was old, one she thought she knew back to front. Instead of working to control it, she let it transport her by letting herself play.

> ***Likewise, the music you choose for the ceremony will do a lot of the work for you.***
>
> The music you choose will help to galvanize your audience, to let them play, to free their minds and hearts, and to guide them to a new place. And if you offer "the grace of your listening"—as my yoga teacher, Nancy, says—it will take you there as well.

We had the good fortune of being friends with musicians. And I must say that to offer the grace of your listening to live music, made by people you know and love, during a major life transition, is *intense*. (Not to mention that it is the best gift one could ever receive.) All of our guests shared in our bittersweet feelings of separation during the processional—as per the Sinead O'Connor ballad "In This Heart"— and joined in our revelrous union during the recessional—as per the selection from Purcell's *The Fairy Queen,* "They Shall Be as Happy." (I had played one of the *non-singing* lovers in that Purcell opera in college and remembered this piece to be contagiously jubilant and transporting.)

> Choose music that rouses you. But keep in mind that over-played numbers are often less *transporting* than they are like

trainspotting—bleak, repetitive, deadening. Standard wedding fare—like "Pachelbel's Canon" and "The Bridal Chorus"—might move your guests to tears . . . of boredom. Rather than revving them to play, to receive, and to be taken somewhere new, "traditional wedding" music could slam the breaks on their imaginations; stifle their curiosity about the meaning of your event; and convince them that they know what to expect—they've *seen it all before*. Or it could just put you all to sleep.

This isn't to say you can't find pieces that remind you of the usual suspects that are similar in style and evoke similar emotions. But you should offer the grace of your listening to discover sounds that catch your ear and songs that offer a brisk surprise—like a fresh inhale of icy air—that awaken, enliven, and will you to be moved. Impacted. Changed.

Also, by *music* I not only mean music. I also mean text: the words, the poetry, the stories you share that stir the imagination. The language you choose that excites them to see you, to take you in, and to join you on a voyage to an undiscovered country.

There was music in our reading from the *Passion of Saints Serge and Bacchus*, which we pulled from John Boswell's, *Same Sex Unions in Pre-Modern Europe*. Their story is one of two friends who "were always together, like stars shining joyously over the earth" and shared deeply in a belief—in their case, a faith in Christ. The two were punished by the Roman Emperor Maximian after refusing to denounce their beliefs. And here's where the language of this reading becomes musical, subversive, and transporting. In the description of their punishment:

[T]he Emperor ordered their belts cut and military garb removed. Women's clothing was placed on them. Thus they were to be parad-

*ed through the middle of the city, bearing heavy chains around their
necks. But when they were led into the middle of the marketplace the
saints sang and chanted together:*
*"Lord, you have clothed us with the garment of salvation; as brides
you have decked us with women's gowns and joined us together
for you through our confession; strengthen our souls that we may not
be separated from you and the impious may not say, 'where is
their God?'"*

And from there the two are tortured and executed for committing
to their faith and to each other. The horrific descriptions gripped our
listeners, recalling a familiar trope of martyrdom. But it also woke them
up to a highly specific version of this trope, one that invited them to
consider our distinct commitment to each other, our struggle for recognition, and our unique love. The language did the work for them,
moving them to a new appreciation of our lives. This was an intuitive,
musical, and playful way of emphasizing how alike we were to everyone present, even in our differences.

The musicality of the reading bled into our vows as well, which
Justin had prepared. He drew them from ideas in the reading, and things
we had said to each other over the years—both lofty and pedestrian.

*Mark and Justin, do you vow to be faithful partners in life? To love
each other unconditionally, and to protect each other, through the
many changes time will bring? To honor and respect each other, to
nurture and nourish the best parts of one another? To support each
other through feast and famine, sickness and health, joy, success,
disappointment and loss? To listen carefully, even when you disagree?
To use kind words but speak the truth to each other?*

*Do you vow to care and provide for your children, when the time
comes? To offer love and support for your parents and families when
they are in need? To always remind each other of your principles, even*

in the face of fear or confusion? To improve the world, together, as a living example of love and compassion? To make each other laugh when you want to cry? Through the many years you are both blessed to live?

Be

As meaningful as vows are, they're less about the actual words and more about the music of the moment. What you're *doing*—or rather how you're *being*—is more powerful than what you're saying. In actor terms: *what's your motivation? Your action? Your intention?* Your text could be the yellow pages, but what actually happens between you and your scene partner, and you and the crowd, *is* the event. The music plays when you listen, when you simply look at each other, stand, and receive the attention. You won't know what this feels like until you're there, but you will find that the marriage contract forms between the lines—in the raw, silent communion between actors and audience—before you even open your mouths.

When I spoke the words "I do," I was not deciding anything. My big, willful choices from the gut had already been made; the actor's homework was done. All I had to do was simply play the scene. And what a great and playful pleasure it was to kiss Justin in their presence, in that theatrical collision of private and public. Letting the transition, which everyone had collectively conjured, happen.

But in my memory, the transition actually happened before the vows—right before. It happened as our friend Brandon played Justin's beloved Chopin solo—you know, the one that *didn't make sense* (yes, I finally gave in). As I listened to the piano, I looked to our guests . . .

. . . and the music ferried us all to a new world.

Part 7

Dancing
In the New World

25 Mingling Tribes: Room of Their Own

I had a cocktail in the room of my dreams at my brother Angus's wedding.

For years, I wanted to live in the Frank Lloyd Wright Room at the Metropolitan Museum of Art: a living room of windows and oak, in which outside and inside seem to converge. And for a moment I did. Or at least a version of it—a replica of a room designed by Wright, tucked away within a labyrinthine warehouse in upstate New York, where Angus and my sister-in-law Summer's entire wedding took place, from ceremony to dancing. Justin and I found the Wright room while exploring the . . . um . . . gallery. Oh yeah, the space was called an "art gallery." And although it contained pieces of art, they were mostly in tall heaps bordering the cavernous space. Don't get me wrong, it was cool, in a funhouse sort of way. But coolest of all was navigating the clutter to discover that room and to realize my dream to freely wander within its walls. With a cocktail.

Angus and Summer chose to host us in a gallery, but they could not have known how the art I found there on my own would impact me. How it would inspire me to dream myself into their wedding; enliven my curiosity, my willingness to meet and be changed by new people; and to extract meaning from the event in my own way.

> *Providing your guests space and time to wander is a gift, for them and for you.*

By giving them the freedom to explore, you increase their potential interest in mingling, engaging, and finding their way into your new world, rather than having you abruptly shove it in their faces. You also get fresh and creative perspectives from your guests: on you, your wedding, and each other; observations and insights you wouldn't have noticed on your own. This is good practice for your future: as hosts, parents, and professionals. You'll be more effective in these roles throughout your lives by giving friends, children, and colleagues room to find their way to you.

Choosing a location that has room to explore within clear parameters will help.

For instance, Angus and Summer's "gallery" provided more space to wander than originally met the eye. The heaps of art were not the only clutter to navigate. How about the nearly two hundred guests, including Summer's double digits of sisters—who basically form their own corporation. (I suspect they rent a convention center when they get together, wear name tags to remember one another and exchange business cards to stay in touch.) One thing they've definitely got down is their weddings, having graciously agreed to cut costs by wearing the same black dresses to each one. As my two younger brothers and I were each hurriedly paired off with a sister for the processional—a long line of gals in black dresses—I felt like I was on an episode of *The Bachelor*. Though not just because of the gowns. I'm talkin' 'bout a lot of frantic output in a crowded space, and no room for taking anyone in, e.g., "Hi I'm Trina, I hope you give me a rose later, okay, bye."

During the cocktail hour, however, after wandering into my dream room—where I rediscovered how to breathe—I approached Trina again. I did not give her a rose, but I now had room to be curious about her and to take her in. I'll never forget the tidbit she shared about her son, to whom she had taught sign language when he was a baby. This increased his agency, freeing him to communicate and explore in his own way.

B

There are unlimited ways to provide your guests space to explore. If you want and can afford it, host everyone at a gorgeous lake resort, like Justin's friend B did. This was the wedding in India we missed due to an overbooked flight. (*Damn you, Delta!*). B's guests got to meet and mix in the majestic ballroom, in lavish sitting rooms, on patios lit with festive colors, and at the turquoise pool, which traveled throughout the resort alongside each of the rooms. Everyone stayed for a few days, which gave them quality time to visit with the folks they knew and to make new friends. B says that several of her pals who met there became better friends with each other than they were with her.

Julie

My friend Julie's French countryside wedding was hosted at a small rural compound called "The Gite." The rustic houses, in which we all stayed for a week, surrounded a glistening pool where the main events took place. But there were days to discover a variety of rooms and lawns while also discovering new people and new versions of ourselves; ways of being, telling stories, and having fun. We became great friends with Julie's cousin, Ruthie, who, as you may recall, would go on take our wedding photos. We also learned never to dismiss rosé wines as being trashy after consuming possibly the best dinner we will ever have. It was just five friends—old and new—a four-course meal, and an endless flow of refreshing rosé at a small inn in the middle of nowhere, overlooking sprawling lush vineyards and a French sunset.

Shana and Darren

But you don't have to fly everyone to India or France to provide fertile ground for your tribes to mingle. Our friend Shana, for example, rented a summer camp over Labor Day weekend (off-season) in Maine, making it financially possible to celebrate the way she and her husband, Darren, wanted to. Without having to spend a lot on a fancy resort, decorations, or rentals, they had a beautiful lake to swim in during the day, a fire pit at night, and a variety of outdoor sports with which guests could entertain themselves. "People just gravitated to what they wanted to do," she said. There was not any of the typical wedding "hoopla," so she and her husband spent the weekend catching up with each of their friends and family members. Says Shana:

> "We didn't have to do any receiving line or cram a bunch of well-wishes into the wedding day because there was more time to be had that night and the next day. An hour before the wedding ceremony we were swimming with friends, and an hour after the ceremony we were playing badminton with my sister in law and nephew in shorts and t-shirts."

Giving your guests time and space allows them to catch up, in meaningful ways, with friends and family they don't often get to see.

This is a nice opportunity for them to mingle at a mostly happy event, rather than the mostly tragic ones that will inevitably bring them together. Consider ways to give them room to connect with their own tribes before forcing new ones upon them in a crowded, unwelcoming venue. They'll be motivated to mingle if they can first connect with themselves—their own dreams, their sense of home—and with the people they know.

When I flip through our wedding album, my eye is gripped by the smiles of people reuniting. That very specific squint and twinkle of the eye, and the slight curl of a happy lip, that seems to say, "This is my_____. I've missed her." The images include my mother knitting by a fireplace, catching up with my sister-in-law Summer. My brothers playing pool in the parlor, like we all did as kids. Justin's mom, Sandy, hugging her sister-in-law, Aunt Corky, in the garden. Numerous college friends laughing: on couches, by the tree-lined river in the backyard, and on the front stoop.

You can save even more money, and still provide them space, by hosting the event at your home and keeping the guest list small. Justin's cousin Emily did this at her house in Vermont, which has a great big yard and an apple orchard ripe for exploration. My friend Yasmine did the same in her NYC apartment. Her family was able to reconnect and to mingle with her husband's family on their own terms, all while enjoying Manhattan views from Yasmine's terrace.

Jesse and Danny

And if they won't come to your home, you can just bring the wedding to theirs. Our friends Jesse and Danny did this as a creative solution to being a bi-national couple. They used the bulk of their wedding budget for airfare and let their families and friends host them in various places. Jesse's family in Montana had a barbecue, Danny's crew celebrated them in London, and for their mutual friends in New York, they had a full day of live music, eating, and late night dancing—at an exclusive, "illegal" basement party (Danny's a DJ and knows what's up). What at first seemed to be a dilemma—their families scattered all over the globe—turned out to be an advantage. As Jesse says, "We were able to give everyone a little face time and a lot of love."

> *When your guests have room for discovery it allows them to take something meaningful away.*

There are, of course, the things you provide. For example, our choices of ceremonial text piqued a great deal of interest amongst our guests. During the cocktail hour, many of them wanted to share their newfound enthusiasm about the existing historical literature on same-sex couples—from Ancient Mesopotamia, to Ancient Greece, to pre-modern Europe. But there are also the tangible objects that are infused with meaning. At my cousin Lindsay's wedding to her husband Paul, who is a chef, they gave us all olive oil they had infused themselves with fresh rosemary. Whenever I use it, I feel the creativity of their home magically permeating ours. It also always feels good to take home the card indicating that the newlyweds have donated to a charity on your behalf in lieu of a favor.

Allie and Wyatt

There are also the things they find themselves. Our friend Allie and Wyatt's entire wedding, for example, was at a beautiful lodge in upstate New York that had an instant photo booth. This proved to be a super-fun way for their guests, myself included, to actively preserve their own memories of the occasion. And to share them: as we and many other guests frequently post such photos to social media sites with hashtags like #allieandwyatt.

And then there is the inspiration *they* derive from your event. Both Allie and my friend Winnie shared with me how our wedding opened their minds to new possibilities and creative ways to plan their own weddings. As women, they were ambivalent about having ceremonies, due to the traditional implications of women as property. But being at ours, absorbing how we subverted tradition to reveal our truth, got them to dream of their own authentic nuptials—events that would make them feel like them. I could not have known at the time how we would inspire these gals to uniquely bust out of the shackles of tradition, but this included both of them making me a bridesman, a powerful symbol of gender roles becoming more fluid and free.

The ideas your guests discover and take away from your wedding are a gift that keeps on giving. Their inspired, creative thinking will not only expand mental and emotional freedom in all the lives they touch—including yours—but also the desire to share this freedom. Take it from me: my experience as a bridesman for those modern brides fired me up to write an article on *how to be a bridesman*, which then led me to write this book.

26 Take It In:
Breathe, Sense, and Remember

It's really happening! At last you can have a good time.
The canal has been carved and the water's flowing through.

> *Sit back and take it in. No, really. Take. It. In. I mean, why bother building this house if not to live in it for at least a min-ute? You've cried enough, so go ahead and suck!*
>
> It doesn't actually matter what happens from this point forward. What matters is how you sense it. How you drink the moment in. And how you incorporate it into your sanctuary of memory: the lighthouse within that you can visit whenever you like.

A Heaven of Your Own

I remember envisioning heaven when I was a kid. My only point of reference at the time was our church: a warm room with big windows, where everyone—or at least everyone I knew from our small village—was welcome. At first I imagined arriving there seeing everyone asleep on the pews—you know, 'cause they were dead. But then my mom said that by that logic I'd be sleeping too. So then I imagined us all awake, happily mingling in the church.

Cut to our wedding reception: as I scanned the ballroom, I saw rich orange, red, and yellow dresses; pumpkins, flowers, candles; and smiling familiar faces, all in one place. I thought: *this is a heaven of our own creation.*

> *The event would happen only once in reality, but it would forever be available, on demand, in my dreams.*
>
> You create your own internal lighthouse/sanctuary/heaven by staying present (that means *easy on the Xanax*), by indulging in each of your senses, and *taking it all in.*

See

You'll have more fun being a spectator than an overseer, so make sure the following technical considerations are worked out in advance.

Your emcee/party planner/reception wrangler is in charge. She knows the order of your reception events; the timing; and when to give you, the caterers, the toasters, and the DJ, specific cues. This way when she introduces you—in the way you choose—appropriate music will be playing, the glasses will be filled, and anyone with an assignment will be confidently awaiting her instructions.

Now you would want the same to be true for your rehearsal dinner, of course, if you plan to have events at that time—or if you even have a rehearsal dinner. I mean, I haven't mentioned it before now because . . . it's just a dinner. Some people think of it as a tradition where "the groom's family pays" or whatever, but nowadays we're way past all that. Right? Some people do still like using that time for roasts or something. And so, I mean, sure . . . go for it. But it's really just dinner. After the rehearsal.

The table assignments for your guests are organized. Even if your dinner is pizza and beer in the bonus room of a B&B (like our friend Tabitha did), you'll want your guests to have a sense of where to be so you can better take them in.

It generally works to group your guests by table, and to let them choose their own seats. As a waiter, I once worked a big reception that had seat assignments and was tickled to watch Barbara Walters move her place card so as to avoid sitting next to another notable television icon (who shall remain nameless). It won't be quite as tickling for you to see the discontent faces of your own guests stuck next to people they loathe. But if you group them, and let them work out the seating, you'll give them some wiggle room and also know where to look for them.

You can also have fun with the table assignments: e.g., using pictures instead of numbers. For ours we painted and laminated pictures that matched our overall American Gaythic theme. There was a tractor, an ear of corn, a horse, a fence, a barn, a farm house, etc. Each program had the guest's name and our branded portrait on the front, and their table assignment illustration on the back. The programs were spread out on a table in the foyer, so they couldn't miss them as they entered the Inn. You could also make place cards with photos of each of the guests and their table assignments on the back, as Jamie and Sean did.

Each table could be a different photo of the two of you from different stages of your lives. Or you might arrange each table with a different themed centerpiece, or a different word, poem, or phrase. But if you do, be careful not to suggest a coded message.

When we accompanied our friend Hurricane Sharon to her sister's wedding, we spent the majority of the dinner distracted by our table assignment. The bride is the only member of her immediate family who isn't gay or single, and so she staked her claim on this day by having a very "normal" wedding. That being said, she had some fun with the tables, which had quotes by famous people. We were seated at the Bono table, along with Sharon's gay brother, single sister, and offbeat, but friendly cousins. The quote read, "[t]o be united is a great thing. But to respect the right to be different . . ." There was more, but I got stuck on the word *different."* It was a nice sentiment, but I couldn't help but think that by seating us there, she was singling us out as "being different," and therefore contradicting the spirit of the quote she had chosen. Also, if we were the different ones, wasn't she then preaching to the converted? Wouldn't the quote have gotten more mileage at one of the tables with the guests who represented the majority? Which in that particular room was a fratty, hetero sort. Just sayin', it will be harder to *take your guests in* if their heads are spinning.

The most crucial table assignment of all, of course, is yours. It was my instinct to rent a small table, just for us; so we could have space to catch our breath. I only discovered later that this is actually quite a trendy thing to do. We had it set close to the band and dance floor, so we could be seen, and more importantly, we could see everything. This is your room, so make sure you have a view.

Once you're seated, breathe. Let your shoulders down and look around. Let your eyes find what they like. And with the absorbing stare of a baby, take it all in. Throw your head back and look at the ceiling or sky. People will be watching you, to be sure, but you don't have to perform. Spectate. And let the images decorate your inner sanctuary.

Taste

I'll never forget my first sip of water after we sat down: the chilled glass on my lips, the ice cubes against my teeth. It was the most refreshing water I had ever tasted.

Food
People always say things like, "I don't even remember tasting the food . . ." and that's because, without a plan or a script for how the events will play out, you'll get swept up in the whirlwind of it all. But with a schedule, someone in charge, and a table of your own, you'll have afforded yourself the luxury to dig in.

> And don't be shy about it. You picked the food, you paid for it, enjoy it. Think of all those celebrities on the Golden Globe Awards who don't mind stuffing their faces in their shimmery gowns, even as the world is watching.

Drink

To save money, our bar had only wine: red, white, and bubbly. We figured everyone could make do with those options. I once catered an obscenely extravagant engagement party in the Hamptons, and during setup I remember hearing the hostess shout out, "Where's all the top-shelf liquors? The guests need to have a choice!" *Really? They need to have a choice between a margarita, a gin and tonic, or a single malt scotch on the rocks, with only the finest spirits? It's a wedding, not the inauguration of the first transgender president!* Everyone was happy with our bar. The great-tasting wines we had gotten were all under fifteen bucks (get recommendations if you need them), and we served a cocktail of sparkling wine with puréed mango. I slowly took in the fruit and bubbles and that was plenty luxe for me. And our guests still talk about that drink, like it was special.

Smell

The smell I remember the most is Justin's—or, rather, the fragrance I bought that weekend. We call it "wedding scent."

I also recall the smell of the fall chill. The roasting fire on the fireplace. The puréed root vegetables—with a swirl of spinach—warming on the buffet. The smell of our mothers' perfumes when they kissed us after making toasts. My friend Allie's perfume when I kissed her, after she sang Tom Waits's "I Want You," right next to our table.

I also remember the smoky breath of this guy who looked like a lumberjack. He was the long-term boyfriend of a guest, and we met him for the first time that day. He tried to corner me to complain about "some bitches"—his words, not mine. He had heard me complain about something random (albeit not "some bitches") and I guess figured he had an entry. It will do you well to avoid this kind of smell, as I did, and to follow your nose to ones more enlivening than destructive.

Feel

There's a picture of me at our table with an imbecilic smile and shimmering tears. I used to hate it, though it's grown on me over the years. It reminds me how it felt to *take in* the toasts and the songs. I felt it, and I let that show. Why not? This is no time for a celebrity awards show "loser face"—you know, the rehearsed smile, nod, and clap the stars deploy so as not to seem disappointed when they lose. React how you will. This is your time to *suck*, and to feel. Your facial responses won't be critiqued on the blogosphere the next day, I swear.

If you choose to do the rounds and talk to everyone, make sure you take in whatever feels good from the encounters and don't linger too long on the bad. My brother Steve said things to me like, "Why are you smiling like that?" *Thanks, Steve.* I focused instead on his compliments about the ceremony—his interest in Serge and Bacchus—and kept moving.

Oh, and speaking of moving, it's time for your first dance.

Our band of friends had arranged a very plucky version of "I'll Be Your Mirror" by the Velvet Underground for us, per our request. As it began, we looked into each other's eyes, started to move, and thought "Oh shit! We didn't rehearse!" I mean, we did. Before the reception . . . like, several minutes before. But you see, the real problem is that Justin and I move to the beat of very different drums. Fortunately we have a default move we call The Christmas Ornament wherein I just hang my arms around his neck and swing from side to side. So we did that. And didn't think about me being several inches taller than him and what that must have looked like . . .

I thought it went okay. And it was better than wrestling each other for a rhythm. Though, when I discussed it with my friend Joy months later, all she said was, "Mark, don't worry. There were so many other things about your wedding that were great . . ." Ouch. I felt that. But you know, it's okay to take in what doesn't work. That's how we stay honest, motivated, and interested in improving ourselves. If we ever renew our vows, or have a big anniversary party, I'd like to spend some time on a choreographed dance for our guests. I think that would be fun now, having lived through a big dance flop. Maybe we'll do a waltz, tango, swing, or maybe a more highly involved camp duet. But certainly something that both feels and reveals our sense of fun through captivating moves as opposed to clumsy ones.

At the same time, it did feel great to live in that moment. To be surrounded by dear friends who used sweet voices, guitars, and a tambourine to celebrate our love and consecrate our lives together. And when my cousin Lindsay toasted us, right after our dance, she said something like, "Watching them dance right now, you can see how happy they are..." So it must have been charming after all. *Right?*

Although . . . she had pre-written her toast. So she was planning to say that anyway expecting (hoping?) the dance would be good.

As you can see, certain threads of anxiety may be forever embedded in the fabric of who you are. Just remember to focus on feeling alive during the reception rather than on what *should* have happened.

Listen

Listening is the key to your own private heaven, your jewelry box of memory. The singing, the laughing, and the toasting.

Here's something technical to help you receive the toasts: inhale what they say, then exhale all of your loneliness, tension, stress, discomfort, worry, anxiety, and fear.

We had requested three toasts each and scattered them out throughout the evening. I loved the variety of voices and how they forged together our tribes.

Hurricane Sharon reminded us all that we were at a *wedding.* Cogent and electrifying, she emphasized the importance of the occasion given the political and social strikes against us. She was fierce, but we don't grow without a little pain; chicks don't hatch without the cracking of an egg. We heard about how we catalyzed transformation in each other and how we encouraged one another's creative ambitions. My brother Mike shared a poem he wrote about being the lynchpin to hooking us up (by telling me to watch *The Real World*). No one else understood the meaning of his verse, but I took it in. From Julie we heard how I missed a professional performance of *A Christmas Carol*—in which I was nephew Fred—because I had been on the phone with Justin all night the night before. How my peers at the time thought, "What an idiot. What's going to happen to his career?" And how Julie thought, "Who's Justin?" How living is more powerful than performing.

And then, out of a dark corner of the room, Justin's brother Chris turned on his phone and a soft green light animated his face. He welcomed everyone. He expressed gratitude for his circle of family growing bigger. He complimented us on having created and cultivated a quality extended family of our own. And then he said this:

> *Together, Mark and Justin have been a consistent and steadfast*
> *source of comfort, decency, inspiration, and joy to me personally*
> *and I imagine to all of you as well. Their relationship has been*
> *an unequalled model of commitment, compromise, sacrifice, and*
> *acceptance—all the hallmarks of a deep, mature love and the*
> *cornerstones of a wonderful marriage. I could indeed be happy to do*
> *half as well.*
>
> *Mark and Justin, I'm sure I speak for all here when I say I love you*
> *both dearly and wish you a long and happy marriage.*

I think that was when the photog caught me with the imbecilic smile and tears. Chris is very cerebral and reserved, and I had never heard him speak with such emotional gravity before this. We would all be changed forever by his speech. I kept it in my head and my heart. And it still nourishes me.

Each speaker in their own way exceeded my expectations, inspiring a new place in my mind and assuring me that there is so much potential love and support waiting in the dark silences of our lives—if we remember to listen.

27 Something Old:
Daddy's Little Boy, Mommy's Little Girl, and Other Nods to Your Past

As I shoved cake in Justin's face, my Uncle Dan—a neatly-pressed, gay professional—hooted like a brute. Now I'm the first to explode stereotypes, but what was happening?

Why were we stuffing each other's cakeholes in public? Why was Dan hooting?

I'm not so sure Dan knew why either. In that hoot, I heard rowdy men from his childhood in the Bronx and also from his grandparents' childhoods in Ireland years before that. Sometimes traditions pass through generations completely unprocessed. Their original excitement and vulgarity remains lustrous and fully intact, but without any immediate context, meaning, or purpose—*what's happening?*

Now, old traditions have advantages to be sure. They provide something to hold onto at celebrations. They are familiar. They make your guests feel at home, they galvanize them, and orient them to the big event. *Where are we? Oh, we're at a wedding.*

But the more mindful you are about the traditions you deploy, the more time, money, and extraneous effort you'll save on the reception and the less likely you are to get caught gobsmacked, staring at the crowd, wondering what's going on.

Breaking down and understanding the meaning of each tradition, and why you're using it, will connect you to its purpose. The most significant of which is to celebrate where you've come

> from—paying homage to those who have contributed to the life and love that you enjoy.

There are a wide variety of festive rituals that honor our family histories, cultures, and tribes.

The hora, for one: a circle dance most commonly seen at Jewish weddings at which the spouses and their parents are raised up in chairs at the center of the frolicking guests. Most non-Jewish people I know want to crib this one for their own because, as a wildly fun celebration of families joining, it's hard to beat. But of course there is the question of context and respect to the people for whom this tradition has specific meaning.

B

There are also numerous traditions involving bowing or touching the feet of one's elders in Eastern cultures. Our friend B, who is Hindu and got married in India, found bowing to the hundreds of elder family members to be even more moving than she expected. Although, she minimized her *moving* while bowing, so as not to throw up—she was two months pregnant. B's mother, who is otherwise stalwart of tradition, stayed by her side during the ceremony, helping to disguise the pregnancy. With an assist from her mom, B was able to make it work. Her secret was obviously out seven months later, but B was glad to have gone through the motions to honor her family and their rich history.

Jamie and Sean

We can also get creative and invent rituals that pay respect to the history of our tribes if none exist. For example, it was important to Jamie and Sean that their wedding reflect their identities as gay men in the context of queer history. So they named the dinner tables after prominent LGBT figures. Says Jamie:

"On each table was a photo of the person with a brief bio on the back so our guests could learn a little bit about our history. Since it's not taught in most schools, we thought this would be interesting for some folks. We had a Harvey Milk table, Oscar Wilde, Sylvia Rivera, Josephine Baker, Alan Turing. It was a lot of fun."

The Parent/Child Dance

Of course, the most evocative nods you make to your past will be the ones toward those who raised you. I learned about the theatrical potency of such moments in a graduate acting class from a posh British acting teacher. An actress, who was black, was working on a monologue about her character's ancestors. The teacher suddenly cut her off—in her posh British way—and said, "Dahling, you cahn't take responsibility for the enti-yah race. Speak the wahds as yoh fa-thah's daw-tah. Then you'll find the pow-ah of the piece." We find a similar power when we acknowledge our primary caretakers at our receptions.

The most popular Western tradition of this kind is the father-daughter dance. Why? Most likely due to that good ol' history of weddings as property transaction, a bride getting passed from a father to a husband. Although, the mother-son dance has almost caught up in popularity over the years. But you see, I would have liked to dance with my father at my wedding, had he been alive at the time.

Feelings? Thoughts? Reactions?

The topic of same-sex parent-child dancing at weddings is never discussed—especially with two men. And on the very rare occasion that it is, our internal normative police are instantly summoned, hand-cuffing us in discomfort, confusion, and fear at the thought of this unprecedented proposition—*I've never heard of that.*

I recently asked our friend Sharon and her wife, Emily, if either would have considered doing a mother-daughter dance at their reception. (They had danced with a father and a brother respectively.) They both winced, as if smelling something foul or getting squirted in the eye with a lemon.

Sharon instantly said, "No. That would be sad. It would suggest that we were two old ladies who had been passed over that nobody wanted."

I'd like to take a moment to reflect on her reaction. As I've mentioned earlier in this book, Sharon is a fiercely intelligent, highly accomplished, superhero in LGBT law and has fought passionately, like a titan, for her own freedom and happiness. In other words, she is known to be incredibly self-reflective. So her statement here is notably out of character. I mean, why would the absence of a man in a parent-child dance indicate either bride was "passed over" and not "wanted"? The whole premise of their wedding was that she and Emily *wanted* and had chosen each other. But this shows just how strong a headlock the gender binary/heteronormativity holds on us *all*, especially regarding parent-child narratives. Even the smartest, most passionate, and insightful among us are easily possessed by such narratives, like a deep sleep from which we are cursed to never wake up.

Emily's response was also delivered from the clutches of fear, though less reactive, and more reflective. She said:

> "My mother had already come a long way as far as accepting me as a lesbian, accepting our relationship, and accepting our wedding—announcing it to all her family and friends. I wanted to respect her efforts, and wouldn't have wanted to rock the boat by pulling her out into the spotlight like that. But, truthfully . . . I wouldn't have been comfortable with it either . . ."

Emily thought of several strong reasons to spare her mother the discomfort of a mother-daughter dance. Yet when it came to her own discomfort, she was blocked.

I'm not saying that she *should* have wanted to dance with her mom. But, as with every ritual we consider, it behooves us to understand all the options and our own feelings about them. This way we avoid saying yay or nay to anything based on a knee-jerk reaction alone (if only Justin and I had this advice before signing up for that cake-feeding incident).

To be fair to Sharon and Emily, their choices in this case reflect great efforts to include their families in their celebration without alienating them. And I'm not sure I would have been comfortable asking my dad to dance, though I would have wanted to. I can talk a big game now, given I didn't have the option, but I likely would have felt a discomfort similar to theirs.

So what is this plaguing discomfort, and how can we get past it?

Celebrating Erotic Development

My friend Lyn—having danced with her mother (who raised her) at her bat mitzvah, but danced with her father (who did not raise her) at her wedding—says, "I think brides in particular want that father-daughter dance so we can feel, I hesitate to say . . . 'normal.'" She then added, "In a . . . heterosexual way . . ."

Emphasis on "sexual."

And therein lies our answer.

The sexual implications of Daddy's Little Girl are considered to be so "normal" that we never even notice them. For instance, my mother's favorite memory of her father—which she frequently, indiscriminately, and proudly shares with any kind stranger who will listen—is of her having breakfast with him as a child, during which he would allow her to call him by his first name, "But only until your mother wakes up," he'd say. (Oedipal theory anyone?) By contrast, with Daddy's Little Boy, the sexual element is *all* we think about, immediately concerning ourselves with words like *incest* and *pedophilia*.

In other words, we consider a child's erotic/sexual fantasies about a parent to be perfectly normal if they are co-ed, but we consider them to be sick, disturbed, and problematic if the sexes are the same. (This might help us understand Sharon's knee-jerk reaction to Mommy's Little Girl and how "sad"—sexless?—she found that idea.)

So, yes, I'm saying it:

The traditional parent-child wedding dance is a tribute to the erotic fantasies the newlyweds once had for one of their folks.

Though this book is the only place—so far—you'll hear it described like that. (Try Googling father-son dance. You'll get a lot of, "huh?") If this had been broken down for me when I got married, and my dad were alive, I would have definitely elected to dance with him. I would then be confident that the implications are no different from traditional father-daughter or mother-son dances.

Now, when I say *erotic fantasies* I don't necessarily mean conscious ones. I'm referring to the process, of child development during which we all, universally, dream ourselves into adulthood. Erotic and sexual feelings are of course a big part of this process and fantasies of this kind show up in our play and in a variety of our behaviors. When our parents are appropriately validating of our erotic dream life, we gain an internal sense of self-worth, and the confidence to one day pursue romantic love as adults.

Case in point:

A photograph of me lying on my dad's chest. I'm about six. I'm nestling my small head in the crevice between his collar bone and his neck. My eyes are wistful. And he's kissing the top of my head. Sixteen years later, I would nap on Justin's chest, soon after we got back in touch. I would nestle my rather large head in the crevice between his collar bone and his neck. My eyes would close. I would feel safe and loved. And that's why I wanted to slow dance with my dad at my wedding.

Winnie

But there are other great reasons and ways to dance with, and pay respects to, your parents at your reception. Winnie, for one, acknowledged her mom—the world-famous choreographer who raised her as a single parent—by dancing the cha-cha together. It was magnificent fun! And one of the most memorably moving moments of Winnie's wedding. It was a far cry from the story of "two old ladies getting passed over." This was a spirited celebration of Winnie's foundation as a relational being, having clearly been the recipient of unconditional nurturing, support, and joie de vivre from her mom.

Chris

Now, not all of us are lucky enough to have those who raised us at our weddings. But we can still find ways to memorialize them. For example, when Justin toasted his brother Chris, he conveyed that the great gifts their mother had given them would survive, though she had not. And when Chris's wife, Ionela, danced with her brother—who had helped to raise her—Ionela's mother danced with Chris, whispering to him, "Mama's here."

Repurposing Random Traditions

And then there are all of those gratuitous reception traditions you'll be forced to consider that don't really honor much more than the multitude of cookie-cutter weddings that preceded yours. That would include the cake cutting and feeding, the bouquet toss, and that garter business. You don't have to do those. But you can subvert and repurpose them in a way that is meaningful to you. For example, Winnie and her husband, Mason, cut their cake with a sword. This was not only a fun bit of theater, but it was also a nod to Mason's service to the US military (the sword was part of his uniform). Winnie also publicly presented her bouquet to her mother, stating, "There is no one whose happiness I wish for more than my mom's." Once again, there was absolutely nothing "sad" about this move. Winnie's intention was so clear, specific, and heartfelt that it allowed her to make this presentation with confident and contagious exuberance.

We too had specific intent when we each danced with our moms. As we swayed to Mama Cass's "Dream a Little Dream of Me," I recalled how my mother sang this to me as a kid when she'd tuck me in at night, preparing me to dream. Her constant encouragement of my dream life was perhaps her greatest gift to me. It inspired me to change the world, so that I could live and love in it more fully and more freely. And I got to honor that with this dance.

28 They Become You:
The Mirror's Many Faces

Every one of our guests came alive on the dance floor, bounc-
ing and whirling in their own queer ways. That's because DJ Concerned was true to his name, intensely concerning himself with our
craving for a good beat. But it was also because they had been made
to feel like an essential part of the day. They were, and continue to be,
essential to our lives.

> As you throw yourself into the party, which you can now rel-
> ish with abandon, capture images of the moving bodies around
> you. These are the faces, voices, and gestures that have made you
> *you*. They will travel with you, guiding you through challeng-
> ing choices and transitions ahead. As the great psychoanalyst Joan
> Riviere wrote, "[e]ach of us is a company of many, and . . . our
> being is contained in all those others we have been and are occu-
> pied with as we live, just as they are contained in us."

Whenever I revisit our wedding, on that proscenium stage in my
mind, I see so many vibrant actors. There's Aunt Connie, twisting and
twirling with her husband, Steve, and inspiring me to stay inspired,
to ask for recognition, and to fail along the way. There's Uncle Dan,
moving to his own beat. Aunt Rita shaking her luminous platinum
pate, radiating the shimmery forcefield in which she had sheltered the
vulnerable girly-boy I had been from rough-and-tumble uncles and
cousins. Aunt Corky and Uncle John, twisting, and laughing, remind-
ing me that there's always a queer, duct-tape dress tucked away in every
normal closet.

I also see the dozens of friends we assembled; the family of our own making. They're gyrating in our honor, emboldening me to take life by the horns, and showing me how that's done. Without them, I couldn't have written this book. I stole not only their stories, but also their humor, sense of play, style, insights, bravery, and compassion.

A great deal of the me that feels like me is a composite of smiles, laughter, words, and dance moves inspired by our people; indeed, stolen from them. These people are the wellspring from which I perpetually draw to create a life, art, relationships, a marriage, and a home.

Learning from Recognition

There will be times when they live through you more obviously than others.

Like the moments my mother-in-law lends me her social grace.

From my own family, I may have learned to be intensely affectionate—and intensely aggressive—though I learned *nothing* about social gestures or manners (e.g., my brothers spent most of our wedding talking only to each other, while hogging the pool table). But Sandy showed me the worth of a gracious, ceremonious greeting; not least by introducing me to the wealth of friends she had cultivated in her community—all of whom attended her beautiful memorial service.

So when I approached Sandy's parents during our reception—trying out my very small small-talk—I felt her smiling over my shoulder. She also thanked me for the effort. Years later, at the wedding of her son, my brother-in-law, Chris's wedding, I would approach her ex-husband—Chris and Justin's father. They had been estranged from him for many years, and he was sitting alone. I would offer him my (only slightly) improved small-talk. And once again feel I could Sandy's smile over my shoulder, though she had died years before. I knew she would want me (us) to make this gesture, even if we cannot sustain a relationship with their father in the big picture. And I was glad I did: for me, for him, for her, for Justin, and for Chris.

Learning from Conflict

But you know, it's also useful to recall what you don't like about your people. The things you don't agree with and that you don't want to mirror, incorporate, or repeat. As psychoanalyst Ken Corbett says, "[l]ife is not only made in recognition. It is often those relationships that are threaded with conflict from which we learn the most."

That means the mothers who tried to plan your wedding themselves, to reign over your parade; the fathers who criticized your choices or checked out too soon; the friends and family who threatened not to show or the ones who really didn't show. All of them help us to define ourselves and to continuously compose that thing we call a self.

One of my clients, Jim, and I recently learned together about the value of conflict.

After nearly a year of therapy, Jim felt he wasn't getting anywhere. He saw me as sitting back, lazily and uncaringly taking his money. My efforts to help him identify and verbalize his feelings went unnoticed. So he decided to terminate. When I suggested we take a month to process this decision, to mine it, to locate the feelings that had clearly been left unaddressed, he accused me of acting like a "used car salesman."

"You can't help me," he said. "We're not the same. We don't talk the same, look the same, or dress the same." (His group therapist wore "hoodies" and was deemed to be "accessible" whereas my attire was more "professional" and therefore unhelpfully "inaccessible"/unrelatable.) He planned to leave this conflict in my office and start therapy anew with his group counselor, whom he felt was "just like" him, on an individual basis.

I reminded Jim that he originally thought *I* was "just like" him when we started, when I was little more than an online description and a fantasy in his mind. I suggested the very same thing would occur with the new therapist and that he would attempt to leave, rather than engage in the conflict. Rather than acknowledge the feelings of inadequacy, discomfort, and hurt induced by his inevitable differences from me. I encouraged him to stay in this conflict with me, to practice putting these feelings into words, to rehearse the negotiating process that is required to truly be in a relationship with another person.

Jim chose to stay. And he also recently told someone in his group how angry that person makes him, something he would have been too afraid to do only a few weeks before. To this he credits our work—our willingness to engage and survive conflict together. He maintains a relationship with the group member, as well, appreciating their differences and freeing himself to own where one person ends and the other begins.

Evolving Together

In addition to noticing the things that make us different from others, as Jim learned to do, also keep in mind that we all grow, adapt, and evolve. So we can expect the images of our people that we hold in our minds to evolve as well.

My relationship with my brothers, for example, has grown as we have grown. The more we become our own people, the less we experience each other through the filter of our mother. The less we take each other for granted, and the more boundaries we set between us the more clearly we can see and appreciate each other as unique adults. This came into focus when we all worked together to plan our mother's surprise sixtieth birthday party. For this we had to creatively collaborate, negotiate, and step out of our comfort zones to embrace a variety of new people.

(As time goes by, I envision my brothers ever so slowly extricating themselves from the pool table at our reception, and creeping, little by little, toward our guests.)

The memory of your wedding will also evolve as new enriching relationships enter your life. There are handfuls of new family and friends that I now superimpose onto the images of our dance floor, as though they had rocked-out in support of us like the rest of them. This reserve in my mind is a nurturing piece of theater with an ever growing cast.

Tangible Memories

You don't have to rely on memory alone to create this reserve. There are of course a number of literal, tangible ways to capture your guests contributions to your life, as well. There's that old standard known as the Guest Book that they can sign, or the more modern, creative alternative of setting up a video camera and having them each record a little message. Or you might ask them to take a little more time to compose thoughts and reflections.

Jamie and Sean, for example, set up an *Anniversary Box* and provided cards with questions on all of the dinner tables. The questions ranged from "What's one wish you have for Jamie and Sean?" to "What should we name our kids?" People filled them out and dropped them into a box that they'll open on their one-year anniversary.

I arranged something similar as a gift to Justin for our first-year anniversary: a box of letters, reflections on him, written by each of our people. This, as it turns out, was one of the most traditional wedding things we did, as the first year is the year of "paper" or something. (A complete coincidence, by the way. I have no idea what the other anniversary gifts are supposed to be; e.g., gold? Silver?) I put each letter in a colored envelope, on which I pasted a photo of the respective author. I then put them all in a decorative box that Justin keeps on a bookshelf. He still hasn't read every one, but he enjoys having them at his elbow, so he can read a letter whenever he wants or needs to.

Life may not only be about recognition, but being recognized can be sweet. And this day, this moment that you've struggled to achieve, is an opportunity to taste that sweetness.

I tasted it the next morning, during our brunch.

(By "brunch" I really just mean bagels, fruit, and coffee. Just a simple way to connect with our guests one last time before they returned home and left us to the one we had newly minted together.)

Justin's grandparents smiled as they gave us hugs, thanks, and congratulations. You might recall that his grandmother had insisted on calling this event a "party" only weeks prior? As they stepped out the door, his grandfather turned to us, winked—in the warm way he does—and said:

"That was a wonderful wedding."

Part **8**

Then Comes . . .

The Honeymoon Is Sweeter for Those Who Wait

"Are you two lovers or brothers?"

He appeared abruptly, out of nowhere. It was CNN anchor Don Lemon.

"We're both," I said, reactively. When I get startled, I try to startle in turn.

"Really?" he replied, unstartled, though slightly interested.

We were at a resort on the island of Vieques off of Puerto Rico. This was not our honeymoon; it had been five years since the wedding and we still hadn't taken it. We did intend to one day visit the smörgåsbord of Iceland, Denmark, and Sweden, for which we had registered as a gift and collected several thousand dollars. The problem was that we had spent those funds on my graduate school training to become a therapist. And we were also consumed with too much work, projects, and family tragedies to organize a big voyage. But we are *husbands* (not brothers or just "lovers"), and we needed a romantic excursion. A paradisiacal beach. ASAP! So we planned, saved, and off we went.

Mini Moon

It has actually become quite common for couples to wait a bit before taking a honeymoon: that significant vacation celebrating your newly wedded-ness. These days, couples want to invest in a special trip they wouldn't ordinarily be able to take. And according to a 2013 article in the *New York Times*, modern marrying couples tend to be older than previous generations and have "more demands in their lives." That means that in many cases both spouses are working, pursuing careers, and/or transitioning to new careers, making it hard to find time and money to take a meaningful journey immediately after a wedding.

As an alternative, many couples first take what's called a *mini moon* and postpone the *moon of honey* (if you will) for a more convenient and affordable time, which is exactly what we did.

As soon as the last guest drove away from our post-wedding brunch, we darted to a family house on the Hudson River and hid for a couple of days before returning to our lives. This was an easy and affordable way to rest, recover from the hoopla, and register what the heck happened. (And eat carbs.)

We then had some time—years, in fact—to prepare for the fantastic Scandinavian adventure we originally envisioned. And in the meantime, we budgeted for little necessary getaways—like the one to the island of Vieques, which turned out to be a pivotal jaunt for us.

Post-wedding, we had gotten so caught up in our goals for the future that we began to lose sight of pleasures in our present. Even after we arrived on the island, we were at first a bit low-risk as far as taking it all in—e.g., we did not rent a jeep. *What a hassle, an expense! Who wants to drive on vacation?!* But that meant being sequestered within the walls of the resort.

Fortunately for us, Don Lemon popped out of the bushes. (In my memory, he magically materialized out of some shrubs by the pool as we strolled by.)

He and his boyfriend generously gave us a lift around the island in their jeep, providing a glorious tour of the shimmery, heavenly, turquoise surrounding its borders. They also reminded us of the vital fun that lurks just around the corner in this life, readily available if we allow ourselves to be startled into waking life.

During lunch, I explained my concept of the Engulfed and the Abandoned to them. Don refused to identify with either . . . though I couldn't help but observe, and share, that the multitude of engulfing texts his boyfriend received from family throughout the afternoon, while Don abandonedly tweeted beachy pics to his thousands of "followers," sort of spoke for itself.

After a day of blue beaches and red snapper tacos, we all settled down in the fire pit at the resort just in time for fireworks. I forgot to mention, it was New Year's Eve. Then Justin and I made a resolution: to finally buckle down and take our honeymoon that year.

As we turned to thank Don, we caught him offering a jeep tour to a straight couple for the following morning; he had startled them with his famous face. Like Puck in *A Midsummer Night's Dream*, he would continue to sprinkle his abrupt magic onto unsuspecting lovers. Who knows? If the CNN gig doesn't work out, he might find great success running a couples' retreat.

But as I first said in this book: love and marriage are ironic; balancing on a core that rocks from side to side. So, even though getting startled back to life, being spontaneous, and taking risks got us to dig in to our honeymoon, it could not have been nearly as delicious without the patience, preparedness, and mindfulness that came first. (And let's be real: we were better able to enjoy the time away having saved enough money and having reached a point in our careers at which we could take time off without being consumed by worry.)

> Taking the time to prepare for this holiday will allow you to enjoy each other *and* take in the scenery at the same time without the mutual exclusivity that comes with taking it too soon or too late. Time and experience will grant you the wisdom to enjoy the big and the small, the mythic and the mundane.

Finding the Mythic in the Mundane

For us, that meant taking pleasure in the "M + J" and smiley face that Justin drew with his finger on the fogged up window of our cab after landing in Iceland; the heart-shaped milk in our lattes in Denmark; and the upgrade to an enormous honeymoon suite in our hotel in Sweden. (Thank you, lovely, elfin, Swedish receptionist.) It meant being awestruck by the dream-like palaces, cobblestone streets, bridges, boats, and shimmery waters of Stockholm. But also allowing ourselves the unadulterated joy of bolting out of the opera after act one, just to have champagne and chocolate-covered strawberries in our room—and then returning to the opera the next night to see something better. It meant having the wisdom to miss Patti Smith and Russell Crowe singing live, right around the corner, simply to enjoy Icelandic beer and take pictures of Icelandic currency. Oh yes, and to take lots of pictures and to also forget to take them.

We took boats to castles along the archipelago by day and danced like sixteen-year-olds in divey bars with cheap-looking disco balls by night. We felt the thrill of a roller coaster drop in Copenhagen's fantastically Technicolor Tivoli Gardens and the rush of humiliation upon seeing the pic they take of you—and expect you to pay for—dropping, screaming like Munch's *The Scream*, while a nine-year-old sits behind you looking bored. We enjoyed exotic foods—like puffin—as well as much-too-proper British accents of fellow tourists talking of "maths" and "sport" and "curd." (And mimicked these words, in said accent, nonsensically, incessantly, like toddlers, making each other laugh.) We delighted in words like *slutspurt* (which simply translates to "sale") while being overtaken by colossal waterfalls with enchanted mist and black beaches with wisps of heavenly fog. We were humbled by geysers, and also bored by them.

We experienced the terrible beauty of swinging above the entire city of Copenhagen—at the height of a skyscraper—soaring over the story-book bridges, pastel houses, and watery reflections on glass buildings; while also being transfixed, down below, by the organized anarchy of Christiania, where teenagers freely smoke pot along tree-lined graces of shimmery water. We had the wisdom to visit Helsingor (Elsinore/Hamlet's) Castle and to indulge our inner dorks by miming the Hamlet/Ophelia wrist-grab moment from Shakespeare's play. We had the good sense to talk to people—we looked up my Danish penpal from high school, Ayoe (thank you, Facebook)—reached outside our zones of comfort, felt the wee breeze of something new, and willed ourselves to be disoriented and changed. But we also had the good sense to stick to the familiar, to curl up in our rustic hotel room (ostensibly waiting for Northern Lights that never came), and acting out eighties music videos in hotel robes.

Oh yes, and we had a lot of sex. Good sex. The kind of sex you get to have after years of committing, communicating, and taking emotional risks. After failing, failing again, failing better, and again. *It gets better!* So yeah, we enjoyed each other and the foreign countries equally without one excluding the other.

But you know, I have to tell you, that's not how the journey began.

The Storm before the Calm

It would be so easy to end this story with us riding off into the sunset, effortlessly, pontificating on how love and romance win against all odds. But that isn't true. And my years-long search for truth and honesty—in my work as a therapist, an actor, an artist, and as a once-closeted gay man—compels me to be honest with you now. You see, far too many spouses just *aren't* honest about the challenges of marriage—with their communities, with friends, or even themselves. This closetedness perpetuates a silent shame for couples who struggle to negotiate emotional and sexual needs as the years go by. (Which is, of course, every pair of long-time lovers since the beginning of time.) So here it goes:

Before we dipped our moon in honey, it was blue.

As much as waiting to take a honeymoon can yield the virtues I described, you'll want to be mindful about waiting too long. At a certain point, your amorous escapade could end up becoming what another 2013 *New York Times* article calls a *Hail Mary Moon*: an eleventh hour, desperate attempt to save the marriage—via extravagant get-away—before throwing in the towel. Six years after getting married, we were walking this line.

While flying the first leg of our journey, I tried to tune out the fact that this was our *thirteenth* year together. And the fact that we both had been working *thirteen*-hour days for the past year, rarely seeing each other. And that the plane was featuring that Meryl Streep movie in which she and Tommy Lee Jones play a married couple facing the painful reality that their sex life is dead. And that my clients—Rapunzel and Prince—whom I had been working with for a year—had just taken a *Hail Mary Moon*—to Iceland!—and came to the conclusion that they should get a divorce.

Our first destination, an apartment we rented in Reykjavik, greeted us with two twin beds separated by a lamp table. *Oh shit*, I thought. *We definitely waited too long.*

The proprietor told us we could push the beds together. But we didn't.

Now, it is universally unrealistic for a long-term couple, free falling in busy schedules, to instantly begin a passionate tango as they first touch the ground. But it felt like we *should*, and that not to do so immediately meant that something was wrong with us. And the mutual comfort in sinking into our own twin beds felt even worse.

Each day began with hope, but ended with tension. Not the sexy kind. The scary kind. The kind where each of us felt too afraid to be vulnerable, to share our feelings, needs, or desires with the other. We were shifting, like the tectonic plates—the tourist attraction we visited without speaking to each other.

Where was Don Lemon now? There was no catalyst to startle us back to life, to give us a tour of paradise, to turn these lemons into (forgive me) *Don Lemonade*. There was only us; seeming more like *brothers* than *lovers*.

Then came that fateful night. We were in our own beds, sharing the lamplight. He was reading *The Swimming Pool Diaries*—an acclaimed novel from the eighties featuring explicit man-on-man sex—while I researched an article I was writing for HuffPost called, "We Need To Talk About Butt Sex." My intention with the article was to eliminate shame among women and gay men; to open communication lines between anyone, really, who is somehow penetrated during penetrative sex. There is often an assumption, reinforced by Hollywood and porn, that one should be easily, spontaneously, receptive to such entry without any mental or physical preparation. It was not lost on me in this moment that I was seeking to eliminate my own shame, my own obstacles, as much as everyone else's.

I couldn't sleep that night. Neither could he. We both lay awake separately in the dark. It was agony. What should I do? To speak or not to speak? In the past, any time I asked if he was losing interest in me ended only in yelling, and both of us getting shut down. But we were sleeping separately in twin beds. This was as explicit a statement of dissatisfaction as spouses could make, and it demanded address and redress. Had I been more confident at the time, I would have just joined him in his bed. Instead, after suffering silently for far too long, I spoke. "What's happening?!" He had to own up: he was ignoring me! It was unfair. He countered by pointing out that I constantly, unabashedly showered unfiltered anxieties onto him; that too was unfair. We argued. We suggested that perhaps we had waited too long. And that perhaps we should separate.

The simple statement woke me up like ice on bare flesh.

The next day we went to the Blue Lagoon: a geothermal spa, world-famous for rejuvenating skin with its naturally heated, mineral bath. It was also the location where my clients, Rapunzel and Prince, decided to get a divorce.

We entered the milky blue baptismal pool together without speaking. No matter what happened next, we would be reborn. We would exfoliate identities and modes of being, revealing fresh new ones. We would be sensitive, raw, and a bit lost in this new state. We would be forced to talk, negotiate, and make hard choices—choices we would simply rather not make; preferring to curl up in avoidance on twin beds. But now there was no turning back.

I thought of my work with Rapunzel and Prince. How afraid Rapunzel was to assert her preferences; how she preferred to be safely engulfed in her tower and for Prince to constantly desire, pursue, and rescue her. How afraid Prince was to rely on her; afraid that if he let his guard down, he risked abandonment and the possibility of her sitting coldly cloistered in her tower, while he suffered on the ground.

I thought of how frustrated I would get when they would enter a session, stare at me quietly, and make light jokes to cover their pain. How I would tell them about my frustration; modeling for them the necessary, albeit frightening, task of putting words to risky feelings when we want relationships to improve. I thought of how I always reminded them that there was no shame in separating and that through clear communication they might discover that remaining married was not their best option. That separating was not a failure if they determined this relationship to have run its course, and that they could support each other even as they moved apart.

I thought about how effective their treatment was, even though they chose to separate. Rapunzel had begun to free herself from the tower, no longer depending on Prince just as he began to surrender the belief that he needed to rescue her to be loved.

Justin and I moved through the hot spring, without eye contact, but in unison—as if connected by an invisible leash. Suddenly I decided to choose my own direction. As I fought against the familiar gravitational pull of being by his side, I began to feel sensitive, raw, and a bit lost, but also strangely exhilarated—an invigorating melancholy. I now understood my own advice, feeling for the first time why people make the choice to separate.

As I moved, following my own lead, the shimmery turquoise pool expanded before my eyes. My eye has always liked shimmer; a flickering light leading me to my truth, to a life that feels alive, even at those times when my truth defies sense, tradition, or the norm.

The pool became a theatrical stage, and this a climactic moment of a performance. A choice would be made on the precipice. Yes, even now I was "so drama!" (The older I get, the more I refuse to have it any other way.) I thought of the theatrical stage of our wedding; all of the mingling, dancing players who had once witnessed me enacting a life-changing choice, and how they (or at least the version of them now imprinted in my mind) would support me in this choice, whatever it would be.

Then I thought again of Rapunzel. Having freed herself from the tower, she would be empowered no matter what choice she made, even if that choice was to stay with Prince, if she wanted. I thought of what Justin had said—about the anxieties I put on him; how I expect him to rescue me from them; and how unfair a burden this is. I thought of how owning up to this would be just as frightening—and perhaps as exhilarating—as separating. How enlivening—thrilling!—it might be to find separateness while together. I thought how damn difficult it is to say "I love you" first.

I turned around. And then willingly, from the gut, and the heart in which I had flown and fallen—again, and again, better, and again—I called out, "Justin!"

30 The Beginning

Enter the future here . . .

Appendix
Example Budget Chart

VENDORS	SERVICE	PROJECTED COST		PAYMENT TO DATE		
		Amnt	Notes	Amnt	Date	Notes
Inn	Rooms & Reception	$5,000	Entire Weekend	$2,700	1/23/2006	Deposit Paid
Paperie and Copy Place	Invitations	$314	Envelopes, Paper (76) Copies	$280	1/31/2006	
Wine Shop	Liquor	$1,404	Red Wine, White Wine & Prosecco only	$1,140	10/6/2013	4, 3, 4
Restaurant	Rehearsal Dinner	$1,280	Rehearsal	$1,030	10/13/2014	
Patti	Catering	$5,898	Dinner, Brunch Staff	$5,898	7/12/2006	Deposit Paid
Rental Co.	Rentals	$1,794		$1,794.40		
Printing CO	Programs	$90	Table cards & Programs	$123	9/16/2006	
Baker	Wedding Cake	$313	Carrot Cake, no filling, autumn leaves design, delivery	$313	9/30/2006	
Electronic Store	Turn Tables/ Slide Projector	$230	DJ & Slide Show	$230	10/10/2006	
Deb		$100	Travel & Stipend	$100		
DJ Concerned	DJ	$550	$550 (payment and travel)	$550.00		
B&B	Room for Musicians	$269	Deb 1 nite $67.20 Dj 1 nite $67.20	$269	7/27/2006	
~~Zondra~~ Ruthie	Photography	$170	$100 stipend plus travel	$650		Ruthie's airfaire
Bed and Breakfast	Room for Singer & Photographer	$494	~~Zondra~~ Ruthie 2 nites $274.25, Allie 2 nites $274.25	$494.00	7/27/2006	

Suit Place	Suits & Ties	$600	Suits, tailoring			
Ring Place	Rings	$690		$690		
West Village Hotel	Engagement Party	$475	Appetizer platters	$475	2/26/2006	
Grocery Store		$75	3 cakes, cake boxes.	$30	2/26/2006	
	TOTALS					
	PROJECTED	**$19,746**				
	ACTUAL	**$20,002**				
	JUSTIN	**$5,002**				
	MARK	**$5,000**				
	MARY	**$5,000**				
	SANDY	**$5,000**				

Resources

Beckett, S. (1983) *Worstward Ho*. London: John Calder Publishers.

Boswell, J. (1995) *Same-Sex Unions* in Premodern Europe. New York: Vintage Books.

Bromberg, P. (1998) *Standing in the Spaces*. Hillsdale, NJ: Analytic Press.

Brook, P. (1990) *The Empty Space*. London, UK: Penguin.

Browne, B. (2012) Daring Greatly: How the Courage to Be Vulnerable Transforms the Way We Live, Love, Parent, and Lead, Gotham.

Corbett, K. (2009). *Boyhoods*: Rethinking Masculinities. New Haven, CT: Yale University Press.

Corse, Sarah. and Silva, Jennifer. (2013) "Intimate Inequalities: Love and Work in a Post-Industrial Landscape" Paper presented at the annual meeting of the American Sociological Association Annual Meeting, New York, NY, Aug 09, 2013.

Eliot, G. (1871–2) Middlemarch. Oxford: World's Classics.

Hendrix, H. (2007) Getting the Love You Want: A Guide for Couples, Henry Holt & Co; Revised and Updated edition.

Lamott, A. (1995) *Bird by Bird: Some Instructions on Writing and Life*. Anchor.

Lévi–Strauss, C. (1969). *The Elementary Structures* of Kinship. Boston: Beacon Press.

Mitchell, S. (2006) *Gilgamesh: A New English Version*. Atria Books.

O'Connell, M. (2014): "Review of A Kid Like Jake," *Journal of the American Psychoanalytic Association*, 62: 363-371.

Rafkin, L. (2013) "A Reluctant Bride Conquers her Fears." *The New York Times*, December 27, 2013.

Riviere, J. (1952) *The Unconscious Phantasy of an Inner World Reflected in Examples from English Literature*. Int. J. Psycho-Anal., 33:160-172.

Sedgwick, E. K. (1993) Tendencies. Durham, NC: Duke University Press.

Seim, C. (2013) "The Hail-Mary-Moon." *The New York Times*.

Wise, I., and Mills, M. (2006). *Psychoanalytic Ideas and Shakespeare*. Karnac Books.

Valhouli, C. (2013) "A Little Getaway After the Big Event." *The New York Times* October 21, 2013.

Acknowledgments

I want to thank:

The great women to whom this book owes its conception: Allison Langerak Tuzo, for my first run as a bridesman; Lian-Marie Holmes Munro, for my second; Aileen Barry, for breathing life into my wedding; Julie Carpineto, for suggesting I write a book; and all of you for illuminating the wonders of platonic love.

My agent, Alice Speilburg, for believing in my work, making it better, finding it a home, and guiding me every step of the way. My editor, Nicole Frail, for always starting with yes (and for saying no when necessary), for working hard to sharpen my most unwieldy of ideas, and for illustrating my concept of Dream Hostage Negotiation: rejecting my proposal for one book while inviting me to write another.

My illustrator, Dan Parent, for your transcendent collaboration. Liza Monroy, for your magnificent words.

My family who provided stories, insights, inspiration, and/or support: Aunt Connie and Steve, Uncle Dan, Corky and John Bond, Mike O'Connell, Steve O'Connell and Sonia Mereles, Angus and Summer (not their real names), Chris and Ionella Deabler, Lindsay Lopez-Rodkin ("Cousin!") and Paul Parillo, Emily Bond and Brandon Weaver, Aunt Rita, Uncle Phil, Sam Bond, John Bond Sr. and the late Vivian Bond. And also the memories of: Mary and Sam Lopez, and Rita and Tom O'Connell.

The friends and friends of friends whose contributions have enriched the pages of this book: Joy Besozzi, Deborah C. Smith, Evelina Shmukler, Sharon McGowan and Emily Hecht-McGowan, Brandon Matthews, Ruthie Brownfield, DJ Concerned, Dani and Jamie Blackbird, Jesse Alick and Danny Taylor, Bill Bowers and Michael Growler, Kaki and Jason Kasdorf, Joy and Jason Marr, Jamie McGonnigal and Sean Carlson, Rachel Skiffer and Marvin Coote, Kim Winslow,

Shana and Darren, Karen Nelson and Jamie Lacy, Jamie and Aaron Weiner, Margaret Beck, Danielle Aspromatis and D'Luxe Events, Wyatt Tuzo, Allison Katz, Fernando Valencia and Michael, Tom Leith and Yael Zeira, Susan Ferrara and Zack Calhoun, Sue Ferziger and Jason Lampert, Liz Rosier and Ruth Sternberg, Catherine Cloniger Koontz and Kristopher Koontz, Rachel and Paul Tracy, Jason Warehouse, Deb Travis and Maya Ciarrocchi, Suzanne Guillette, Nancy Elkes-Culp, Drew Munro, Ida Rothschild, Sarah Shaddy-Farnsworth, Su Ciampa, Lee, Fernando Rodas and Jessica Moskowitz, and B and Lyle (not their real names).

My clients who have allowed me to share glimmers of your inspiring work. My mentors: Ken Corbett, for guiding me to my own sense of creative play; Al Sbordone, for teaching me the only way out of family conflicts is through; Brian McEleney and Stephen Berenson, Annie Scurria, Julia Carey, Eliza Anderson; and all of you for helping me appreciate how truth lives in multiplicity.

Fiona True and Virginia Goldner for salvation.

The editors who have allowed me to be a writer and made me a better one: My friend Kasia Anderson; Peter Scheer at Truthdig; Noah Michelson at Huffington Post; Lybi Ma at Psychology Today; Rosemary Balsam at Journal of the American Psychoanalytic Association; Chris McIntosh at Journal of Lesbian and Gay Mental Health; and Anna Peirano, at dot 429.

The memory of my mother-in-law, Sandy Deabler, for showing me the beauty of seeing other people.

The memory of my father, Stephen P. O'Connell, for making me feel worthy of being loved.

My mother, Mary O'Connell, for being brave enough to process these musings with me, and for always encouraging me to dream.

And finally, my husband Justin Deabler, for failing with me—again and again—for seeing me, fighting to see me better, and for making me laugh.

Index

organization, 99–100
OTP (Overtly Toxic Prejudice), 102, 112
Outside Providence (film), 43
Overtly Toxic Prejudice (OTP), 102, 112

P
"Pachelbel's Canon" (song), 223b
parent-child dance, 245–47, 247–49
Parents, Friends and Family of Lesbians and Gays (PFLAG), 194
Patterson, David, 3
Patti (caterer), 113–14, 190, 196
Paul (cousin-in-law), 159, 216, 232–33
Peter (client), 38–39
PFLAG (Parents, Friends and Family of Lesbians and Gays), 194
Phelps, Fred, 194
Phil (friend), 218–19
Phil (uncle), 24
photo booths, 233
photographers, 110–11, 118–19
pictures, 199–205, 199b, 200b, 201b, 202b–3b, 204b, 216–17, 231–32
planning, 90, 99–100
Plato, 220
point person, 105
Pokémon (TV show), 53
polyamory, 163
potential moves, 185–87
preferences, 104–5
presenting, 212–15, 216–19, 217b
Prince (client), 41, 263, 264–65, 266
The Princess Bride (film), 111
Project Runway, 16, 67
Proposal Week, 82–85
proposals, 78–79, 78b, 79–81, 80b, 81b, 82b
Proposition 8, 3
Puck (fictional character), 260

Q
queer weddings, 14
queerness

hidden, 72–73
truth and need, 67
weddings, 2, 71

R
Rachel (friend), 214
Rain Man (film), 190
Rapunzel (client), 41, 263, 264–65, 266
The Real World: Hawaii (TV show), 12, 17, 43, 63–64, 156, 162, 183, 188
Reality Bites (film), 161
receptions
cocktail hour, 228, 229, 232–33
dance, first, 239–240
dance, parent-child, 245–47, 247–49
drinks, 238
emcees, 235
food, 237, 237b
mingling, 228b–29b, 231–32, 231b
photo booths, 233
seat assignments, 235–37
toasts, 130–32, 131b, 240–42
traveling, 232
recovery, 11–12
Red Lion Inn, 61, 65
registry, 124b–25b, 125, 125b
regrets, 92
rehearsal, 183–87, 184b
rehearsal dinner, 235
Rehearsal Master, 183, 184b
rejection, 22
relationships. *see also* marriage
abusive, 10–11
choices, making, 104–5, 105b
collaboration, 220–22
communication, 9b, 36–38, 37b
conflict, 11–12, 17–18, 148–150, 150–51, 180–81, 253–54
emotional roles, 28b
evolving, 254–55
failure in, 16–17, 16b, 181
Growing Apart Conflicts (GAC), 153–54
separation, 10–11
subjectivity in, 152
releasing emotions, 176b, 177b

responsibilities, dividing, 95, 95b, 97b
reuniting, 231–32, 231b
Richard (uncle), 14
Rilke, Rainer Maria, 220
"Ring of Fire" (song), 218
rings, 85, 187b–88b, 188–89
Rita (aunt), 72, 157, 251
rituals, 83b, 142–43
Rivera, Sylvia, 245
Riviere, Joan, 251b
Roberts, Julia, 20
Roche, Lucy Wainwright, 126
Roche, Suzzy, 126
Romney, Mitt, 2, 54
Ross, Katharine, 9–10
Runaway Bride (film), 150
Russ (friend), 163
Ruthie (photographer), 118–19, 204, 230
Ryder, Winona, 161–62

S
Same-Sex Unions in Premodern Europe (Boswell), 101, 223–24
San Domino, 23
Sandy (mother-in-law)
centerpieces, 127, 179, 182
coffee, 114
email to her mother, 167–69
family, 70
Gilgamesh reading, 215–16
Italian vacation, 29, 42–45
Justin, author's fight with, 148–49
LGBT activism, 194
photograph of, 231
pictures, 203–4
relationship with, 83, 191–93, 196
social graces, 252–53
Savage, Dan, 2
scents, 205, 238
SCOTUS (Supreme Court of the United States), 1
screaming, 176b
sea themed wedding, 25b
Sean (friend), 236, 244–45, 255
seat assignments, 235–37
security, 51–52
Sedgwick, Eve, 19, 21–24
self-expression, 68b
sensory awareness, 234b, 235–242

About the Author

Mark O'Connell LCSW is a New York City–based psychotherapist in private practice. As a *Psychology Today* expert he writes the column Quite Queerly, regularly contributes to the *Huffington Post*, and has been published on Truthdig.com and in *Out* and *Dot 429* magazine. His scholarly writing has been published by *Journal of the American Psychoanalytic Association* and *the Journal of Gay and Lesbian Mental Health*. His website is: www.markoconnelltherapist.com